W9-BTP-771

Praise for *The Second Decade*

"*The Second Decade* is a synthesis of the author's observations, scholarship, and insight into the period of transition from childhood to adulthood. Dr. Helveston provides a roadmap for parents to help their children see what opportunities are available to them and guide them on the journey to become their best selves. He identifies important milestones of decision-making that he regards as foundations to lifelong personal and professional satisfaction.

"This book will prove to be an enjoyable and practical guide for shepherding children through these formative years, and will be equally useful to parents and those in their 'second decade' who read this enjoyable and valuable contribution by Dr. Helveston."

KIRK PARR, MD, CARDIOLOGIST AND PARENT OF TWO SUCCESSFUL CHILDREN
NOW IN THE BEGINNING YEARS OF THEIR OWN MEDICAL PRACTICE

"Gene Helveston has done a real favor for the parents of ten- to twenty-year-olds. He has written a guidebook that, in addition to highlighting the usual recommendations, shines a spotlight on an area that receives little attention in similar books. That area is WORK. Not homework, not family chores or extracurricular activities, but age-appropriate work outside the home. Work like babysitting, mowing lawns, and restaurants.

"In my experience, young teens are eager for this opportunity. Dr. Helveston does a marvelous job of discussing the many facets of this important area and preparing parents for their responsibilities."

PATRICIA A KEENER, MD, PROFESSOR EMERITUS OF PEDIATRICS,
AND ASSOCIATE DEAN, INDIANA UNIVERSITY SCHOOL OF MEDICINE
FOUNDER OF SAFE SITTER

"Who amongst us as parents of teenagers couldn't benefit from a practical guide to help us ensure that our children would grow up to be happy, self-sufficient adults? *The Second Decade* is a welcomed addition to the self-help section of the library, and provides a practical approach to raising children in those critically important developmental years. A noted scholar in the medical and health arena, Dr. Gene Helveston uses his highly analytical mind to strongly make the case that parents must necessarily introduce the concept of work into their children's lives so that they may gain a proper understanding of and appreciation for the value of education and occupation."

Marvin R. LeRoy, Jr., President & CEO
The Institute for Philanthropic Excellence

"This is a well-researched, readable, and very informative treatise on childhood; making good choices; and educational alternatives. A great resource, not only for parents, but also counselors and college consultants."

John C. Robertson, Retired Vice Chancellor,
St. Louis Community College (1965-1988)

THE SECOND DECADE

Eugene M Helveston

THE SECOND DECADE

Raising Kids to be Happy, Self-Sufficient Adults through WORK

EUGENE M. HELVESTON, MD

MARLI BAR PRESS | INDIANAPOLIS

© Copyright 2016 by Eugene M. Helveston

MARLI BAR PRESS
Indianapolis, Indiana

All rights reserved. No part of this book may be reproduced in any manner or form whatsoever, by any means, electronically or mechanically, including photocopying or recording, or by any information or retrieval system, without the expressed, written permission from the publisher, (www.marlibarpress.com) except by a reviewer, who may quote brief passages for reviews or articles about the book.

Library of Congress Cataloging-in-Publication Data

Helveston, Eugene M., 1934–

The second decade : raising kids to be happy, self-sufficient adults through work / Eugene M. Helveston.

First edition. | Indianapolis : MarLi Bar Press, [2016]

Includes bibliographical references and index.

ISBN: 978-0-9972230-0-2 | LCCN: 2016900831

Parent and teenager. Teenagers—Employment. Teenagers—Education. Experiential learning. Education—Evaluation. Mentoring. Teenagers—Family relationships. Adolescent psychology. Teenagers—Life skills guides.

HQ799.15 .H45 2016 | 649/.125—dc23

Eugene M. Helveston, MD, is available for speaking and consulting. To invite him to your organization, group, or school visit www.marlibarpress.com.

Manufactured in the United States of America
First Edition

Cover and text design by Mary Jo Zazueta (tothepointsolutions.com)

To my girls, Barbara, Martha, and Lisa

CONTENTS

Preface xi

Acknowledgments xv

Introduction xix

1   Getting Started. 1

2   The Inclusive Middle Class 9

3   The First Two Decades. 27

4   Necessary Life Skills 41

5   How Smart is Smart Enough? 57

6   The importance of High School. 67

7   Finishing the Second Decade 87

8   W-O-R-K 115

9   Cultivating Skills & Achieving Accomplishments . . 133

10   Parenting Styles 141

11   The Armed Services. .147

12 Take Advantage of Opportunity. 153

13 Find a Mentor. 159

14 The Major Leagues of Life 173

In Summary 179

Appendix A: My First Real Job 181

Appendix B: An Unorthodox Path
to Success. 187

Appendix C: Volunteer Work 189

Appendix D: Suitable Job Prospects. 191

Notes 193

About the Author 237

Index. 239

PREFACE

T HE SECOND DECADE IS FOR ADULTS WHO CARE ABOUT CHILDREN and want to do what they can to guide children to attain happiness and success in life: parents, grandparents, teachers, and mentors.

While it is universally agreed that a formal education in school is essential for success, working during the years between ten and twenty is one of the best experiences and character-building exercises your child can have during these formative years. Working at a meaningful job beyond the confines of family life adds valuable lessons to what is already being offered at home and in school. Summer vacations, Christmas and spring breaks, after school during the week, and weekends provide abundant time for most teens to work part-time. Social activities and extra-curricular programs, including athletics, are important, but not all-encompassing.

If you want to help a child, encourage him to find a suitable job to fill the void of free time.

Exposing youth to the benefits of work—earning money and gaining independence while taking on responsibility and embracing accountability—will inspire them to find their own jobs, which is a knack that can last a lifetime and will lead them to happiness and self-sufficiency.

I, along with many others who have written about the years between ten and twenty, call it the "Second Decade."[1] The term is capitalized because it is used here not only as a measure of time but also as a proper name for what is arguably the most significant ten-year period of a person's life, the decade that takes youth into adulthood.

The Second Decade encompasses three important and distinctly different juxtaposed times of life.

They are: those last years in primary school leading to the teens, including the "high-octane" event that is puberty (ages 10–13); earning a high school diploma (ages 14–17); and seriously preparing for life as an adult (ages 18–20).

Although lifestyles and society changes with each generation, the path to happiness and self-sufficiency remains a constant. Let me explain.

There are three components to every action: *what* you do, *how* you do it, and *why* you do it.

Since the time of your Second Decade, the what and the why have remained pretty much constant. Generally speaking, what we would like to do in life is be the best we can while earning our livelihood and being a productive member of society. The why is the value in being a self-reliant and useful citizen. In contrast, the how has changed; and it will continue to do so as technology and our everyday lives evolve.

I have had a front row vantage to this phenomenon, contrasting my childhood with the challenges that face youth and their parents today.

During my Second Decade, I went to school fulltime and also worked at a wide variety of jobs. Not all of these positions are still available today—but technology has created new opportunities for youth! The jobs I worked included:

▼ Assembly-line worker in an auto factory

▼ Babysitter

▼ Busboy

▼ Carpenter's helper/laborer

▼ Carpet layer's helper

▼ Cook's helper

▼ Delivery helper for a furniture store

▼ Gas station attendant

▼ Golf caddy

▼ Grounds-keeping and forestry

▼ Lawn care and snow shoveling

▼ Manager of a drive-through carwash

▼ Painting houses

▼ Paper route

▼ Saxophone player in a dance band

▼ Setting pins at a bowling alley

▼ Soda jerk

▼ Waiter

There is no question in my mind that the knowledge a youth gains from the regimented, academic experience and study in school, called *cognitive skills*, is essential. But to complete the road to success, which can be summarized as earning a sufficient amount of money that provides a productive and satisfying life, these cognitive skills need to be augmented by acquiring *savvy*, which has been called "executive skills," to better navigate in society; and *grit*, which is defined as courage, resolve, and strength of character.[2] I can think of no better way to acquire these two skills than by working at a job, while engaging people of all walks of life, during that impressionable time called the Second Decade.

The climate for education, jobs, and technology, is ever-changing; and it is easy to dwell on how much "better" it might have been in the "old days." The truth is that most things that we thought were so great then have been replaced by something that is even better today.

Together with your child, you must take full advantage of the opportunities at hand today. *You*, the caring adult, must be the agent of change. You cannot simply wait for good things to happen. You must take charge and do your part to help youth succeed.

Read on to learn how.

ACKNOWLEDGMENTS

THANK YOU TO MY GIRLS ON THE HOME FRONT. BARBARA, MY wife, has been cheerleader, critic, reader, and most of all the finest example of what a mother should be like.

Thank you to our daughters, Martha, and Lisa, who brought their generation to life and also produced four wonderful children, Henry, Charlie, Caroline, and Freddy; who, along with their friends, provided me insight into the world of Generation X and the Millennials.

Thank you to Shelly Buchanan, who offered encouragement and helped me begin to navigate the complicated publication process.

Thank you to Mary Jo Zazueta, my editor, who worked efficiently and with consummate skill to get my words just right. She transformed my manuscript from a memoir to the book you now hold in your hands—the book I was intending to write for the audience I hope to reach. Her help and encouragement have been indispensable.

My sincere appreciation to those Second Decade youth willing to work and grow from their own efforts and who shared their experiences: Caleb, Travance, Hannah, Joshua, Elina and her two smiling grade-schoolers, Tara, Zak, Mary, Allie, and Maggie.

Thank you to the countless grocery baggers, carwash attendants, stock boys (and girls), golf course attendants, young computer savants, fast-food workers, wait staff, and other youth who I never actually met but who taught me by their actions. They demonstrated pluck and talent; they are the hope for the future.

Thank you to Rick Strieff, football coach extraordinaire, for sharing his insight on high school students, both in the classroom and on the athletic field.

Thank you to the teachers who put up with me and especially those who inspired me during my twenty years from kindergarten through medical school.

Very special thanks to my adult mentors: Professor Arthur Louis Dunham, Florian H. Hiss, Malcolm A. McCannel, and Gunter K. von Noorden.

Lynda Smallwood has been a vital part of this project from its inception, as she was for several other of my publishing projects in the medical field. Without her work at editing; formatting; arranging; and yes, even rescuing, this book would have been impossible to complete.

The Community College Career Track by Thomas J. Snyder explained the value and challenges of this school choice, and Melissa Wolter provided insight into the student aid and scholarship process.

I want to give special thanks to my family: remembering my parents, Ann and Gene Helveston, and my older brother Tom and also my younger brothers, Ron and Joe.

I also want to thank those departed "bosses": "Uncle" Carl; Caesar the Caddy Master; my neighbors with snowy sidewalks and overgrown lawns; Bill Lake, the construction foreman with O. W. Burke; Mrs. Bacon from the Nu Sigma Nu kitchen; Dave, owner of Mac's Speedy Wash; Mr. Van Lockeren, owner of the furniture store; Walt and Marv, who trusted me with their Sunoco gas stations; Vic, the carpet layer; *The Detroit News*; *The Detroit Free Press*; *The Michigan Daily*; Benny Cucuzza and the team at the City of Detroit's Department of Parks and Recreation; Jimmy Hendricks, the orchestra leader; Red at the Phi Delta kitchen; Mr. Abby, who asked us to build a pond in the shape of the Great Lakes; Dave at the drugstore; Chrysler Briggs Body; Reska Spline; Wally and Ceil, owners of Woods Florist; and everyone else who gave me the opportunity to work for them during my Second Decade, thereby giving me invaluable and life-changing experiences.

INTRODUCTION

FROM THE BEGINNING OF CIVILIZATION UNTIL THE START OF THE Industrial Revolution in the mid-eighteenth century, there was little change in how children were treated. Boys born into working-class families toiled in the fields with their fathers or were hired out to neighbors. This group included all but the few who were born into wealthy families or the aristocracy.

Work, mostly agricultural, began at an early age, often before ten. Other boys, usually between ten and fourteen years old, were taken on as apprentices to learn a trade while working under a master. Girls performed light agricultural work and carried out the domestic duties of cooking, cleaning, and mending—general household chores—in their family's home or they too were hired out.

During most of the nineteenth century, the main focus for children was simply survival. The infant mortality rate was high and a child's chance of living until five years of age in the United States was on the order of 60 percent; this compares to a child having a 99 percent chance of living until five years of age today.[1]

In the years leading up to the Renaissance, children who lived beyond infancy were considered to be small adults. The church designated, with some provisions, age seven as the "age of reason."[2] Artwork from this period depicts baby Jesus and angels in religious paintings, but these were likely to be the only portrayals of infants who actually looked like infants.[3] Were families loath to record images of young children only to watch them die? In the 1600s, paintings by the Dutch Masters and others showed children of wealthy families and nobility attired in adult clothing with serious countenances and resembling older people. When the Barbizon School of Art began showing people working as peasants in the fields, children were not likely to be included.[4]

All of this changed during the Industrial Revolution. With the advent of machinery to carry out the heavy, repetitive, and dangerous functions of manufacture, it became clear that children could tend machines and, in some cases, because of their small size, do things more effectively than a larger and bulkier adult.[5] Additionally, children were paid less and could be more manageable than adults. So, for about 150 years, children as young as seven and through their teens, toiled in factories, mines, and fields, performing dangerous and monotonous activities at low pay, for as long as twelve hours a day, six days a week. Because of the pervasive nature of these practices, child labor was considered commonplace and expected.[6]

In contrast to there being few images of children from the eighteenth century and earlier, there are many photographs from the nineteenth century that show young children working in mills, mines, and factories while doing heavy and sometimes hazardous work. In these images, children often posed as adults with a jaunty tilt to their hat while smoking a stogie.[7]

By the beginning of the twentieth century, the inherent danger and inappropriateness of having children do this kind of work was recognized. This led to laws limiting the age of employment, as well as the hours and type of work that could be done by children. In 1820, children under fifteen made up 23 percent of the manufacturing labor force in the industrialized northeast.

On average, their pay was just 7 percent of that earned by an adult.[8]

After new child labor laws were enacted in the late nineteenth and early twentieth centuries, child labor was dramatically reduced. The extra "free time" children had, and increased awareness of the value of a formal education for all, led to the establishment of public high schools in the United States. By 1910, nearly 20 percent of children aged fifteen to eighteen attended high school, and 10 percent graduated. The number of high school graduates increased steadily over the century, with around 80 percent graduating today.[9]

Starting with child labor laws, and continuing with changes in manufacturing, along with the outsourcing of many jobs overseas, employment opportunities for teenagers in these areas have been significantly reduced—down nearly 25 percent since the 1950s.[10] Why is this? Is there less meaningful work for a young person today?

Given the scope of our global society led by advances in technology, the answer is a resounding no. There are more options, but the "more" is likely to include activities other than physical labor; and finding work requires planning, thought, and preparation. In this "different" world, meaningful work might even include volunteer activities that are unpaid but nonetheless offer important lessons in preparing children for life as productive and self-sufficient adults.

In this sea of change, there remain immutable factors. These start with the essential role of family and adult mentors. (The word *family* appears frequently in this book. Realize, I use it to mean the nuclear family [father, mother, and children], extended family [grandparents, aunts and uncles, and cousins]; and any adult who provides stable, loving support [teacher, counselor, family friend, etc.]).

Sadly, many children lack the presence of a responsible parent, guardian, mentor, or other adult in their lives. And even when parents are available, eager, and willing to help their children, they might lack the objectivity necessary to prepare their child for the world outside the home. For parents today, the process of guiding children through what, at times, can be characterized as the minefield of the Second Decade, could be more challenging than ever.

As you face decisions, you aren't automatically endowed with the right answers. Finding the right high school for a child takes work on the part of a conscientious parent. (See ch. 6) After high school, there are two basic choices for youth: work or more education. Two thirds of high school graduates elect more education,[11] with about one third of them choosing to attend a community college. These institutions, which number 2,000 in the U.S., offer vocational training, making it possible for a youth to obtain a marketable skill in as little as nine months. Other community college students earn an associate degree in two years and either get a fulltime job or transfer to a four-year college to earn a bachelor's degree.

Any youth called on to navigate the maze that is the educational system, beginning with high school, needs adult help. This can be from the family, or from school counselors, or others—but help is needed!

Also necessary is a strong desire to succeed on the part of the youth, and an understanding of the adult society they are entering, and realistic goals with plans on how to achieve them.

This book addresses the challenges today's youth and the adults who guide them face during the important Second Decade. I discuss the physical and psychological changes children experience during this time frame; as well as the responsibilities of and opportunities for parents and mentors to help children succeed. Although there is no foolproof formula that meets every child's needs and circumstances, the information in this book works.

The Second Decade is based on my experiences and observations of generations. It is intended to encourage and inform parents as they guide their children. There are also some sections adults should share with children about the challenges ahead and the solutions available. Solutions are not described in terms of major societal concepts, government edicts, or entitlement programs. Solutions are based on actions that can be carried out by anyone:

▼ Plan ahead for a quality education pursued with an eye on the future.

▼ Learn life lessons and useful skills from the work you perform and the people you meet.

▼ Seek advice and inspiration from mentors throughout your life.

▼ Recognize that nothing is accomplished without time and effort.

▼ Pursue honest and productive work.

This book is not about economics or politics, nor is it simply another self-help book on parenting. What follows is an argument about the important role of work, attitude, and opportunity in attaining a place in what I call the *inclusive middle class*. It is about youth getting the best education they can. It is about having children work at a job to gain skills and to earn money while building on what they are learning in school.

The Second Decade offers a game plan for navigating two of the most important challenges facing today's youth: gaining academic skills through a quality education at school, and acquiring practical skills learned by working at a job.

Let's get started.

THE SECOND DECADE

1

GETTING STARTED

"The only place success comes
before work is in the dictionary."
VINCE LOMBARDI

B ETWEEN THE AGES OF TEN AND TWENTY, CHILDREN CHART
the course that will profoundly influence the rest of
their lives. This Second Decade can be thought of as a
launching pad. It is when children are ready to take on more
responsibility for their lives while making important decisions
that have far-reaching and everlasting consequences. In these
years, a parent's relationship with his child changes from one
of nearly complete authority to one of guidance, bordering on
partnership.[1]

The Second Decade starts with most children pursuing
studies in the fifth grade. From this rather common beginning,
unfolds a wide spectrum of possible endings. Where will the
twenty-year-old find him or herself?

As a parent, you should be aware of the five most important
"checkpoints" in the life of children as they navigate their usually turbulent and always crucial Second Decade.

These checkpoints are:

1. *Family.* At age ten, your child is dependent on family for most things, but as the years progress, he will learn, mature, and grow; thereby becoming more independent. The nature of the parent-child relationship changes as children gain more autonomy, but the depth of your commitment as a parent should remain solid. Children will make more of their own decisions but family should be there with them.

2. The *friendships* children make during this period can become lifelong relationships. Encourage your child to choose his friends well and be selective. Peer pressure is a strong force in the Second Decade.

3. Being successful at *school* and earning a high school diploma is the most important goal your child can accomplish. Although this diploma does not guarantee success, it promises opportunity. Being a high school dropout takes away this promise and the lack of a high school diploma is one of the most reliable predictors of a person failing to achieve success.

4. *Activities* outside of school, like sports, clubs, volunteering, etc. are important, but not to the exclusion of meaningful work at a paying job. (In a few select cases, an elite athlete or a youth with a special talent will be so involved in that activity, which can lead to a life's work, there is no time for a job.)

5. *Household chores* done as part of a family unit are important and should be expected of any child. *Work* done outside of the home is more important and is an essential ingredient to personal growth for a meaningful Second Decade.[2]

After working for forty years as a pediatric ophthalmologist, having three brothers, raising two children, and observing four grandchildren and their numerous peers, I am convinced that the fuel for the fire that produces success in life is: preparation, attitude, character, and hard work. I believe the spark that ignites the desire and aptitude for hard work takes hold during the Second Decade. I also believe the American dream for a better life remains alive and is attainable for those who are willing to work for it.

As parents and grandparents, it is our role and obligation to offer guidance to children as they take the steps that will lead them to a happy and successful adulthood. The ten short years of the Second Decade are critical in laying the foundation for the edifice children will create as self-sufficient adults. I believe the experiences obtained during this period can be the most important predictor of success later in life, which is why it deserves to be called the *formative decade*.

While there will always be late bloomers, your child cannot take the chance of seriously underachieving in his Second Decade. If children fail to take advantage of these years, there is no convenient or readily available do-over. There is even a risk they might never recover. The Second Decade is when youth should develop the skills and attitudes that prepare them for life's long-haul adventure. And they need our help. (See ch. 9)

Moreover, all of this development is happening as a child experiences the kaleidoscope of change, with new things happening almost every day. Remember, things that might seem routine for adults are oftentimes experienced by children as firsts.

Events occurring for the *first time* for our children take place on a blank canvas and can have an enduring effect. As a parent, you can't shield your child from every bad experience, but you can and should guide your child with care.

For example, I saw my first dead person at age five. I was in the backseat of the car one evening when my mother pulled into a gas station. It was cold outside. The attendant, a young man, came out of the station and, with a hop, sailed over a well-dressed, middle-aged man who was sprawled on the ground just outside the door. My mother quietly told the attendant that the man needed attention, got out of the car for a minute, and came back without getting any gas or saying anything to me about the incident. Later she told me the man was dead of an apparent heart attack. My mother had elected not to burden me at that time with the realities of death.

As a child's Second Decade progresses, he will spend more time away from home without close adult supervision. More time away from the immediate family introduces a peer group and even older individuals that will expand to include people who are not so tightly aligned. This wider group of associates will be encountered at church; school; after-school activities, including sports and clubs; travel; and, importantly, a variety of jobs.

A significant feature of this growing network is that it is likely to include an ever-increasing number of people who come from different backgrounds.

Many things I learned from and experienced dealing with adults other than my parents during my Second Decade, starting with my first paid job, have remained with me (see appendix A). Sometimes it is as if these events are emblazoned on a large movie screen in front of me; they are alive and persist as significant and indelible influences in my life. In this aspect, I am not alone.

Disappointments, frustrations, and embarrassments during the Second Decade might persist in some form because they occurred when there was no other significant competition or any reassurance based on experience to mitigate these momentous events. They were our first big disappointments and they were real, or they were our first real pleasures and they are remembered with joy. It is only after gaining more life experience that we learn no matter how bad things seem at any given moment, life will go on and we will survive to live another day.

In time, some of these stories of early disappointment are the ones we are most likely to share with our children, or our children with their children, softened with time and likely to be accompanied with a good laugh.

Teach your child how to use her time in the Second Decade productively. Help her make the most of her successes and to learn from, but not be burdened or intimidated by, any failures.

For your child, these years between ten and twenty are the stepping stones to her future. Help her use them wisely.

The *Declaration of Independence* states:[3]

"We hold these truths to be self-evident, that all men are created equal, that they are endowed by their Creator with certain unalienable Rights that among these are Life, Liberty and the pursuit of Happiness."

This *Declaration* means that neither circumstance of birth, title assumed, nor decree makes one person inherently better than another. It can be argued that by being equal, we are born free of having our aspirations limited by statute or caste or of being placed in a lesser status than anyone else born in our country.

However, once a person comes into being, this concept of equality is challenged by the circumstances of one's birth; which could include privilege and wealth or challenging circumstances. We are equal in that we are not limited by statute or law, but physical limitations, innate abilities, and environment do influence the path each child is provided.

The status of birth isn't anything other than luck.

It is undeniable that even when some people work hard and do the right things, their ability to achieve the life they want is made more difficult by the environment they were born into. But, *difficult* does not mean *impossible*!

Without a doubt, some people have a better start than others.

The one thing we all have going for us, however, is that there are no hard-and-fast limits as to what a citizen can accomplish in the United States. Achieving success might take a great deal of effort and even require some luck, but it is never denied by rule of law.

It is up to each individual to take advantage of opportunity and manage adversity—which is why parents must teach these skills early and well to their children.

The silver spoon a child is born with, on the face of it, might be considered a positive; however, that is not always the case. Having too much too soon in life can deprive a child of the knowledge and satisfaction that comes from personal accomplishment. As with many things, a common ground between extremes is best. Regardless of finances, a supportive and stable home is one of the best things you can give your child.

I was raised in a blue-collar family. I never felt poor or put upon. All of us were expected to work. We knew people who had more possessions than us, but envy was not a prevailing attitude in our home. Sometimes we wondered about the wealthy and how they had obtained that financial status, but we never felt as though we were victims of inequality or that we were owed anything by those who had more. Whatever we absolutely had to have, we somehow acquired. Likewise, much we thought we couldn't live without but couldn't afford to buy, we got along without just fine.

My friends from high school, who were also raised in blue-collar families, did well. Including me, three became medical doctors, one a dentist, one a policeman, one entered business, and one had a lifelong career as an officer in the U.S. Air Force. Six out of seven graduated from college and four of us obtained professional degrees. None of our parents were college graduates—but my friends and I shared optimism. None of us felt constrained when it came to the freedom to make choices about how we would live. There were no imaginary lines we could not cross, no goal unattainable because of who we were or where we came from.

I believe these same opportunities remain today.

Agreed: life is not always fair.

I recognize that too many children lack the basic foundation of a stable home and need assistance from sources beyond their biological parents; however, your first obligation as a parent is to impart the best values you can in *your* children. After that, you can reach out to other youth who need support and encouragement.

First of all, though, do everything in your power to help your own child learn how to be self-reliant and self-support-ing. Realize there is no better way to do this than to help her find a meaningful job outside of the home. By doing this, you will introduce her to the "real world" at a time when she can learn from her experiences in a safe and controlled environment, learning lessons that will be with her for a lifetime.

Next, let's take a look at what it means to find a place in the inclusive middle class.

2

THE INCLUSIVE MIDDLE CLASS

"It is to the middle class we must look
for the safety of England."
WILLIAM MAKEPEACE THACKERAY

WHEN I WAS A KID LIVING IN A MIDDLE-CLASS FAMILY, I WAS able to start my work life at the age of nine. My first jobs were on a freelance basis and arranged informally. Like most of my pals, I worked just about every time the opportunity arose. The pay was usually whatever the customer felt the job I did was worth. Even if it was less than I thought I deserved, getting paid something was better than having no money at all!

At the start, I worked close to home in my neighborhood. The jobs included shoveling snow; mowing lawns; and when I was a bit older, delivering newspapers. For the girls I knew, and even for me sometimes, it was common to take a job as a babysitter. Unfortunately, most of my babysitting was caring for my two younger brothers while my mother sold ladies' and men's apparel door to door. No pay for me; it was just part of doing family chores.

What was life like for a middle-class kid like me? We mostly stayed on the move; riding bikes, walking, or taking a bus—our mode of transportation depended on the distance we travelled and how we felt that day. Having continuous sidewalks made it much easier for us to get around. There were sidewalks galore, alongside paved streets that filled a seemingly endless grid! This meant our neighborhood and the adjacent ones were limitless, at least within reason. We had the advantages of safety, mobility, and independence—which led naturally to opportunity. Our bikes were for serious transportation, not just play and exercise.

Life is different for youth today. They lack much of the independence made possible by the unfettered mobility I enjoyed and, to some extent, what my children enjoyed. Families that live in or near inner cities today, where there are sidewalks, might fear for the safety of their children because of traffic or, in some cases, because of concerns for personal safety. Sidewalks in today's affluent residential neighborhoods are likely to be limited to busy streets, and tend to be non-continuous. They are usable for walking the dog or a short stroll, but not for serious travel on foot or on a bike. Homes in many suburban settings today have lawns that extend to the street's edge, lack the canopy trees long a hallmark of the city, and the streets that curve through these sidewalk-free neighborhoods often end without warning in a cul-de-sac—security but also limiting.[1]

Does this lack of accessible mobility isolate today's youth? The answer is yes and no. Social media has come to the fore, making it possible for youth to get around virtually, using text messaging, Twitter, YouTube, Facebook, e-mail, a variety of apps, online games, and more. Today's youth are mobile but in a different way.

Instead of a central downtown with scattered and easily accessible small businesses in neighborhoods interconnected with sidewalks, today's communities have large shopping centers and malls that are safely accessed by bus, when service is available, or by auto, but not safely by bike or on foot. Mammoth parking lots and multilevel garages surround these commercial sites, making them essentially unapproachable for the pedestrian or biker.

Yes, lifestyles have changed over the last fifty years, but the importance of some things has endured. Foremost is the need to get the best formal education possible, and close behind is the importance of learning essential life skills by working at a job. The effort to succeed at attaining these two goals starts with having the right attitude. "Yes, I will do the things necessary to prepare myself for success."

The life most people would be satisfied attaining is a place in the middle class. The *middle class* can be defined by using guidelines of income and wealth. These measures are objective and the numbers are readily available.

The middle class can also be defined according to subjective measures, like a positive attitude, a feeling of satisfaction, and a sense of responsibility.

These characteristics are subjective and while you may be able to recognize them in a person or a family they can be difficult to measure.

The middle class is diverse—made up of people representing a wide range of incomes and lifestyles. Though it should not be measured exclusively in terms of dollars and cents, it is most often characterized that way. With more than 75 percent of the U.S. population considered middle class, both its numbers and its diversity make this segment of society important as well as socially and economically challenging.

The middle class is discussed frequently by economists, politicians, and sociologists.[2] But all too often, those talking about the middle class do so without clearly defining who they include in this category. Depending on who is talking, some in the middle class, mostly those who are in the top 10 percent of earners, are felt to be taking too much, others are the object of concern because they may be losing what they have, and some are pitied, or even denied respect, because they have too little.

The boundaries of the middle class are blurred by the behavior of those in it. This lack of clear demarcation happens when the subjective element of attitude overrules the objective elements of income and wealth. Those people considering themselves middle-class, in spite of having an income level that is extremely high or relatively low, do so more as a state of mind than on the "bottom line" of economics. Being in the middle class depends on how you think of yourself more than how others think of you or even how much money you have. (These issues are discussed in detail later in this chapter.)

The middle class receives lots of coverage in the media. A recurring theme is that something must be done for the people who are "victims of economic circumstances over which they have no control." In spite of this attention and loudly voiced concern, no societal solution has been forthcoming. When pressed during a recent U.S. presidential campaign, one of the candidates, quite accurately in my opinion, described the middle class as "more of a feeling than a statistic."[3]

Life in the middle class is not without challenge, but overall people in this social standing are satisfied and consider themselves to be in a good place.

They probably have an income around the median, are likely to be optimistic, and consider the glass half full. Individuals in this position are likely to garner little attention.

A segment of the middle class frequently discussed by politicians and economists are those who earn at a level below the median income, or possibly below their expectations, but above the arbitrarily determined level of poverty for the United States. They may have experienced a reduction in income, either on a relative basis (not keeping up with inflation), or they could have lost their job, relegating them to a lower rung, or they may be elderly or disabled, but still cling to their place in the middle

LIFE LESSONS

During my medical training, I was driving from Baltimore to Philadelphia to attend a symposium on dyslexia. My companion, Fernando, was studying medicine as a Pan-American scholar from Chile. He was bright, hardworking, pleasant to be with, and above all proud of his country. His wife's family had a successful manufacturing and distribution business, and Fernando's father was a physician. Both families had a solid social position in Chile. I suspect they were even considered rich.

After finishing his fellowship, Fernando was looking forward to beginning his career in Chile as an ophthalmologist. During the first two months we were co-fellows at the Institute, he never missed a chance to extol the virtues of his homeland and how eager he was to return. He wasn't bragging but was proud and satisfied.

During this two-hour ride, our conversation touched on the subject of life insurance. Fernando asked me how it worked. I was up to date on the subject because my father-in-law was a great believer in this product. (See ch. 13)

After a few minutes of my explanation, during which Fernando was quiet and seemed thoughtful, he said, "The thing I envy about Americans is that even an ordinary person can work hard, send money to a company like you describe, and expect to get the promised amount back thirty, forty, or even fifty years later." Then he added, "You seem to be happy and have confidence about the future!"

Fernando, no doubt in the upper class at home, pretty much summed up my concept of the inclusive middle class in the United States, a class that included me, my family, and most of my friends—all of whom were confident and many of whom were upwardly mobile.

class. Others may lack the skill to obtain a better paying job and are doing the best they can. As a group, these people are likely to be less satisfied and are sometimes described as victims. Many need help. For this segment, the glass is half empty, but they are not without help. According to Brad Plummer in the *Washington Post*, forty-nine percent of the population receives some type of government assistance.[4]

These varying classifications within the middle class are based primarily on income, which in turn depends mostly on the job a person has. This concept notwithstanding, people in the middle class, including those at the extreme levels of income and those in the middle range, have the opportunity to improve their lot. A spot in the middle class is not guaranteed, but the chance to improve one's place exists for those who work at it. Likewise, anyone in the middle class is potentially at risk of losing his place because of adversity including being unable to work.

The reality is there is no quick fix for the problems that face the segment of society living with lower income levels. Even with massive programs like the War on Poverty, their numbers have increased.[5] Although looking for such a solution is beyond the scope of this book, it is tempting to point out that, as is often the case with many of life's problems, the best fix is not cleaning up a mess but rather preventing it. In this case, the best way to attain a solid footing in the middle class is to get a good education and develop a sound work ethic during the Second Decade—and that is what this book *is* about!

According to the National Bureau of Economic Research, the reason that as many as 25 percent of the population falls below the arbitrary classification of middle class is lack of education. One third of the people in this country have no education beyond high school, and 13 percent (40 million) lack a high school diploma.[6] These are the people most likely to be at the low level of the middle class and below.

With many jobs shifting from manufacturing to technology,

those individual and families with low levels of education could be stuck where they are. This can be an incentive for those who are able to return to school; for example, taking vocational courses at a community college (See ch. 7) or doing the necessary work to get a GED, which is a high school diploma equivalent. (See ch. 6) Those who earn a GED or obtain job skills at a community college or other training program might be able to move away from this dependency and into the middle class on their own and then retain their place with consistent hard work.

The middle class is fluid and there remains the opportunity for anyone to work harder or land a better job seeking a larger share of the total economic "pie."

People who take no action to advance their education or improve their workplace skill set will most likely remain stuck in place.

For those who need help and have nowhere else to turn, assistance is available from the government in the form of unemployment benefits, food stamps, income tax credits, mortgage assistance, Medicaid, and more.

A problem that is discussed at the big-picture level of economics is that wealth in our country is already unevenly distributed, with the top 10 percent of the population having 85 percent of the wealth.[7] Even with this being true, a hallmark of our society is that everyone has a chance to move up. This upward mobility has traditionally been called "generational leap" (See ch. 7) with children doing better than their parents, who also did better than *their* parents.

But wait! Two problems—first, the point of diminishing return means there can't be a giant leap for every generation forever. Second, if that happened, the world would be way too full of "superstars." Things have to level off, and I have seen this clearly in my grandchildren's generation. When it comes to generational leap, it should be replaced with the admonition that all youth should simply do the very best they can. A good start is to get a solid education and to learn how to work effectively. The best time to start on this path is in the years between ten and twenty.

Let's look at the wide-ranging middle class metaphorically.

Joey was excited. He was going to his first NFL game with his dad. The game would be in the new stadium in the center of the city. Joey knew it had a movable dome that could be closed in bad weather. The sun was shining. The dome would be open today. Joey was all eyes and ears—the kind of fellow who noticed everything.

Outside the large stadium was a wide walkway. Lots of people milled around. Some people sat on the curb, facing away from the stadium; and a few were drinking out of a bottle wrapped in a brown paper bag. There was also a small group listening to the pre-game show on a portable radio held up to the ear of one of them. However, most of the people, like Joey and his dad, had their tickets out and were heading toward the entrance.

Once inside the stadium, Joey saw an immense ring of seats. Then he looked up and checked the large hole in the roof. "That hole is really cool!" Joey exclaimed. "It would be neat if I could see them close it."

"Not today," his dad said. "Let's enjoy the sunshine while we can."

"Wow!" said Joey. "I bet that roof cost a lot."

"Yes, it did," said his dad. "But don't worry, we are paying for it with the price of our tickets."

Joey was on to the next thing. "This place must hold thousands," Joey said. "Where are we sitting, Dad?"

"Just a few rows up from here."

His dad was referring to the level where they entered from the lobby, which was about twenty rows up from the field.

"My pals say sitting on the fifty-yard line is best," Joey said to his dad.

"Hey, don't complain," his dad replied. "The thirty-yard line isn't too bad. This is where the players' wives and girlfriends sit. It is also behind the home team's bench."

"Cool," was Joey's response.

When they sat down, Joey realized his dad had done a pretty good job with the seats. He could see the field clearly. He could read the players' numbers and even their names on the backs of their jerseys. Joey took a closer look at the seats below them that were closer to the field. He noticed they had a little more room between them and had cushions on the backs.

"I bet down there by the field they can hear the players smack each other," Joey said, but his dad didn't hear. Then he looked up and saw what looked like fifty rows of seats higher than his. At the top, it didn't look like the seats even had backs. They were bleachers, like the stands at his school's ball field.

Looking up a bit higher, Joey asked his dad, "What are those things way up there, around the top of the stadium, with glass in front?"

"Those are special seats called sky boxes. They cost a lot of money."

Finally, the game started and all conversation turned to the game.

On the way home, Joey's dad said, "Joey, you noticed a lot about the stadium besides the game."

"Oh, did I?" Joey said. "Like what?"

"Before I start, Joey, I want to ask you if you know what the middle class is," said his dad.

"Yeah, Dad. I heard my teacher say we were all middle-class, but I am not sure what she meant."

"Well, the things you asked about made me think that going to the stadium is a pretty good metaphor for what we call the middle class. And, don't worry about that big *word, it just means another, more picturesque way of saying something.*

"Remember those guys sitting on the curb outside the stadium?" said his dad. "They are poor folks, really poor people, and they could use our help. You noticed they gave up even trying to see the game, and some were even asking for money. And the men listening to the radio in a group, they were interested in the game and had enough money for a radio, but they couldn't afford a ticket. They probably all have a job of some kind or another but not enough money to spare to buy a ticket to see the game. Sometimes people give them a spare ticket. I gave a couple away free last year, and when I was a kid like you, a man gave me a fifty-yard line seat free at the stadium in the town where I grew up. That day I didn't have to sit in the bleachers that cost seventy-five cents.

"All of those people with us inside the stadium had at least enough money to see the game in person. But some had more money to spend, or at least were willing to spend, and they were the ones who sat closer to the field or on the fif-ty-yard line. Others who had less money to spend sat farther up in that place you called the bleachers. When you think about it, the stadium looked a little bit like what your teacher called the middle class. Where each of us sat was a pretty accurate measure of how much money we had to spend on something like going to the game. The important thing is that we could all see the game and cheer when our team made a touchdown. Some of the people who were closer to the field and on the fifty-yard line might have seen part of the game better than us, and we saw the game better than the people in the bleachers, but the important thing is that we all saw the game. Besides, the hot dogs tasted the same to all of us, that's for sure.

"We could change our seats if we wanted to, but it would cost more to move closer to the field. If we wanted to save

money or didn't have as much to spend next year, we could buy a less expensive seat and still see the game. My point is that inside the stadium, there are lots of choices and levels, and lots of ways things get done."

Joey was getting into the conversation. "What about the people in the sky boxes?"

"Good question, Joey! Those people paid a lot of money to sit there. Do you remember Mr. Gale, the man who owns the dealership where we bought our car? He is a wealthy man who worked hard to build five or six car dealerships. He has lots of money and I heard that he has one of those suites—he can afford it!

"Anyway, even in the sky boxes, the hot dogs and sodas tasted like they did for the rest of us, but they also had wings, and cheese balls, and other fancy stuff that cost more. There are televisions in the sky boxes, to help them see the game and the replays, but you know, we saw the game as well as they did—and maybe even better. Isn't that a hoot! Those sky boxes are pretty nice for them ... but remember, we saw the same game from our seats as they did from up there."

Joey looked at his dad. "That was a great game. I wish we would have won."

At that they were home and the conversation ended as Joey ran into the house, excited to tell his mother about the game.

The reality is that most Americans, about 75 percent, who live below the pinnacles of wealth and above the depths of poverty, consider themselves in the middle class. The greater portion of these people form a group that I call the *inclusive middle class*. This group includes a diverse population that lives anywhere from slightly above the income level that defines poverty to earners in the top 10 percent and higher.

Probably the most important characteristic of the inclusive middle class is the combination of the following: a solid work ethic; formal education, including at least a high school diploma but most likely beyond; and underlying confidence combined with some healthy optimism.

Just about everybody who claims a place in the middle class must work to earn money in order to maintain or improve their status.

Unfortunately, for a variety of reasons, not everyone who works can claim a place in the middle class. Those who comprise the "working poor" might not qualify for a job that pays a wage sufficient for their needs or they have a good job but are strapped with financial obligations beyond their earning power.

Whatever the level, healthy characteristics of people in the middle class include: a positive outlook for the future, appreciation of the importance of a formal education, and a willingness to work, even accomplishing a "generational leap," especially for those at the lower end.

Maintaining status or taking a small step forward might be a goal for those already solidly situated in the middle class, but that will take effort too.

The inclusive middle class can be defined with some confidence at the lower end when inclusion is related solely to income; that is, above the arbitrarily determined poverty level. So I'll start by describing what the middle class is *not* when it comes to income.

The inclusive middle class excludes those near or below the poverty level of approximately $12,000 annual income for an individual and in larger increments depending on the number in the family; for example, $24,250, for a family of four. [8] A common characteristic of those low-income individuals failing to qualify as middle-class is that they may only qualify for a job requiring the lowest skill level which in turn offers low pay. They can be the working poor or they may have no job at all. They are likely to be people with low levels of formal education, and those who depend on government largess. These people are often discouraged and may be in despair about their station in life. Lacking confidence and sufficient job-related skills, they could believe they have little or no hope for a better future. Income and attitude are usually closely related at this lower level.

The upper level of the middle class is more difficult to identify. What do you call people who are just above the income level of middle class—wealthy, rich, upper class, privileged, empowered, important, etc.? I am not comfortable with any of these labels and will explain. If those exceeding the income level of the upper border of the middle class are called "upper class," it suggests a qualitative value not just quantitative wealth. Upper class sounds too much like royalty and we got rid of that a long time ago! Likewise, the term "lower class" carries with it an unacceptable stigma. Better terms such as "lower income," "below the middle class," "working poor," and even "below poverty level" are not great but are less pejorative.

The difference between a middle-class high earner and someone who considers himself in the upper class can be blurred by attitude. For example, an otherwise ordinary fellow can be smart, work hard, have an income near the top 2 percent ($250,000) or 1 percent ($388,000), and have many possessions usually associated with those who are rich, but retain an attitude and assume a behavior that clearly identifies him as part of the middle class. This person works for a living, stops earning money if he stops working, probably comes from a clearly middle-class family, and feels both proud and lucky to be where he is now. The great middle ground between the arbitrarily determined poor and rich, according to income, attitude, or aura contains most Americans and it is the inclusive middle class.

People on the cusp, at the lower level of the middle class, might have a high school diploma, trade school certificate, or on-the-job training. They might be a family with two parents in the home or be headed by a hardworking and stressed single parent. The breadwinner(s) are employed with reasonable assurance of retaining their jobs. In families with two parents working, childcare costs can be a drain on the family income, but this is considered worth the expense by those who engage in this practice.[10] For this and a variety of economic and social reasons, those in the lower end of the middle class might have reasons for concern about the future, but they still maintain a level of confidence that keeps them going.

The median household income in the United States is around $50,000. Below this number, half make $25,000 or less and half

Regardless of income level, attitude remains a common denominator of the middle class. Kim Peterson, of *MSN Money*, agrees that the middle class may be a state of mind. She writes: "It is [the middle class] average Americans, not the ones at the ideological or economic fringes [who make up the bulk of our population]. The ones who drive their kids to band practice, who slog through long workdays, cook at home, and don't have time for much else." She lists the following nine characteristics as a way to determine if you are in the middle class:[9]

▼ You make between $40,000 and $100,000 (or more) a year, but have likely exceeded the income level of your parents, and identify with the middle class.
▼ You shop at Target and Costco [but still visit Sam's and Walmart from time to time]
▼ You are saving for your kids' college tuition.
▼ You take annual vacations.
▼ You own (or are purchasing) your home.
▼ You have a secure job.
▼ You have health insurance.
▼ The closer you are to the bottom, the more likely you will lean Democratic.
▼ You are saving for your retirement.

make between \$25,000 and \$50,000. Above the median, the spread of income level is greater. Slightly more than half make between \$50,000 and \$100,000 and slightly less than half make between \$100,000 and \$200,000 or more. This means that the household income level below the median, that has half of the population, is in a range of \$50,000 and those above the median are in a much broader range of at least \$150,000 but with no stipulated upper limit.

Within the middle class, the most reliable predictor of an individual's income is the level of formal education completed. (See ch. 7) The most reliable way of moving up in the middle class is to obtain more education. To be sure, this is not the only way, but a person is taking a big chance bucking this trend. To this stipulation could be added the caveat: there is a no more predictable way to take advantage of the education you worked so hard to achieve than to get a good job, one that you enjoy doing, and earn enough money to live a satisfying life.

No one is stuck in place.

Each person is free to improve his position in society; and while doing so, even pull others up, like the family he grew up with or the new family he forms. Although there can be strength in the family (team) unit, ultimately a child's level of success depends on how he does as an individual—which is why it is critical for adults to encourage children to accomplish the two most reliable predictors of success and happiness, things that a child must eventually do on his own: get an education and pursue meaningful work.

Right here let us agree that money alone is not sufficient to make a person happy.

To name just a few, there are also family, friends, self-esteem, and good health. At the same time, a lack of money and the pressures that strained finances put on a person and family can be crippling, to the point where a person and his family are robbed of a place in the middle class, not only financially but also when it comes to the all-important feelings of confidence and optimism.

There is nothing in the *U.S. Constitution* or our laws stating we must stay in the station where we were born or finish where we started. We can move along the statistical curve and make whatever of ourselves we have the will, persistence, and talent to accomplish.

HARD WORK AND THE MIDDLE CLASS

Joe was a husband, a father, a grandfather, a friend, and an employee who was like family to me. He never made a lot of money but was always willing to work and thus, always steadily employed. In addition to his regular job on the night shift, Joe regularly found time to do yardwork, handyman chores, and whatever else he could to help someone.

I never heard Joe complain about anything but the weather. He didn't envy people who had more nor did he disparage those who had less money or ambition. He worked so hard, one morning he perforated a stomach ulcer while shoveling dirt to grade a lawn. (He never complained to the person who put him on the job—me!) Another time, he essentially died from electrocution at his regular job, but survived to go back to work for more than a decade.

Joe believed in a hand up in favor of a handout. He and his wife, Bonnie, formed a team that provided for their two children and, when needed, for their grandchildren.

Although Joe's income might never have technically qualified him as being more than barely in the middle class, his work ethic, attitude, self-reliance, and dependability put him as high in the middle class as anyone I ever met.

Joe was an inspiration and exemplified what America is all about.

But the future offers a two-way street. A position attained is never guaranteed. A person can accomplish more or accomplish less. Success can be in the form of financial security or with attainment of other worthwhile goals. In either case, it takes effort to keep and possibly improve one's place in society.

Figures for poverty that include $12,000 for an individual and $24,500 annual income for a family of four are derived from wages earned and do not include non-cash entitlements. According to U.S. Department of Labor statistics, these could be as much as $18,000 per year. (Op.cit. 4, 7) Nearly 15 percent of the U.S. population is said to live in statistical poverty, but receive significant aid mostly for life's essentials that most of the population is likely to take for granted.

The current federal minimum wage is $7.25 an hour, which would allow an individual to earn about $15,000 annually—just above the poverty level. But some states have increased their minimum wage.[11] And one large retailer recently increased its minimum wage for most of its workers to $10.00 an hour, for an annual salary of nearly $21,000 a year for a fulltime employee. However to avoid certain requirements dealing with healthcare and other benefits, many employers limit employees to thirty hours of work a week.

With your guidance, children will be better able to make decisions, enabling them to find a more favorable place in the inclusive middle class or beyond. There are many things you and your children can control and take advantage of now; especially a formal education (See ch. 5 and 6) and a meaningful job (See ch. 8) that teaches life lessons and provides income.

Wealth can be a nice comfort, but there are no guarantees. Even great wealth can be lost and that is an unpleasant way to enter the inclusive middle class! This phenomenon has been described as "going from shirt sleeves to shirt sleeves," a fate that befell the Stroh family of Detroit. Kerry Dolan wrote of their misfortune in *Forbes* magazine.[12]

"The Stroh Brewery as a family business or even a collective financial entity has [sic] essentially ceased to exist. The company has been sold for parts. The trust funds have doled out their last pennies to shareholders. The last remaining family entity owns a half-empty office building in Detroit. While there was enough cash flowing for enough years that the fifth generation still seems pretty comfortable, the Stroh family looks destined to go shirtsleeves-to-shirtsleeves in six generations. This family started modestly with Bernhard Stroh in 1850. The Stroh family owned it all, a fortune that (in the 1980s) FORBES then calculated was worth at least $700 million. Just by matching the S&P 500, the family would currently be worth about $9 billion."

Next, a look at the first two decades of life—where it begins in lockstep with others and culminates in unique, individual choices and paths.

3

THE FIRST TWO DECADES

"Parents can only give good advice or put them on
the right paths, but the final forming of a person's
character lies in their own hands."
ANNE FRANK

ADULTS WHO COMPARE THEIR CHILDHOODS WITH THOSE OF young people today will see many differences. Because so much of what is different can be difficult for parents to understand, like texting instead of having a phone conversation, it is tempting to conclude today's youth face tougher challenges—but is this really so? The truth is that what is challenging for adults is the norm for our youth. New technology and different lifestyles have been the rule for past generations and will be for generations to come.

Social and economic conditions are constantly evolving, and it should be no surprise that our children and grandchildren face lifestyles and choices that are unlike what we experienced. Like us, our children will cope. People always have and always will.

However, in this sea of change, life does have *constants*. One is the need for parents to do all they can to support and guide their children. This includes helping youth achieve the most they can today while looking ahead and preparing for the years to come.

There is no time than during the formative years of the first two decades when it is more important for effective and informed parental involvement.

When I was growing up, having a job was important to me. That's how I am wired. I have been employed almost nonstop since I was ten years old. I found it rewarding to meet and interact with people and to accept the challenges of different jobs; and, of course, I appreciated being paid for the work I did. This pay could be monetary or simply the satisfaction that comes with doing something well and useful. My approach to work might not be suited for everybody, but I believe all children should have the benefit of doing some meaningful work in their formative years.

High school, including sports; college; social activities; and work, completed the list of activities I pursued during the Second Decade. I was a Cub Scout briefly at ten years old; mostly because my friends were and my mother agreed to be a den mother. At twelve, it was time for me to become a Boy Scout—which I enjoyed for two years while we dismantled and rebuilt our Boy Scout cabin on the Clinton River. When this project was completed, scouting became less interesting for me. I realized that without the physical activity and labor leading to accomplishment, I wasn't getting much out of being a Boy Scout; so I ended my scouting career.

As it is for most kids, my first ten years "set the stage" for the performance of a lifetime—the Second Decade. By age ten, all of the props are in place and the stage is ready—assembled with care under the close supervision of parents and other adults. The Second Decade is the time for children to practice their lines and polish their performances in preparation for opening night: adulthood. The Second Decade is when youth expand their contacts, hone their skills, define their attitude, and experience physical maturation—all culminating in exponential social growth.

Let's start at the beginning …

All humans are born with an innate level of intelligence and physical and behavioral traits that are determined by the DNA supplied by their biological parents. Also the circumstances of the family in which youth are raised plays a significant role in their future success. Thus, even though Americans are endowed with equal rights under the law, a child's chance of taking full advantage of this promise can be profoundly affected by the circumstances of his birth and childhood.

Parents' economic status, education level, and nurturing skills; along with other characteristics of family life, influence the actions and lives of their children. This is especially true when it comes to the quality of education a child receives in school and the type of social training they receive at home. All of these factors are intertwined and remain important when it comes to a child being able to make the right choices and remain focused on his future.[1]

A child born into a stable and loving family has a better chance to learn, thrive, and mature, while gaining important life skills, compared to a child who lacks this foundation.[2]

A child typically spends most of his time being closely supervised at home until the start of primary school, which used to be kindergarten at age five. Today an increasing number of children are entering pre-school as young as three years of age.[3] Recognizing the value of pre-kindergarten, some parents and governments are now making this educational opportunity available to most, if not all children in their communities.[4]

For many other children, the first time away from home and parental supervision is when they are taken to daycare. Daycare differs from pre-kindergarten in that it can start with much younger children, including infants, and is primarily custodial or play-based.[5] Very early daycare can result in an unavoidable tradeoff between having enough money to sustain the family and potential harm from separating a parent from an infant or toddler for long periods.

The first decade, continuing in primary school to the fifth grade, provides a narrow and prescribed experience that, for most children and their families, is more alike than different. This experience can vary in quality and quantity, but the intent and parameters remain the same.

By the end of the first decade, children have in common an array of basic skills attained in school; as well as thoughts,

---

In February 2011, the Washington State Department of Social and Health Services described ten-year-olds as:[6]

▼ Rough and tumble (especially boys)

▼ Curious

▼ Capable of abstract thinking and reasoning

▼ Trustworthy (at least capable of being so)

▼ Having a conscience

▼ Knows right from wrong

▼ Enjoys team sports/games

▼ Having increased body control and strength

▼ Able to manage complicated and work-related tasks

▼ Displays individuality

▼ Able to read, write, and use a computer, tablet, and smart phones

▼ Able to function in groups (mostly same-gender)

▼ Establishing their independence

▼ May have some behavior problems

---

habits, characteristics, and beliefs, many of which were acquired at home. By age ten, a child has grown from total dependency as an infant to having acquired a set of life skills: academic (reading, writing, math, science, etc.) and social (communication, hygiene, manners, etc.). These skills are the foundation for appropriate behavior in a child, including the ability to deal with new people and novel experiences beyond the familiar surroundings of home.

The first decade witnesses most of a child's physical growth and early socialization. This physical and social growth, along with academic attainments from six years of primary school education, provides a more or less common product in our society: a ten-year-old ready for the exciting ride that is the Second Decade.

By age ten, a child's aggregated physical, intellectual, and psychological potential is bursting at the seams, poised to be passed onto that youth on the brink of adolescence. The baton is passed to that mostly awkward, but eager, boy or girl about to begin the Second Decade, those ten eventful years that see a child hurtling toward adulthood.

More than any other time in life, the crucial Second Decade holds the key to your child's future.

At this age, children encounter myriad opportunities and countless challenges and pitfalls. How they react to and deal with these events can influence the rest of their lives. How children behave and the choices they make during their teen years are critical.

The years from ten to twenty abound with change. Youth have countless opportunities to learn and develop skills that will be with them for life. The children who benefit most during this period are those who look for, recognize, and take advantage of all that is available.

The Second Decade can be divided into three distinct parts:

From **ten to thirteen**, puberty is the big event. Physically, children are no longer "little kids" and socially each is becoming his or her own person. They are starting to observe and interact with life beyond the scope of their parents and immediate family.

At this age, children, mostly under some adult supervision, begin to explore the world outside of the home. New activities tend to be approached with a level of caution by children and privileges are usually granted to children by parents when earned. Youth who deserve these privileges may be given more freedom, and with this freedom they take on more responsibility while learning about life. More is expected of them.

By the age of thirteen, nearly all children will have reached that unique rite of passage—puberty. In doing so, they confront their parents with those special, if sometimes tumultuous, teenage years; a time filled with obvious changes in how children look and even more in how they feel. Changes in your child's size and shape are significant, but even more important is how your child's body and mind function as they assume a new outlook on life. In short, children are becoming young men and women. The game has changed! Richard Lerner explains:

> "... although the perinatal period exceeds adolescence as an ontogenic (developmental) stage of rapid physical and physiologic growth, the years from approximately ten to twenty ... include the considerable physical and physiologic changes associated with puberty ... a time when the interdependency of biology and context development is readily apparent."[7]

Morphological changes, characterized by increased physical stature and muscle development, proceed on a continuum that slows down and culminates in the Second Decade. Puberty is a watershed event, an explosion that changes everything. This complexity of the growing and maturing child is emphasized by E. J. Susman and A. Rogel:

"There are said to be over 70 trillion potential human gen-
otypes and each of them may be coupled across life with
an even larger set of life courses, trajectories, and social
experiences."[8]

In other words, no two children are the same. As children
mature and experience things that are unique to them, the
changes they undergo only multiply. Nobody else has dealt with
or has been exposed to *exactly* what your child has. Stay alert. As
a parent, you have an even greater responsibility now that the
options for your child have expanded. But—this parenting role
in the Second Decade is to counsel and guide rather than rule
and direct—not always an easy task!

From **fourteen to seventeen**, a great deal happens in a
child's life; but none is more critical than graduating high school
and earning a diploma. (See ch. 6) By this time, your child should
also have had one or more jobs outside of the home and been
engaged in some combination of extracurricular activities, such
as sports, a school club, volunteering, a civic group, etc.

Another defining milestone in this segment of a child's
Second Decade occurs when she is eligible to receive a driver's
license. This event is likely to be consummated in the first hours
or days after she meets the minimum age requirement, usually
sixteen, and after she passes a written and practical driving test.
This achievement is probably the best example that teenagers
can get the job done (on time) when they want to.

The privilege of driving a car is a rite of passage that brings
with it new responsibility. Most youth meet this successfully,
but a few, tragically, do not. Driving a car requires maturity and
responsibility.

Between **eighteen and twenty**, your child begins a new
and different phase of life. During these years, a child graduates
high school, becomes eligible to vote, and can enlist in the armed
services without parental consent.

Graduating from high school can be compared to the cork coming out of a champagne bottle. It can happen in an ordered way, under control, or it can be chaotic. Whatever happens, graduation is a crucial milestone. Life moves forward and change is happening fast.

It is now time for young people to embark on a path that supports the goals they have for life as an adult, which requires self-motivation. A paradox is presented to the eighteen- to twenty-year-old: now *free* from the more-or-less charted course through high school, he is *shackled* with the responsibility to make decisions on his own, without a parent or someone in authority telling him what to do.

It is reasonable to say that what a young adult does in this two-year period portends the life he is likely to pursue.

Some in this age group will decide to marry, but according to Pew Social and Psychological Research Trends, youth of today are "in no rush to marry" with the average age now for men marrying being twenty-eight and for women it is twenty-seven.[9]

Two thirds of youth enter college after high school and, for the first time, most will live at least part of the year away from home, on their own. Youth who complete high school but do not go to college or seek further education, such as an apprenticeship or a vocational skill at a community college, will be expected to work. This entry-level job is likely to be a learning experience and the first of many jobs a person will have throughout life.

For those who dropped out of high school, looking for a job will be a sobering experience. Applicants will discover that a high school diploma is expected in most cases, even for an entry-level position. Moreover, in cases where an employer has a choice, a high school graduate is likely to be selected over a dropout.

A few in this age group will become single parents. When

this happens, responsibility is typically thrust on the female, who will usually live a life of hardship, need, and frustration.

It is difficult to imagine a more challenging way to complete the Second Decade than lacking a high school diploma or having a child to raise alone—unless it would be both simultaneously. Young people in this state need help, which might come from a

---

While each child is unique, the following is a list of events that typically occur between the ages of ten and twenty:[10]

▼ Body weight doubles

▼ Height increases by nearly a third

▼ Puberty (along with its physical, psychological, and emotional changes)

▼ Greater independence is achieved with less time spent at home

▼ Mobility and unsupervised activities increase

▼ Circle of friends expands

▼ Increased interaction with adults—teachers, employers, mentors, etc.

▼ Sets goals and makes plans for the future

▼ Graduates from high school

▼ Pursues education or training beyond high school

▼ Obtains a driver's license

▼ Can enter the workforce

▼ Can enlist in the armed forces

▼ Experiences increased peer pressure (tobacco, alcohol, drugs, sex, etc.)

▼ Obtains the right to vote

▼ May get married

▼ May have a child with or without marriage

---

family member, an employer, a social agency, or simply from the person's own grit.

It is essential that youth build toward a future that will find them gaining independence while pursuing a happy and productive life. At eighteen and beyond, children are more likely go to their parents for advice and encouragement—on their terms—and not ask for permission.

A potentially life-altering challenge that occurs during the Second Decade is the social and peer pressure of alcohol, tobacco, drugs, and sex.

Remarkably, even kids in elementary and middle school are exposed; so it is up to parents, teachers, and other adults to make youth aware of the seriousness of these activities as well as the potential dire consequences.

Falsely glamorized examples of risqué lifestyles pervade the media and entertainment our children are exposed to—and the Internet makes it available 24/7. The best you, as a parent, can do is to tell your children what is safe and what to avoid, and then show them how it can be done by living a lifestyle that provides a healthy example.

There is no way for a young person to avoid exposure to these temptations completely. To deal with the harmful lifestyle issues they face, youth must develop their own coping mechanisms. This can be done with the support and guidance from parents and other adults, but the challenge of dealing with drugs, in particular, is mostly on the youth.

Drugs are far easier to obtain than most adults suspect—including prescription and over-the-counter medications that can be abused. My advice for parents and grandparents: stay informed and be watchful for signs of possible drug use in your children, i.e., behavior changes, a drop in grades, different friends, physical changes, etc.

In addition to formal education, children learn from experience. Important first impressions, many of which remain for life, can be made well before youth celebrate their twentieth birthday. Most adults can remember things that happened in their childhoods that remain with them as if they happened yesterday.

For me, two of these memorable events are my first day of kindergarten and my first experience going through a cafeteria line. A vivid memory of the latter is triggered every time I slide a tray in front of a wide array of foods that call for good decisions made on the spot.

My cafeteria line experience highlights a concept that starts to take hold for most children early in the Second Decade. (see page 38) It is called *future time preference*—the ability to turn down an immediate reward when there is reason to expect a larger reward later. Future time preference is a tangible form of patience. Using this technique, a child expressing future time preference can remain calm while waiting and planning for better things to come.[11] Complex and subtle manifestations of future time preference are learned gradually and are not easily acquired—even for some adults!

In the Second Decade, thoughts about long-term life goals can give rise to ambitions expressed by youth which are at times abstract and idealistic, or they may be concrete and practical. Regardless, a young person's ideas and future plans at this age are subject to change; and as a parent, this can be when it is best to avoid overreacting and not playing your cards too soon. Patience on these occasions is a form of future time preference. Sometimes it is best to roll with the punches and wait for a better time to act. Let me share a story:

> *George, a young man of nineteen, attended a prestigious Midwestern liberal arts college that stressed the importance of a broad and truly liberal education. In the middle of his sophomore year, he announced to his father, a successful business executive, he had decided on what he intended to pursue for his life's work. With defiance, and anticipating some pushback for this idea, George told his father that he*

did not see any value in living a pedestrian life in business. His disapproval of his father's line of work was not further stressed, but the message was clear. Then, with pride more fitting accomplishment than intention, he announced that his goal in life was to become a poet. Wisely his father replied simply, "George, it's your life. Just go ahead and become the best poet you can be."

LIFE LESSONS

The first time I was exposed to the concept of future time preference (of course, I did not realize what was going on at the time), was in a cafeteria line when I was twelve years old. I was a member of the Detroit Police Boys Band and we were playing a concert at Boblo Island, near the entrance to Lake Erie at the south end of the Detroit River. Our reward for performing was a free lunch at the amusement park's cafeteria. I looked forward to this wonderful dining experience, which would be a first for me.

As I pushed my tray down the line, I helped myself to a crisp salad, cherry pie, molded gelatin salad with fruit, and cottage cheese. I didn't even want some of this but it looked too good to pass up.

Then, with a tray that was already full, I arrived at the roast beef, hamburgers, hot dogs, chili, fried chicken, rolls, and a lot of food I was really hungry for. A helpful and somewhat amused worker helped me remove most of the food from my tray; actually everything but the cherry pie. Now, I had room to add a hot roast-beef sandwich, mashed potatoes and gravy, green beans, a roll, and a glass of iced tea.

I never repeated this faux pas. I learned my lesson about the benefits of patience.

After receiving his liberal arts degree two years later, the not-so-positive graduate decided to hedge his bets by enrolling in an equally prestigious university where he received a graduate degree in business. Following this, George enrolled in law school and earned his JD. At forty-five years of age, the "poet in waiting" is the president of a commercial real estate company and raising a family. His life is a near perfect duplication of his father's. (I am not sure George even reads poetry now.)

This story points out two things: First, George's father did the right thing by not finding fault with his son's immature and idealistic statements. He knew his son well enough to be confident that it would be best to restrain from objecting now. When the time came to offer sound parental advice, and it did, George's father used his influence to good effect. When George returned later with a more realistic career option, his father offered support and encouragement. This is an example of "picking the right battle"—one of the most important strategies of parenting.

Second, the liberal arts college was in no way lacking. It accomplished what it promised. It gave George a sound foundation that prepared him for further educational pursuits that would eventually qualify him for a life of work that suited him, not immediately, but when the time was right. In George's case, it was more schooling and a career in business and law—not poetry. However, a word of warning: unless your child has the staying power and you have sufficient money, it is a good idea to choose a college degree that will prepare your child sooner rather than later. While going to college "twice" is a wonderful way to both broaden the mind and teach a practical skill, it is also costly and could lead to crippling debt for the unwary.

Pivotal landmarks that parents should recognize and deal with in an appropriate way are:

Birth to ten: It all starts here. Have fun and nurture the best family you can. Life should be relatively smooth sailing for the first dozen years with Mom and Dad still in charge.

Puberty: A game changer for everyone and a watershed separating your child's first two decades. Keep your eyes and ears open and be sensitive to any special needs of your child.

Diploma: A high school diploma is your child's most important accomplishment when it comes to preparing for a happy and productive life as an adult. This is serious, don't let them blow it.

After High School: The immediate post-high school period, during the last years of the Second Decade, should be a time for your child to continue working toward the attainment of a productive and fulfilling life. These years can be carefree and fun, but there should also be serious behavior. Your child should not waste these years. Freedom can be "seductive" and lead to putting things off. These are not the years for your child to take his "foot off the gas."

Next, let's look at some soft skills and behavioral patterns that can be learned during the Second Decade that will best equip your child for a more successful and happy adult life.

NECESSARY LIFE SKILLS

"All too often we are giving young people
cut flowers when we should be teaching
them to grow their own plants."
JOHN W. GARDNER

T HE SECOND DECADE SETS THE STAGE FOR THE REMAINDER OF a person's life—fifty plus years for people living in the United States.[1] These years provide a crucial window of opportunity for growth and learning that will have a profound and lasting effect on the quality of your children's remaining productive years. In order to best help them prepare for success and self-sufficiency, the following are some basic life skills they should achieve by the age of twenty. These, of course, aren't everything they should know, but rather they are the minimal and reasonable expectations:

Communicate Effectively

Barring disabilities, all children should be able to communicate verbally, nonverbally (by their body language and behavior), and in writing. They should speak Standard English—forgoing slang for essential and formal communication, and avoid other fads and bad habits. These language lapses can imply defiance, hostility, indifference, or even stupidity.

Your child should be able to provide instructions, give directions, and tell stories in a clear and understandable way. A mile is a mile, north is north, an ounce is an ounce, etc. It is not necessarily the size of one's vocabulary that makes a person smart. A person can be considered literate if he has the ability to use 20,000 different words and understands another 20,000, which together make up about one fifth of the more than 170,000 words in current use and found in the *Oxford English Dictionary*.[2]

It isn't how many words you know or how many facts you have at hand that make you sound smart. It is far more important to use the words you know properly and avoid expounding in areas where your facts are shaky. More important than the number, is the use of words while speaking clearly and using proper grammar.

Consider how important clear communication is for a 911 operator or an air traffic controller. In these cases, lives depend on accurate communication.

The spoken language is used to inform, entertain, convey emotions, and much more. This communication can be formal, informal, or personal. A child's words, beginning on average with about fifty words at eighteen months are, after all, a manifestation of his first thoughts and feelings. Your child should be taught to use these words carefully.

Starting early, and continuing during your child's formative years, you should teach your child to avoid using slang, vulgarity, and profanity. It is never too early to instill the habits of using correct grammar. Some examples of words and phrases you might urge your child to avoid, or at the least not overuse, are: *ya know*, *like*, *friggin*, *freekin*, and *youse*. Excessive use of these words and other slang can result in a person not being taken seriously.

The proper use of language is critical when it comes to

LIFE LESSONS

Eddie was spending the summer with his grandparents. He was a big, good-looking, and intelligent young man who knew how to work hard, make friends, and have a good time. But there was one problem. He had the habit of saying, "Me and Joe are ..." and various other ways of avoiding the "I" and substituting "me" instead.

Worried for Eddie, who might use this poor grammar in a job interview or other formal circumstance, his grandmother gently pointed out the error to Eddie. She explained the proper usage, and said that if it was okay with him, she would remind Eddie whenever it was necessary.

With a good-natured grin, Eddie said, "Okay. Go ahead; I'll get it, Grandma!"

And by the end of the summer, he did.

that all-important first impression, including job interviews. "Coaches" stress the importance of dress, body language, and the assumption of an air of confidence, but these are all things that can be "tuned up and straightened out" on relatively short notice. They are important but they don't reveal as much as how a person speaks and the words he uses.

Yes, you should encourage your child to dress appropriately (behavior) and help him develop self-confidence, but above all, teach him to speak properly. Urge your child to eliminate those words and phrases that are most offensive and "grating" to you. Chances are these words are likely to offend or give the wrong impression to others.

We all have our favorites, the ones we least like to hear, especially coming from a son or daughter. For me, it is the word *whatever*, especially when spoken in a dismissive manner. Maybe this is just my quirk, but I think it is disrespectful to respond to an offer with a shrug and "Whatever." To me it implies that both options are so uninteresting that it couldn't possibly make a difference. The responder just doesn't care. Instead, how about saying: "I'll think about it." "Sounds good to me." Or anything that indicates the offer had enough merit to call for a thoughtful answer.

One of the best ways to introduce your child to language and the proper use of words is by reading books to them. Reading to children has many important and positive ramifications above and beyond introduction to language, but if language appreciation were the only plus, it would stand alone as being of high value. Reading to a child can start anytime the parent chooses, as early as six months of age.

It isn't only words that we use to express ourselves.[3] Body language delivers a powerful unspoken message about personal feelings, opinions, and emotions. Such a message can be intended, but all too often is not. A good rule is: if you are not willing to say what is on your mind, don't act it out by saying

LIFE LESSONS

During visits to our home, our five-year-old grandson would entreat me with an unusual request: "Grandpa, teach me some big words." This led to a discussion of words like: *discern*, *corroborate*, *horticulture*, and *obfuscate*. Freddy's fascination with words and how to use them never left him.

Fifteen years older and a successful college student working at the school's radio station, Freddy had enough words to announce a girls' soccer match and make it sound interesting—no small feat! Later that year Freddy was honored as the College Sportscaster of the Year in his state by the Associated Press.

it with your body. Teach your child how to control his body language.

Body language can betray a person by revealing his true feelings while something else is being said. These actions can be reflexive, and include: avoiding eye contact, slouching, shuffling your feet, pointing your finger to emphasize a point, fidgeting, speaking in a monotone, using more words than necessary, etc.

These can be interpreted to mean: "Get serious!" "You expect me to believe that?" "Wow, not that again." "Let's get on with it." "You bore me." "Stop wasting my time." Etc.

Another unspoken communication that is delivered loud and clear, is to arrive late for an appointment. Being even a couple minutes late can send a negative message about the little importance you assign to a person or an activity.

This indication of a lack of respect or reduced importance is a powerful negative that can be detrimental to established relationships and limit your chance when trying to forge new ones.

Arriving late for a job interview creates a negative image that can dim or even rule out any chance of being hired.

Yes, the reality is we will all be late for something at some time in our lives, and at other times we will act out in some way, sending a message we wish we hadn't. In these cases, make an apology if you feel one is necessary. Amends made in a timely manner are likely to be well received and appreciated, thereby salvaging what could have been an unfortunate situation.

A positive example of body language that I used extensively when I was a caddy during my teens was "strategic" eye contact. When the caddy master came through the door of the caddy shed to select one of us to go out on a loop (carry a bag for nine or eighteen holes), I consciously made direct eye contact with him if that bag promised a good golfer, a pleasant person, or a good tipper. This worked. I was usually chosen. When I did not want the bag, I slouched and looked at the floor, and was rarely chosen. This tactic really worked for me and it was a good thing.

An example of not-so-good eye contact was what I did just before kickoff at a high school football game. As a 160-pound lineman, I was relegated to the second string. I got a reasonable amount of playing time but I had never started, and that was a big deal. It was my senior year and it looked like I would never start a game.

The lights were on and the stadium was packed when the coach came over to the sidelines and told us that the regular starting right guard was sick and couldn't play. He looked at me and the fellow next to me, who was also a second-string guard. As the coach was talking, I looked down to avoid eye contact, and the other player was selected. I missed my chance because by not looking the coach in the eye I "told" him I lacked self-confidence.

In today's world of instant communication, the issue rarely is that someone is not "in the know." Instead the issue may be that someone, and that includes a lot of people, may know too much. Facebook, text messaging, Twitter, e-mail, LinkedIn, and many other possibilities give us what may be far too many opportunities to share information quickly, and sometimes without enough forethought.

Slow down! Once a word is uttered or the send button is hit, there is no going back. (A new feature in Gmail offers the option to un-send an e-mail during a delay that is set by you.) Teach her to use restraint when using e-mail and social media. After writing a message, especially one that she is unsure about or might not be willing to say to a person face to face, offer this strategy: Compose the message and then save it as a draft. Consider it for hours or overnight, and then if it still seems like a good idea, go ahead and send it.

Caution your child about communicating in haste or acting impulsively.

I have discovered that simply writing down what is on my mind may be all that it takes to come to grips with an issue. A few hours later, or the next day, what riled me at the time seems far less serious. Ask your child if she would send the same e-mail if it had to be written on a piece of paper, stuffed in an envelope, addressed, stamped, and then put in the mailbox.

A simple rule for anyone to follow before e-mailing an important or possibly contentious note is to compose it offline in a Word document or equivalent. This offers the opportunity for easier editing and is a way to save the message and revisit it later before pasting it in an e-mail and hitting send.

A person should not send any e-mail that could be easily misunderstood or that conveys a message that would embarrass you later. Realize that attempts at humor can be misunderstood. And remember, once an e-mail is sent, it is fair game for unlimited forwarding by the recipient. So be careful!

People have been wounded as a result of mean and inappropriate messages; and ill-advised selfies have ended political careers, damaged the reputations of celebrities, and have even led to suicide.

And the obsession with the need to communicate has resulted in tragedy for those people who have caused death or injury to themselves and others because they were texting while driving.

The bottom line for employing any of the powerful communication tools available to us is to use good judgment.

Instill this caution in your children.

Wear Suitable Attire

Suitable attire for young men and women starts by dressing a slight notch above what is expected for the occasion. This is especially true when the event is a "first" for your child. This might include a job interview or a meeting with an adult on any occasion taking place in a formal setting.

For females, a good rule is to keep covered the parts that should be covered; no bare midriff, don't show cleavage, the skirt should not be too short, and either slacks or a skirt should be well-fitting and not too tight.

Young men can never go wrong wearing a suit coat and a tie, but a clean sport shirt without a tie, trousers, and leather shoes are appropriate for less formal occasions.

For both genders, sweats, yoga pants, flip-flops, tennis shoes, shorts, and other comfortable clothes are great for home and with friends but this should be considered informal attire and used as such!

I realize it is difficult to come up with an agreed-upon standard of dress for every occasion. For example, during the 2012 presidential campaign, both candidates for the nation's highest office seemed to try to outdo each other when it came to *not* wearing a tie at campaign functions. Appearing in an open-neck dress shirt may have been their attempt to look casual, be a regular guy, one of the people, and not stiff and formal. Although this more casual attire tends to take away some of the seriousness from a situation, at least for the older generations, lack of a tie for politicians is becoming de rigueur.

In a similar manner, some TV personalities have made not wearing a tie their trademark, again probably to look cool, especially if an additional button is left undone and maybe a gold chain is in evidence. Assure your child that dressing like that may be okay for a celebrity, but it is not a good idea for a college or job interview.

There is a big difference in rules of dress depending on who you are and where you live. On the West Coast, it has been said that the person in a business meeting wearing a tie must be the chauffeur. However, on the East Coast, a jacket and tie are standard business attire—except in some cases where special rules are in place, such as casual Fridays. Steve Jobs, the founder of Apple, could get away with wearing no socks and a well-worn t-shirt at high level business meetings—because of who he was.[4]

It is clear there is a steady move toward informality. A good rule is to get an idea of what the local norms are and for first impressions dress up rather than dress down. Those with the genius, clout, celebrity, and attitude can get by attending a formal business meeting wearing a t-shirt—but the rest of us must earn our stripes! For your children, a more conservative approach is in order.

An example:

> *Pete was going to the country club with a group of friends to celebrate their "formal" night of the summer. As he was going out the door, his mother asked him where they would be eating.*
>
> *Pete, who was wearing shorts, replied, "In the grill."*
>
> *She told him that while suitcoats were no longer required, she was sure that shorts were worn only in the informal dining area and were not accepted in the formal dining room.*

HOW YOU DRESS MATTERS

First impressions are immediate and difficult to amend. For example, on the evening of our first meeting, my future father-in-law, a successful retail jeweler and old-school gentleman, asked if I wore attached collars. He obviously noticed I was wearing a dress shirt and tie, and his comment might have been a reflexive indication of tacit approval (what I was hoping for as a young suitor). Incredulous, I said, "Yes, I do." I later found out that he had sold collar buttons since he was a young man, and although they were no longer available for sale when we met, he had an ample supply and still used them daily. To look fresh, he commonly changed his "collar" after a day's work, wearing the same shirt in the evenings but with a fresh collar held in place with a collar button.

Dutifully he grabbed a pair of long trousers, just in case, and headed out still wearing shorts, saying it was too late to warn the others because they had already left their homes.

Later that evening, when Pete returned home, he told his mother that the group was seated, all wearing shorts, with no comment from the staff. The dining room, he said, had only one other table occupied and the informal area was packed. The dining room staff was not going to turn away more than half of their business for the night. That night Pete learned a lesson in pragmatism. Things change. So much for arbitrary rules. His mother also learned that some things are different form her youth. She should remain flexible.

It should go without my saying that "shock" behavior should be avoided. This includes Mohawk haircuts, visible body piercings, tattoos, the Goth look, pants with the crotch at knee level, etc.[5]

Fortunately, all is not necessarily lost if there is a slip-up. Several years ago, I encountered a young woman as a patient, who dressed in a garish all-black outfit with hair, makeup, and even black fingernails that made her look like Dracula in drag. A few years later, and looking much different, she earned her PhD and is now an executive for a large corporation.

Sometimes children simply threaten to shock us. At a family dinner, our nineteen-year-old grandson announced that he would be letting his already longish hair grow for three months. If he made it that long, his friends, who he would be with at spring break, would pay to have his hair put in cornrows. But, if he got a haircut before then, they would give him a reverse Mohawk, with his hair shaved down the middle. The response by the adults at the table was, "Oh." Nobody took his bait.

And yes, table manners are important.

Your child might not be tested on whether the bread and butter plate goes on the left and the water glasses on the right but his demeanor at the table will be observed. It is important that your child use a knife and fork properly. And a napkin. It is too easy to make a wrong first impression at the table. You might not get many points for doing it right, but you will get low marks if you don't.

Basic Knowledge of U.S. History

By the time a child is a teen, she should know basic U.S. and world history. That doesn't mean your child should be an historian, but a basic knowledge of how we got here is a requirement. Following are ten simple questions to ask your child. There are many more that I am sure you can think of—she should be able to answer at least seven of these questions correctly:

1. When was North America discovered and by whom? (In 1492 by Christopher Columbus.)

2. Where did most of our earliest settlers immigrate from and why? (Europe. To gain religious, political, and economic freedom.)

3. Name the document written by colonists that announced their intention to sever ties with England and the document that described the form of government they would establish. (The *Declaration of Independence* and the *U.S. Constitution*.)

4. How long has the United States been formally recognized as a country? (Based on the U.S. being formed with the signing of the *Declaration of Independence* in 1776, in 2016, it will have been 240 years.)

5. Name four major wars—national and international—in which the U.S. has fought. (Revolutionary War, War of 1812, Civil War, Spanish-American War, World War I, World War II, Vietnam War, Iraq War, etc.)

6. What is the population of the United States? (In 2013, there were 317 million people living in the U.S. Answer should be within 10 percent.)

7. In what hemisphere is the United States located? (The Western Hemisphere.)

8. How many states are there in the Union; which one was admitted last? (There are 50 states; Hawaii was the last to be admitted.)

9. Name six countries in Europe (France, Germany, Italy, Spain, Greece, Portugal, Switzerland, Austria, Ireland, Poland, United Kingdom, Netherlands, Romania, etc.)

10. Name three countries in South America (Brazil, Argentina, Colombia, Chile, Ecuador, Peru, Venezuela, Paraguay, Uruguay, etc.)

Basic Understanding of U.S. Government

Before graduating high school, children should be able to correctly answer at least seven of the following questions about the U.S. government:

1. What is the form of government in the United States? (A federal republic—a group of states governed by an elected government. A common answer, not quite right, would also be a democracy.)

2. How many terms can the U.S. president serve? How long is one term? (Two four-year terms, for a total of eight years.)

3. Name the three branches of government. (Executive, legislative, and judicial.)

4. What right of a citizen is protected by the First Amendment to the U.S. Constitution? (The freedom of expression and speech.)

5. How many U.S. senators are elected from each state? (Two.)

6. What are the terms of office for members of the U.S. Congress? (The U.S. House of Representatives is two years; the U.S. Senate is six years.)

7. What is the title of the chief officer in state government? (Governor.)

8. Money to sustain the United States government comes mainly from what source? (Income taxes.)

9. How many judges serve on the U.S. Supreme Court? (Nine.)

10. What assigned number identifies you as a citizen of the United States, or an employed noncitizen authorized by the Department of Homeland Security? (Social Security Number.)

Ethical Behavior

Ethics can be defined as the rules that guide our behavior and conduct. Stated more simply, it is doing what is right.

It is living by the Golden Rule: Do unto others as you would have them do unto you.

Knowing right from wrong and possessing the will to do the right thing is essential to a child pursuing and maintaining an appropriate role in and being an effective member of society. This basic moral duty is paramount for the individual as well as for society.

It is important for children to mature into a lifestyle that is consistent with their faith—but not to impose their beliefs on others or to criticize people who believe differently.

Children face their own challenges. As they become older, they will see more of the world and be exposed to provocative sights, irreverent sounds, and potentially destructive temptations in ever increasing ways. They should be encouraged, by example, to deal with these issues in a healthy way.

A newly emerging factor in our society is bullying. While teasing and even overt acts of physical conflict on playgrounds have always been with us, a new type of social misbehavior called cyber-bullying is reaching almost institutional levels.[6]

Pervasive social networking has made it possible to inflict severe and widespread personal abuse without confrontation or the need for usual gossip.

Young people must be made aware of how important it is for them to use social media with care. They should be urged to recognize the enormous potential for harm if it is used irresponsibly.

Moreover, they should be taught that once a message is sent the same responsibility for judgment applies regardless of the age or gender of the sender. Social media is unisex and "age indifferent."

There are currently no federal laws dealing specifically with cyber-bullying, but legal issues dealing with civil rights violations, libel, and defamation can come into play protecting victims and punishing perpetrators.[7]

As a parent, you should be aware of the symptoms from being bullied ...

including dropping grades, unexplained injuries, loss of appetite, sudden loss of friends, avoiding social situations, loss of self-esteem, difficulty sleeping, complaints about health, and self-destructive behavior.[8]

There is no more important time in your child's life when it comes to building a foundation for their future.

The Second Decade can be fragile years, when kids are subjected to far-reaching damage from events that would not be so consequential if they occurred later in life. As parents, grandparents, and mentors we need to be sensitive to any special needs of our children. This time of life is not all fun and games for youth.

As children encounter many firsts, they also have the stress of managing peer pressure and making decisions about their future. How much education and training do I need? Can I find a job that will pay enough to support a family someday? Can I find a job that I enjoy and want to keep working at it? Will I have a date for the big dance? When should I get serious about getting married?

This and a whole lot more is heavy-duty stuff!

Next, let's discuss IQ and how smart is smart enough!

5

HOW SMART IS
SMART ENOUGH?

"Half of being smart is
knowing what you are dumb about."
SOLOMON SHORT

INTELLIGENCE CAN BE MEASURED CLINICALLY BY USING A BATTERY
of tests that produce a number called the Intelligence Quotient—more commonly referred to as IQ. The test used most
widely in the United States is the Wechsler Adult Intelligence
Scale (WAIS). Introduced in 1939, it has been revised several
times in the ensuing eighty plus years.

An advantage of this test is that it is designed to measure
a broad range of intelligence, including: memory, organization,
processing, vocabulary, digit recognition, picture comprehen-
sion, and symbol coding. It also assesses verbal and performance
ability.[1]

This unique combination of tests is thought to provide a reliable measure of intelligence, at least in most cases.

**But no single test or even combination of tests pro-
vides an accurate assessment in *every* case.**

The average intelligence score with the Weschler is 100. This is an arbitrary number given to the median raw score of individuals who are tested. It is simply a convenient number dividing the population equally. That is, half of the population has an IQ greater than 100, and half has one that is lower. Results expressed in a bell curve, show most people having an IQ at or around 100. For example; 68 percent have an IQ between 15 points above and fifteen points below the median. Stated another way, two thirds of the population has an IQ at or near the median.

An IQ of 85 (fifteen points below the median) or higher, includes 84 percent of the U.S. population. All of these people are thought to be intelligent enough to earn a high school diploma.

Factors other than intelligence are likely to contribute when it comes to the approximately six percent of children who enter high school and fail to graduate.

Fourteen percent of the U.S. population has an IQ between 70 and 85. Those at this level are said to have a fifty-fifty chance of graduating high school. Those with IQs between 70 and 75 have a lesser chance and those with IQs between 75 and 85 have a better chance.[2]

The approximately 2 percent of the U.S. population with an IQ below 70 is considered to have no chance to complete high school under any circumstance, and only some of those could be trained for simple tasks like domestic work and agriculture. This means that in a country of 317 million people, as many as 20 million could be destined to a life of unskilled and low-paid work at best, or no job at all, based on limited intelligence, educability, and trainability.

Measured intelligence and level of achievement do not always coincide.

There are other important factors when it comes to achieving success, including: self-motivation, hard work, and opportunity.

However, this IQ/achievement disparity is more likely to be observed when a person's attainments do not live up to their potential as determined by IQ. In these cases, people with a similar IQ may attain widely different levels of success because one person worked harder and did more with the gifts he possessed. It is probably rarer to see a person with a confirmed low IQ succeed to an unexpected high level; these example are hard to come by, the idiot savant or Forrest Gump notwithstanding.

The IQ considered a reliable indicator of the intelligence level needed to graduate high school, 85, is roughly equivalent to the IQ considered necessary to serve in the United States Armed Forces. Ninety-nine percent of army recruits and 100 percent of marines have earned a high school diploma. But even with this diploma, recruits are required to meet certain standards on the Armed Forces Qualifying Test to be considered fit for service. This means that an IQ of at least 90 is more likely to characterize the typical recruit.[3]

Eighty-four percent of children have an IQ of 85 or higher, and all at this level are considered to have sufficient intelligence to earn a high school diploma.

Of the 14 percent of children with an IQ between 70 and 85, about half could graduate from high school with special help and a more basic course of study. Many of those unable to complete high school, about 7 percent, will benefit from some basic skill training, preparing them to work at a job like domestic help or agriculture. The 2 percent with an IQ below 50 are considered to be borderline educable and are treated on an individual basis.[4]

A high school diploma is also the requirement for ninety percent of the jobs available in our country. A high school diploma, therefore, functions as an important watershed predicting a measure of success for the holder. (See ch. 6)

To obtain a professional degree at the level of MD, DO, or PhD, an IQ of at least 125 is thought to be required. About five percent of the population is in this category.

People in the 98th percentile on the IQ scale, which is around 131, are eligible to take a separate examination to qualify for membership in an organization called Mensa—the largest and oldest high-IQ society in the world.[5] This organization was formed in 1946 in Oxford, England, and has chapters worldwide, with the largest chapter in the United States. The main reason for Mensa seems to be that it offers smart people an opportunity to associate with other smart people.

Since a high school diploma or GED (General Educational Development, a government-sponsored test for high-school-diploma equivalency.) is a requirement for submitting an application to join the police force, the armed forces, and most other jobs, it can be inferred that 84 percent of the population meets this minimum intelligence requirement. Those in the 14 percent of the population with an IQ between 70 and 85 and who worked hard enough to obtain a high school diploma are likely to be relegated to lower level jobs based on pre-employment testing. Those at the lowest level, with an IQ between 50 and 70, are capable of carrying out domestic duties, agricultural work, and other similar tasks.

While by inference an IQ of 85 is necessary to apply, the average IQ for police in the United States is estimated to be 104, or slightly above the median.[6] The armed forces, in addition to requiring a high school diploma, evaluates recruits with the Armed Forces Qualifying Test (AFQT) that has five major levels giving results that equate to IQ scores. Applicants scoring at level 5, representing an IQ below 81, are considered unfit for service. Military personnel with AFQT levels of 4 and above are assigned to jobs, at least in part, according to scores attained. The AFQT is calculated from the math and English subtests and is the most important part of the Armed Services Vocational Aptitude Battery. Recruiters and military job counselors use scores on these tests, along with other factors such as job availability, security clearance eligibility, medical qualifications, and physical strength to match potential recruits with military jobs. As an example, these job "areas" in the Marine Corps would include: infantry, avionics, logistics, vehicle maintenance, aircraft maintenance, munitions, and so on. Inside of each job area is a specific job description. This process functions with some variations in the Army, Air Force, Navy, and Coast Guard.

Success in the military requires a basic level of intelligence that can be determined with considerable accuracy using standard testing. When the Army temporarily began accepting applicants who scored at the 5 level on the AFQT, implying an IQ of as low as 81, they found that these individuals were unable to perform satisfactorily, even at low-level jobs.

Since it has been established that an IQ of 85, which includes eighty-four percent of the population, indicates sufficient intelligence to join the military, most youth have this option.

It is likely that for someone who meets the physical requirements, joining the military is the most readily available job in the United States today. Service in the military can range from a two-year enlistment to a twenty-year career or longer until retirement. (See ch. 11)

As far as I know, no one in my family, including myself, has reliable knowledge of their IQ. (The topic has never been discussed in my presence.) It is likely that this type of testing has been done at some time on all of us, and that the results were used by others to judge each of us. People are tested for performance and aptitude multiple times for a variety of reasons during school years and at pre-employment evaluations. But, to the best of my knowledge, no one in my family has been stigmatized for having a low IQ or lauded for having a high one. I expect this is the case for most other families as well.

Two widely known standardized tests used for college applications are the Scholastic Aptitude Test (SAT) and American College Testing (ACT). Test scores that have been achieved on these tests by several prominent people have been published online. For example, Bill Gates is reported to have scored 1,590 out of 1,600 on his SAT.[7] He missed one question. What else would you expect? Many of the things Bill Gates did to achieve success are things that can be predicted with a test taken at a desk, but that is only part of it. Gates offered the following when questioned about getting good grades: "I failed in some subjects, but my friend passed all of them. Now he works for me as an engineer and I am the owner of Microsoft."[8]

There can be no doubt, it is beneficial to be smart—but is there something more than a high IQ that is required for success and self-sufficiency?

What part of success is achieved by hard work and persistence? What role do common sense and problem-solving skills play when it comes to attaining success?

During thirty-five years as a professor of ophthalmology at Indiana University School of Medicine, I interviewed hundreds of medical school graduates applying for a university ophthalmology residency, and dozens more fully trained ophthalmologists applying for a fellowship in pediatric ophthalmology. During this time I did something that is probably common for most people in my position, I learned from my mistakes. All of the applicants who interviewed for these positions had impressive credentials from respected academic institutions. That was a given. They also came with the trappings of "formal" book smarts. Then, with the advent of computers and software programs like Microsoft Word, each produced what tended to be overly long and padded "I can almost walk on water" personal statements. The funny thing was that some of the applicants couldn't even remember the "wonderful" volunteer work they listed on their resumes, which included things like feeding the poor, working at a shelter, or mentoring underprivileged kids. When asked about these activities, the answers I received were sometimes vague, often unconvincing, and I rarely probed.

A National Football League (NFL) quarterback, who was selected five times as the Most Valuable Player in the NFL in his seventeen-year career, and considered one of the greatest quarterbacks of all time, is said to have achieved a mediocre SAT score of 1030. In contrast, a journeyman NFL quarterback and a Harvard graduate, Ryan Fitzpatrick, has a reported SAT score of 1,580—impressive in the "smarts" department.[9]

The 1030 quarterback is considered a "coach on the field" and, according to some, Peyton Manning, with only an average SAT score, may be the best player to have ever performed at the most complicated and intellectually demanding position on the field.

It seems logical to consider those young men and women with the most impressive applications to be the ones most likely to succeed—but over the years I came to realize this was not necessarily so.

What were the other characteristics I could uncover during the interviews and after studying the written applications that would be most likely to indicate the best applicants? In the process of reducing a roster of fifty applicants to seven who were selected for residency, I ranked those candidates higher who gave evidence that they had learned not only *inside* the classroom but *outside* as well. Applicants who convinced me that they had learned something while working at a job could be rewarded with that all-important tie-breaker when it came to a close call.

All of the applicants were smart; everything else being equal, those who had experience working at a variety of jobs, in my opinion, were better suited to successfully complete the training in our program. Skills that made a candidate stand out for me included evidence of problem-solving skills, flexibility when dealing with a variety of situations, working with different people, innovation, and initiative. All of these are skills that can be acquired best at the kind of job where a person can both *earn* and *learn*.

LIFE LESSONS

The month I graduated from medical school, I received a call from the chairman of the Ophthalmology Department at Indiana University. He asked if I was interested in coming to Indianapolis to be interviewed for a residency position. I had submitted an application earlier in the spring, and after being turned down at the University of Michigan and Wayne State University in Detroit, I was not sure I was cut out to be an ophthalmologist. Maybe I couldn't get a residency anywhere.

It was only a five-hour drive to Indianapolis and I had a few days off before the start of my internship, so I told him I would be happy to interview.

The interview went fine and a week later, I was offered a residency position at Indiana. I was delighted but also realized I was the last one selected. I felt I had a lot to prove, which didn't bother me because I knew I was a hard worker—maybe that impressed the chairman. It was time for me to prove my worthiness.

Twenty years later, I would become Chairman of the Ophthalmology Department.

An example of why you shouldn't put all of your trust in any sort of evaluation or a test score or a grade that someone assigns to your performance, even to the point of changing career plans, was demonstrated to me by a colleague. John (not his real name) shared this experience:

In John's first year of medical school, he received a D in biochemistry and was required to repeat the course in summer school. Before summer classes started, he was offered the chance to undergo psychological testing, which would be entirely voluntary and done at no charge.

Even though the test was not required, he agreed to participate. In truth, John looked forward to hearing the examiner say he was so smart it was hard to imagine how he could have gotten such a low grade, even in a difficult course. He was sure he would be told he just needed to get down to work, study harder, and use the good brain he was lucky to have.

After a long day of testing, John said he was surprised the test had so many parts and at how diverse, and sometimes difficult, the tasks were. He definitely didn't feel as smart after finishing as when he started.

A week later, John returned to the clinic to hear the results. The psychologist, who he described as a white-haired man of about sixty, who wore a long, white lab coat, and not much in the way of expression, invited John to sit down. Without much ado, the psychologist informed John that the test indicated John wasn't smart enough to finish medical school. The news hit John like a ton of bricks.

Looking at the psychologist across the desk, John asked if the results meant he would be kicked out of school.

"No," the psychologist said. "I am only saying the results indicate it is unlikely you will be able to graduate, and I am advising you to consider making different plans for your future."

After a moment of thought, John replied that he didn't have any other plans and if he wasn't being kicked out of medical school, he would go to summer school as he had planned and return to classes in the fall and try to do better.

The psychologist said, "Your decision."

And that was it.

John graduated from medical school and went on to pursue

a distinguished career as a cardiac surgeon. He authored dozens of research papers and published a well-received textbook. In spite of the dire warning John had received when he was a floundering freshman, a combination of sufficient intelligence and a sound work ethic resulted in him compiling a career to be envied.

Next, let's discuss the importance of a diploma and how successfully completing high school impacts a person for life.

THE IMPORTANCE
OF HIGH SCHOOL

"As a high school dropout, I understand the value
of education: A second chance at obtaining my
high school diploma through the G.I. Bill led me to
attend college and law school and allowed me the
opportunity to serve in Congress."
CHARLES B. RANGEL

THERE ARE MANY THINGS CHILDREN CAN DO, ESPECIALLY WITH the guidance of involved parents, to increase their chances of obtaining and sustaining a successful and satisfying adult life—the most tangible is getting an education. Even though education offerings vary throughout the country, existing standards ensure that all U.S. children are provided a quality and free public education. (Ninety percent of enrolled students attend a public school or are home-schooled; 10 percent attend some type of private school.)

In most states, formal schooling starts with kindergarten at age five; and in some cases, pre-kindergarten is available for children as young as three years old.

For every child in the United States, education from the first through twelfth grades is *available* and *free*.

Some cities place such a high value on post-high school

education they offer financial assistance to qualified high school graduates in their districts who attend public universities and colleges in their state. The State of Georgia uses income from their state lottery to assist qualified students with tuition, in some cases providing nearly the entire cost of their college tuition.[1]

The formal primary school and middle school educations that most children receive adheres to a prescribed curriculum according to the local schoolboard's policy. Skill sets achieved by boys and girls in grades one through eight include both social-ization and academic: reading, writing, spelling and vocabulary, basic math, some history and geography, beginning computer skills and introduction to music and art along with organized group activities including supervised sports.

Courses in high school range from advanced placement aca-demics for those able and interested, to basic vocational training for those with special interests or needs. In high school, students can select from a wide array of courses with the common thread that all students must successfully complete selected basic courses that are required to graduate and receive a high school diploma.

Compared with grades 1 through 8, students in high school are able to pursue a more challenging and potentially varied course of study as long as they complete the required courses for graduation.

High school is where your child gains the necessary; more complex; and, in some cases, practical skills that will prepare him to deal with both the opportunities and challenges that arise for all teens after high school graduation.

As a parent, grandparent, or mentor you owe it to the children you might influence to do everything in your power to help and encourage them to continue with their academic education or vocational training. For starters, that means helping them in any way you can to earn their high school diploma.

For a person in their Second Decade, no accomplishment is more emblematic of success than achieving a high school education.

A person before the age of twenty can be a gold medalist in the Olympics, a Wimbledon champion, or sell a million albums, but wonderful as these accomplishments are, they stand beside and not above the high school diploma that every one of these highly successful individuals is expected to receive.

There are so many things going on in a child's life at the start of the second decade, an array of activities must compete for attention. It is simply not in most children's DNA at ten, eleven, or twelve, to be thinking about things as seemingly distant as high school. Remember, your child is experiencing the "big three event" at this time: puberty, the teenage years, and finishing grade school. During these years, it is time for you, the adult in the picture, to step up.

The steps you should take are represented by the concept of *concerted cultivation*. Annette Lareau, PhD, discusses concerted cultivation in her book *Unequal Childhoods: Class, Race, and Family Life.*[2] Lareau describes how some parents supervise their children's activities, help them make decisions, and when it seems right, will make decisions for them. (See ch. 10.)

Dr. Lareau states: "Worried about how their children will get ahead, middle-class parents who practice concerted cultivation are increasingly determined to make sure their children are not excluded from any opportunity that might eventually contribute to their advancement."

This is a perfect description of the parent who takes an active role in selecting the right high school for her child.

This parenting style contrasts with how the majority of lower-middle-class and poor working-class families raise their children. Parents in these households are more likely to pursue a natural growth philosophy for childrearing. *Natural growth* can be defined as using the inherent sense of right and wrong to guide a child growing and developing into maturity. With this parenting style, only the absolutely necessary and usually minimal planning on the part of parents is required.

Natural growth allows children to have more freedom. They do more things on their own without supervision or even knowledge of parents. These children are more or less left to sink or swim on their own. In this type of family, school decisions are likely to be in the hands of school authorities. Students will tell their parents where they are going to high school because that is where their friends are going and they expect to go there too.

Regardless of parenting styles, the *effort* to actually earn a high school diploma must come from the child. Success at school is an individual contest. No "participation" trophies are awarded. In the case of high school, you make it or you fail. Yes, adults can provide encouragement, stability, shelter, etc.—but achieving a high school diploma is personal. It requires setting a goal and then achieving it.

A high school diploma is necessary for growth and success.

Children on their way to earning a high school diploma must attend classes, complete the work assigned, and pass tests that demonstrate the material has been learned and skills mastered. Earning a diploma indicates that a young person has taken the first step on a road they hope will lead to a successful life. There is much more to be accomplished, but this diploma enables your child to apply, with confidence, for entry-level employment and can be considered the "price of admission" when it comes to higher aspirations, which for two thirds of graduates is pursuing a college education.

"What is amazing is, if young people understood how doing well in school makes the rest of their life so much more interesting, they would be more motivated."

Bill Gates

To make the most of the opportunity provided by a high school education, timely consideration and planning are necessary. This planning includes time and effort on the part of both the child and parent(s). Planning for high school should start with exploring the options. This means considering which of the many high school opportunities available would be best for your child. It is not too early to start researching high schools when your child is in the seventh grade.

The first decision to make about high school is the *type* of school that is best for your child. This is not a trivial issue. There are many choices available today compared to a generation or two ago when the decision was more likely to be made for you and not by you. For the most part, the choices for high school for baby boomers were limited to:

▼ The local, public high school that includes college preparatory courses

▼ A private school, parochial or secular

▼ A public vocational school not necessarily in your school district

Until recently, most children who completed the eighth grade in a public school would attend the public high school that served the district. These children were "assigned" to a specific high school. For example, in Detroit I lived just one block removed from the boundary for attending Denby High School, one of the newest and best equipped high schools in the Detroit Public School System. Even though it was the closest public high school to my home and most of my primary school classmates would go there, I was at the outermost reaches of the Southeastern High School District, and that is where I was assigned. That was the way it was. We complied and thought no more about it.

But things are different today. Because there are so many choices, more thought and planning is required to make the best decision. While this planning should include the prospective student, parents should be prepared to take the lead.

Making the right choice for high school can mean your child, and you as parents, will have a more rewarding four-year experience.

Types of High Schools

Let's compare the high school choices for generation Z (this includes those born around the millennium):

Public high school: For many students and families, the local public high school remains the best choice. Reasons for choosing this school include: staying in contact with friends made in primary school, familiarity with the locale, a curriculum that meets the needs and ambitions of the student, and no tuition costs. But the decision to attend the local public high school should not be made by default or in a vacuum, without awareness of other possibly more compelling options.

A large public high school, especially if it is the only high school in the district, could be, in effect, a magnet school (see below) that offers a wide variety of both academic and vocational courses. While the large public high school might offer the courses a student seeks in a magnet school, the public school could have the drawback of lacking the focus and atmosphere of a magnet school.

If your child is not planning to enter the workforce immediately after high school and has not arrived at a specific career interest, the local public high school could be a good choice. This school should provide a basic education, including college-preparatory classes sufficient to allow your child to apply to a two-year community college or a four-year college after graduation.

Magnet school: A common alternative to the local public high school is another public school called a magnet school.

A student and his parent are likely to make the extra effort to enroll in a magnet school only if this school offers a unique curriculum that meets the student's needs and interests. A magnet school is a public high school that offers special instruction and unique courses that might not be available elsewhere in the school system.[3] There is no tuition fee for magnet schools because they are publically funded. They are available to *any* student who applies and who meets the admission requirements, of course admission is subject to space availability. In some cases, otherwise eligible students are turned away because school is oversubscribed.

The concept of the magnet school was originally intended to attract a more diverse, less segregated student body by increasing the area for drawing students. With diversity now better established in public high schools, the magnet high school's most important contribution is to offer a concentration of special courses not available elsewhere in the district, thereby offering its students a unique educational experience.

A magnet school can draw students from single school districts, multiple school districts, or even be statewide. In some cases, magnet *programs* are offered at a local or district public high school. In this case, the school can be referred to as comprehensive (with expanded offerings) but not technically magnet (drawing from a wider area). These self-contained, magnet-like schools can have several "schools" or concentration areas with unique curricula within the school.

For example, a high school might offer four years of Japanese language study, or other equivalent specialty academic concentrations, and also have a career center that teaches vocational skills. If such a high school is the only one in a given district, it is likely to have a large and diversified enrollment. These magnet-like schools can be a good compromise when a school district has only one large public high school.

Most magnet schools concentrate on a particular discipline or area of study, while others—for example, International

Baccalaureate (IB) schools—concentrate on a higher level academic philosophy, with a wider and eclectic focus.[4] A magnet school usually has, in addition to all of the courses needed to fulfill graduation requirements, a unique academic focus; such as, mathematics, natural science and engineering, humanities, social science, fine arts, and performing arts; or may offer technical and vocational/agricultural education. The Indianapolis public magnet schools, similar to other large metropolitan areas, offer the following programs in ten separate high schools: agricultural and environmental sciences, arts and humanities, career technology, health professions, international baccalaureate, law and public policy, math and science, medical, multiple intelligences, and new technology.[5]

Because enrollment at magnet schools can be limited and admission is usually on a first-come, first-served basis, it is wise to apply early.

Charter school: A charter school is technically a public school.[6] Like other public schools, charter schools are supported by public funds. These funds are provided to charter schools according to the number of students enrolled in a dollar amount per pupil that is approximately two-thirds that given to a traditional public school. On average, charter schools receive just over $6,000 per regular pupil compared to approximately $10,000 for public schools. But there are other differences. These baseline numbers can become much larger depending on the district and the needs of the pupils.[7]

In contrast to traditional public schools, most charter schools do not receive public funds to cover the cost of building or maintaining a facility, which means that an individual or organization starting a charter school must secure a suitable facility on its own. This might be purchasing or leasing an unused public school building or other existing space, or building a new structure.

Starting a charter school can be daunting, but many groups have succeeded and these schools have offered a popular option in many communities. Since 1991, with enactment of the first charter school legislation, more than 6,000 charter schools have been established in the U.S. These schools serve two million children, 4.6 percent of public school students, and comprise 6.3 percent of all public schools.[8] Charter schools have more freedom in areas of curriculum and teaching methods, but like any other publically funded or private school, these schools must prepare students to meet established standards. Charter schools, though having more latitude than traditional public schools, are graded according to the success of their students. Some advantages of charter schools are: smaller class size, a more personal approach to education, and the possibility for more parental involvement. However, compared to other public schools, test scores can be better, the same or worse. Charter schools are a bit like private schools, but without tuition.[9]

Private school: Private high schools have, in some cases, been a haven for the wealthy and privileged, and for a few gifted students who have been able to secure financial support. They are also the choice of many who scrimp and save to provide their children a parochial education, usually at a Catholic school. These schools can provide a fine education and, in many cases, are attended by students as a way of carrying on a family tradition. Tuition costs are usually high, but the quality of education and/or prestige associated with many of these private schools is deemed worth it for those parents who choose and can afford to send their children to these schools.

A private high school is likely to be owned by a religious or a not-for-profit group. These schools are not supported by public funds, but as with any school conferring a high school diploma, they must meet prescribed standards. Similar to charter schools, private high schools have significant latitude when it comes to teaching materials and methods, and this can include religion courses. About 10 percent of high school students are enrolled in some manner of private school.[10] Tuition fees can range from just over $5,000 per year in Alaska to nearly

CONCERTED CULTIVATION

Eleana is a single mother of a ten-year-old boy and an eight-year-old girl. She works as the property manager for a large urban household storage facility. As the daughter of a single mother who she described as a "domestic," Eleana was reared in the natural growth parenting style.

Working on her own, Eleana managed to graduate from high school and attended a community college for a year. In addition to her regular job, which she chose mostly because it was near her home, Eleana works part-time as an administrative assistant at a small business.

When her son regularly came home from school saying he didn't like school because the teacher spent all of her time disciplining an unruly class, Eleana decided to take action. She found a nearby charter school that offered a special math and science curriculum and immediately enrolled both of her children. They now enjoy going to school.

Recently, Eleana proudly showed me report cards that each had brought home. There was one B for her daughter and two B's for her son; the rest were A's.

Eleana is pursuing concerted cultivation as her child-rearing strategy as she makes the choice to send her children to a charter school—and her children are benefiting from her involvement. There is no doubt that what Eleana has begun in primary school will continue as her children progress with their education.

$30,000 per year in Connecticut.[11] A private high school could be in the local community or distant, with residential housing provisions; in which case the total cost would be considerably more. School vouchers providing government assistance for private education are available to assist qualified students on a selected basis.[12]

In addition to offering a curriculum that meets prescribed standards, private schools offer a wide range of added educational, social, and life experiences. Private high schools, like their public counterparts, offer a college-preparatory curriculum, including arts, honors, and advanced placement courses. Private high schools are not likely to offer vocational or career courses aimed primarily at preparing students to immediately enter the workforce after graduating.

Nearly all private high school students plan on attending college, and private high school students are twice as likely to attain a bachelor's degree as those who attend public high schools.[13]

Homeschooling: Another option for completing high school and receiving a diploma is with homeschooling. Abundant educational and school-related material available online has helped make this the choice for a small but dedicated group of parents and their children. For homeschooling to work, both teacher (usually a parent) and student must be motivated and disciplined.

Moreover, there are perceived advantages when it comes to homeschooling. A survey of reasons for choosing homeschooling revealed that 91 percent of respondents said that concern about the unwholesome environment in other schools was a significant factor.[14] Another reason for homeschooling was the high tuition costs for a private school that would be a parent's choice over a free public school. A factor in favor of this method is that funds saved while homeschooling in primary school and high school could be used for college expenses where homeschooling is not feasible unless a student elected online courses.

Contrary to what some people believe, home-schooled students do not have to be isolated from their peers and potentially lonely. Homeschool associations are established to promote social interaction, and sports competitions that can include statewide home-school athletic conferences. Under the best of circumstances, athletic, social, and volunteer interactions can give home-schooled students a real sense of community. About 3 percent of students in the United States in 2011–2012 were homeschooled.[15]

Parents *and* children have many opportunities when it comes to making decisions about the all-important high school education.

Statistics available now are useful to highlight current trends but are subject to change. The information provided is intended

A school voucher is a certificate of funding that a parent can use to pay tuition necessary for their child to attend a private school. Use of the voucher system is currently limited, with just over a dozen states and the District of Columbia participating. Private schools must meet minimum standards set by legislatures in order to accept voucher recipients. Legislatures also set parameters for student eligibility that typically target low-income students that meet a specified income threshold, those from chronically under-performing schools, and several other categories.

Vouchers are the subject of hot debate between supporters who believe this program will help children and be a stimulus to improve education overall, and detractors who feel that vouchers take away from and are harmful to the public school system.

to be a start. As has been stated throughout this book, you and your child are not averages or statistics; you are individuals and should behave as such.

It has been said that "All politics is local." Without stretching the point too far, I think it is also fair to say that "All education is local"; especially when it comes to high schools.

For that reason, it is the responsibility of parents to help their sons and daughters by researching the choices.

Go online, get on the phone, and even make a personal visit to a school to gain the information you need to make the best decision in concert with your child. This is a time when it is okay to be a bit selfish. Being that way now, as you make it possible for your child to have the best education, may be the most generous act you can do for your child and for society as a whole.

Experiences gained in the classroom while interacting with teachers and fellow students, participating in sports and clubs, extracurricular activities, and a variety of other experiences unique to attending high school are unique.

These activities for the high school student should also include working at a part-time job during the school year and a fulltime job in the summer.

The wide range of activities available during high school adds to what makes these years rich with experience. High school can be considered the "sweet spot" of the second decade. What a child accomplishes during these four years can launch him to a successful career; and what he fails to accomplish deploys a sea anchor that will hold him back when opportunity beckons.

The following is a useful checklist when considering a high school for your son or daughter:

▼ Know the options and opportunities before you discuss the subject with your child. Contact the schools for information. Go to the website of every school you consider a valid choice. Education remains a hot topic that is evolving. There are likely to be a few changes each time a new school year comes around. Education policy is fluid, so be sure your information is current. Remember, you are likely to get the latest information by speaking with a person compared to online or in print. Don't hesitate to phone the school or request a personal visit. Study the information they provide and listen to what they say.

▼ Talk with parents of children who have attended the schools you are thinking about. Get their impressions of the school experience.

▼ Consider your child's strengths and weaknesses. Is there any chance your child will not want to attend college? Is vocational training best for your child—or what about an apprenticeship?

▼ Does your child require extra help at school? Will he or she continue to benefit from this kind of assistance with classes in high school? If so, some schools are better equipped to provide tutoring and other help. This is the kind of information you are likely to have to dig for.

▼ After doing your research, have a discussion with your child. He or she is likely to have gone no further with the issue of where to go to high school than talking with friends and finding out where they will be going.

▼ If you are considering anything other than the local public high school, apply early. Most other schools have limitations when it comes to enrollment. In some schools, applications exceed available places by large numbers. Magnet schools usually accept all qualified applicants on a first-come, first-served basis, but they can be oversubscribed and forced to turn away otherwise qualified applicants. Charter schools may give preference to family members or other special categories, but usually make a significant number of places available on a first-come, first-served basis. Since charter and magnet schools are likely to have more applicants than positions, early application is especially important. Better to apply and decide against a choice than fail to apply and miss out.

▼ Have a viable backup in case your first choice for a high school falls through.

▼ Be realistic about finances. Don't allow your child to begin at a high school that you will not be able to afford for the entire four years. Encourage your child to apply for available scholarships if a tuition school is selected. Find out if school vouchers are available in your district if you are seriously considering a private school that you are not able to afford.

Finally, don't cease your interest and involvement when your child starts high school. Be aware of your child's grades. Help him select the best courses for his current and future needs. If trouble is on the horizon with one or more courses, don't hesitate to find a suitable tutor. There is no shame in admitting that a tutor is needed. In many cases, a small amount of help and encouragement will keep trouble in one course from dragging down grades in other classes.

There are no hard-and-fast rules for success when it comes to which high school a child should attend. Family resources, scholarships available, encouragement from teachers, availability of schools, and the child's interests all play a part.

Success, regardless of which school is chosen, is achieved by the child who works hard in school, selects the right courses, participates in after-school activities and engages in and learns from meaningful work.

All of this can be accomplished in the local district high school if that seems the right choice, but it behooves any student and family to at least be aware of the other options.

The GED

Each year, more than 6 percent of high school students drop out before earning their diploma. This produces nearly three million dropouts annually. These numbers contribute to current estimates that as many as 15 percent of Americans, or more than 40 million people in the United States, lack the all-important high school diploma.[18]

If you know a teenager who has dropped out of high school, steer him toward earning a General Educational Development (GED) certificate. The GED, which has been in existence since 1942, offers four assessments: literacy (reading and writing), mathematics, science, and social studies.[19]

A GED is "officially" equivalent to a high school diploma when it comes to applying for 90 percent of jobs and applying to 90 percent of colleges, but it is not the same as actually attending high school.

The GED format was updated and improved in 2014, and the test is now taken on a computer. A new scoring system also has the added feature of indicating strengths and weaknesses. This profile demonstrates specific areas of competence

To learn everything you need to know about preparing for and taking the GED do a web search by typing in "GED test [and indicate your state]" in the browser. Each state has a listing with complete information for you.[20]

Dropouts

If you still don't believe how critical a diploma is, consider the daunting reality high school dropouts face:[21]

1. **Stiff Competition.** When competing with applicants who have earned their diploma, it is possible that a person

College entrance after high school is based mostly on grades, recommendations, and test scores achieved with the Student Aptitude Test (SAT) or the American College Testing (ACT).[16] In 2013, 65.9 percent of high school graduates entered college.[17] More students graduating from private high schools enter college, but these numbers are more likely to reflect expectations of the students who enroll then the quality of the education.

without a high school diploma or GED will not even be considered for an available position.

2. **No chance for further formal education.** In order to study at a community college, university, accredited online university, other online courses for credit, or begin an apprenticeship, a high school diploma or GED will be required.

3. **Limited career opportunities.** Without a high school diploma or GED, the chance of finding a rewarding career that pays a living wage is lower. With a high school diploma or GED, young adults can seek employment in a variety of entry-level careers that do not require additional formal education, but allow on-the-job training and the possibility of advancement.

4. **Lower income.** A high school dropout will, on average, earn as much as $300,000 less over a lifetime compared to a person who has earned a high school diploma or GED. About half of all welfare recipients are high school dropouts.[22]

5. **Less job security.** A person without a high school diploma or GED is more likely to be unemployed.

6. **Reduced self-esteem.** Failure to complete high school or earn a GED is tangible evidence of failure at a task that is completed successfully by 90 percent of youth who start high school. A person who lacks a high school diploma has failed to achieve the first significant and widely recognized sign of accomplishment for a person in his second decade and is likely to be the first step leading to failure in the workforce.[23]

8. **Increased chance to end up in jail or prison.** Dropouts comprise a disproportionate percentage of those who are incarcerated. This includes about 75 percent of our state prison inmates, 59 percent of federal prison inmates, and 69 percent of local jail inmates who did not complete high school.[24]

A high school diploma should be the goal of every capable child, and it should be accomplished in the Second Decade. Statistics show a person over twenty-five years of age who is

Reasons given for dropping out of high school include:[25]

▼ Lack of parental engagement

▼ Poor grades

▼ Need to work

▼ Lack of support and mentoring outside of family

▼ School and academics do not relate to "real" work

▼ Lack of individualized attention

▼ Lack of engagement in peer group and school activities

▼ Making poor choices about lifestyles and friends

employed fulltime with some high school, has a median income of only twice the poverty level.[26] It should be recognized that "some high school" may be just a nicer way of saying a person is a dropout.

On a practical level, it is easy to speculate that if a teen drops out of high school at sixteen, he or she is not likely to have learned much in the short time they attended school and were just waiting to be sixteen so they could quit. The median annual income for a person with a high school diploma in 2012 was $35,170.[27] This compares to a median annual income of a high school dropout lucky enough to have a job which is $20,110. Moreover the high school dropout is half again more likely to be unemployed.

At every education level, from a high school diploma to a professional degree, there is a steady increase in income.

These levels include: a two-year college (associate degree, trade school, or apprenticeship), four-year college (bachelor's degree), graduate school (master's degree), doctorate (PhD), and professional degree (MD, DO, JD, etc.). The median income for those at the highest level with a professional degree is ten times the poverty level.[28]

Thus, the most important *job* for youth during the second decade is attending high school. The most important *work* is study. And, the *paycheck* is their diploma.

Because children can opt out of school at sixteen, sticking with high school requires motivation. As children reach the last half of the second decade, there is less time to make up for lost ground. If an eighteen- to twenty-year-old is floundering, there will be people who graduated from high school coming along behind them and getting the available jobs. Each person coming of age has the right to compete for their own place in society. A dropout can lose this chance and be passed along the way. Getting back in the game may not be easy.

A high school diploma gives youth the opportunity to start making decisions that shape the course of their own lives.

It provide choices and officially signals the successful completion of twelve years of compulsory education. A diploma is tangible evidence that a young man or woman is now ready to take over the controls that will guide them in their long life ahead.

There is much going on in a young person's life— but none is more important than earning a high school diploma.

An involved parent and mentor can have a powerful influence when it comes to education. Don't miss the opportunity to encourage your child or any youth you can influence to finish high school and earn their diploma.

Next, we will discuss the choices that arise near the end of the Second Decade.

7

FINISHING THE SECOND DECADE

"That's the value of a college education … I don't
know anywhere in the world where you can make an
investment and [realize] that kind of return."
GASTON CAPERTON

S TUDENTS ANTICIPATING THE END OF HIGH SCHOOL ARE FACED
with the question: Should I further my education or not?
Two-thirds of high school graduates will elect to attend
some type of college. Of those, two-thirds will enroll in a traditional four-year college with the aim of earning a bachelor's
degree. Fifteen percent of these students will continue on for
one or two more years to pursue a master's degree. One third of
college-bound students will enroll in a two-year or community
college.[1] Those high school graduates, one-third of the class, not
furthering their formal education at a college will be expected
to enter the workforce immediately, usually expecting some
on-the-job training.[2]

During the last two years of high school, all youth are called
on to make an important decision that will have far-reaching
consequences for the rest of their lives: "I will start working at a
job as soon as I graduate and work my way up" or "I will go to

college now and hope for a better start with a higher-paying job and move on from there."[3]

With guidance from parents, teachers, counselors, mentors, and in some cases even from peers, all teenagers should start planning for their future while still in high school.

This is when a child should consider where she wants to start in the workforce and where she hopes to end up.

A compelling reason for continuing formal education beyond high school is supported by statistics that indicate the quality of a person's job, as well as the total income earned throughout life, is closely related to the highest level of education a person achieves.[4] Moreover, high-paying manufacturing jobs, long a bastion of the high school graduate, are giving way to service and technical jobs that require more specialized training than can be accomplished either in high school or on the job. This is giving rise to the need for additional formal education or training of some kind.[5]

Discussions with your children about their education plans should begin with aims, but eventually be tempered by reality. This means that planning for your child's future should include a realistic assessment of what he hopes to accomplish and how likely he is to achieve this goal. There should also be a plan for how to pay for this education.

After going over these preliminaries with your child, and dealing with the benefits of further education, you now must answer two important questions: Is my child considering the best course for him/herself? How can this education be obtained without creating a burdensome debt?

A high school diploma is just a starting point that is achieved by 80 percent of people in the U.S. (Statistics for high school graduation in the United States depend on how many graduate considering the whole population; this number might be close to 80 percent. However, if graduation statistics are based on how many of those who begin high school eventually graduate, the number is closer to 90 percent.)

A diploma can be compared to starting blocks for runners in a track meet. Like a runner in starting blocks, a high school graduate starts with the advantage of a solid foundation from which to push off. But looking side to side, there are lots of other youth on the starting line with the same "advantage." Looking ahead, the same track is there for all graduates, each using the resources they have (no two people are exactly the same), hoping to do well in the "race" of life.

Obtaining additional training beyond high school—before starting this "race of life" is like moving the starting blocks farther up the track, creating an early advantage that could lead to a better job, more satisfaction, and higher pay. The course of life is long. It takes effort and resolve to succeed with a good start and even more effort and resolve to successfully overcome a poor one.

A young person near the end of his second decade, having earned a high school diploma or GED is qualified to do the following:

▼ Apply for an entry-level job with on-the-job training, and some hope for advancement or based on this experience move on to a different job.

▼ Enlist in the armed forces; receive job training and other educational benefits, both during and after service (See ch. 11)

▼ Enter an apprentice program that will require an additional two to five years of combined practical and classroom training and then enter a trade.

▼ Enroll in a community college for vocational training, earning a vocational certificate in about a year or complete a two-year associate degree before entering the workforce or transferring to a four-year college.

▼ Enroll in a four-year college or university to pursue a liberal arts degree, preparing for further study toward a graduate or professional degree; or major in a wide selection of specialties like business, nursing, architecture, teaching, journalism, etc., with or without moving on to earn a master's degree before entering the workforce.

The options for the high school graduate are many and varied. Pursuing any of the above options represents at least a tangible step toward gaining control of one's life as an adult. Though college is the choice for most high school graduates, there are many reasons why a youth would choose to forego college. Some who intend to go to work immediately after high school, and this includes about one-third of graduates, do so for reasons that could include: lack of interest, no example or encouragement at home, or the work in college would be too difficult. Others are not fully aware of their options, didn't do well in high school, or they are simply tired of going to school, and have had enough of the classroom. Some might want to

In the United States, the distinction between a college and a university is not always clear. *College* is a term used by most for any post-high school formal education. This term could include a community college for vocational training or a two-year associate degree and also Harvard College which offers a liberal arts curriculum that allows a graduate to enroll in one of twelve graduate programs at Harvard University including: medicine, education, law, business, international affairs, etc. A state university is likely to designate all of its undergraduate divisions as colleges; for example, calling the liberal arts curriculum the "College of Literature, Science, and the Arts."

continue with their education, but are denied the opportunity by circumstances beyond their control, including family and financial reasons, or because of life choices they have made.

Whatever work your child chooses to do after high school in favor of continuing his studies, he should be thinking about what he wants to do in the long term. The following is an example of a "dead end" job:

> *For Brian, a nineteen-year-old two years out of high school, lugging heavy furniture as the low man on a household moving crew, is a perfectly acceptable job today—but will this be the case in a few years? Should he be doing something now to prepare for a better or more suitable job later on, or should he have gotten training even before starting this work?*
>
> *I raised this subject, tactfully, while I watched Brian on the job during our daughter's recent move. It didn't take long to conclude that this young man was focused only on the present as far as his job was concerned. He was satisfied with his job and pay and felt that it would suit him for the foreseeable future. When the time was right for him he could change, but not now.*

Was he being shortsighted? I think so! As a parent, you should help your child with decisions like this rather than expecting him to face them alone. This includes urging your child to pursue formal education or vocational training as soon as possible after finishing high school. This may be the most important advice a person between eighteen and twenty can receive.

It is hard to argue against the value of a good education, especially when it is achieved based on a strategic plan. But there is never a guarantee. Where a person starts does not always determine where he will end up, but having a sound plan in the immediate post-high-school years and sticking to it can be a reliable predictor of success.

With a high school diploma in hand, a youth can look forward, in theory at least, to a future with nearly unlimited options. The

LIFE LESSONS

Rachael had her first child shortly after graduating from high school, and a second child a year later. Between the ages of seventeen and twenty, she was busy caring for her two children, with little time for anything else. Now, at age twenty-five, with one child in the first grade and the second in kindergarten, Rachael, who is working as a waitress, would like to go back to school to become a social worker. Money will be a problem for this single mother. She is planning to start at a two-year community college, costing less than one-third the amount of a typical four-year college, and will apply for grants and scholarships that could pay most of her tuition, fees, and book expenses. Rachael missed her first and best chance to prepare for life ahead, the years immediately after high school, in favor of starting a family. Her work is cut out for her, but with persistence and taking advantage of the financial help available, Rachael has at least a chance of reaching her goal. However, experience at community colleges has shown that older students like Rachael, who have pressing family and personal needs, are at high risk for dropping out. Those who stay the course and succeed are rewarded with a chance for a better job, but unfortunately this tends to be the exception more than the rule. Less than half of older students who enroll in a public two-year college complete their course and receive a degree.[6]

regimentation of the K through 12 years behind, a young person is now free to make his own decisions, but this is an opportunity that can invoke mixed emotions.

The joy of being free to make your own decisions is tempered by the sobering reality that you are now required to make good decisions—many that will have life-long consequences.

Each fall, more than twenty million high school graduates make the decision to attend college. About 7.3 million will attend a two-year community college and 13.7 million will attend a traditional four-year college. This means that nearly two-thirds of all eighteen year olds in the United States have made the decision to enroll in a college of some kind.[7] Deciding to embark on a college career is an important decision for a youth. It is one of the first of many that must be made before entering the workforce, and it is the final years of their Second Decade when this decision is made by most.

The years immediately after high school are likely to be the first time since birth when a child is not expected to do practically the same things as her peers. All kids learned to walk, were toilet trained, were taught how to get along with others, completed grade school, completed high school, etc.—at pretty much the same time. These expectations were universal and the challenges tended to be similar for all.

At age eighteen, life changes.

Now a young person can vote, is legally emancipated, and can enlist in the military or marry on their own recognizance all while beginning to assume shared responsibility with parents; youth this age are taking more responsibility for their own care and well-being.[8]

The last years of the Second Decade are a period of transition, a time when children should be listened to when they talk about their concrete plans as well as their idealistic dreams.

In a supportive family, this transition could have begun earlier in the teen years. In that case, the transition is likely to take place gradually, and continue over several years. This transition from youth to young adulthood can be influenced by how much time a child spends at home, and how well parents grasp the importance of this time in their child's life.

In other cases, this transition can be chaotic and end sadly, resulting in a life of chronic under achievement, poverty, and even incarceration.[9]

The time and effort put forth by parents, teachers, and mentors in the years leading up to and during those final years of the Second Decade can pay huge dividends when it comes to a child's success later in life.

There are a number of reasons children give for not going to college, including:[10]

- ▼ Lacks a role model. (No one in my family ever attended college.)

- ▼ Lacks guidance and/or initiative. (I don't know how to find or choose a college.)

- ▼ Lacks self-esteem. Some children are just not cut out for higher education. (I didn't do well in high school; college-level courses will be too difficult. I don't like the idea of more school.)

- ▼ Lacks self-confidence. (I could go but I am afraid I won't fit in at college.)

- ▼ Can't afford the tuition and/or books.

- ▼ Chooses to join the armed forces.

- ▼ Complacency and lack of parental guidance. (My parents don't have a college degree and they did okay.)

▼ Doesn't realize the financial benefits of higher education. (I already have a job.)

Of the eight reasons listed above, five are related to lack of guidance and mentoring. With better counseling at school and more support at home, a few more children could be influenced to attend college, but it has to be expected that some qualified individuals simply will miss the chance. Should they? I am not aware of any sound argument supporting the absolute value of foregoing further formal education, or at least vocational training, especially for a person who has the intelligence to better prepare for a life at work. With the exception of those with the lowest IQ, any child can benefit from learning a work-related or vocational skill beyond high school. (See ch. 5)

An IQ of about 100 or a little above, which includes close to the top 50 percent of the population, is said to be required to complete the least-demanding courses at a four-year college, at least with some comfort. This is supported by the statistic that just under one-half of the population in the United States has a bachelor's degree.[11] This leaves a broad swath of the population, nearly half, that would not be expected to fare well at a four-year college. However many kids who would be considered borderline or likely to be unqualified for a four-year college could function adequately at a community college and earn an associate degree. In addition, there are more who could successfully complete a vocational certificate, enter the military, or become an apprentice.[12]

Most high school graduates who decide to go to work in lieu of attending college, land the type of job that provides on-the-job training as brief as one day or as intense as a month or longer. These jobs include fast-food, low-end retail, maintenance, unskilled labor, etc. They are low-paying and often short-term. But steady work at any job requires know-how and a level of commitment. Short of some type of formal training, it is up to each individual to get this knowledge the best way they can and, in these cases, it is likely to be "learning" while at work.

Excellent training that promises a well-paying and steady job can be achieved as an apprentice working in a trade, like electrical; plumbing, heating; and air conditioning; automobile mechanic; pipefitter; carpenter; and more. These apprenticeships, lasting for as long as five years, also include significant periods of classroom training, but these opportunities are limited. Those interested in this career path should discuss it with their counselor or inquire locally. (Information about apprenticeships can be obtained by contacting the U.S. Department of Labor at: www.careeronestop.org/credentials/trainingoptions/apprenticeships.aspx.)

If your child begins work immediately after high school, by the end of the Second Decade she could be in her third year at a job she enjoys and is good at. Ideally she is earning a steady income with benefits, including health insurance, and is looking forward to advancement either with the same employer or moving on to something more suitable. She could be earning $25,000 annually, along with additional health and retirement benefits. For the future she could be looking forward to an average peak income of $35,000, or she could be juggling multiple low-paying part-time jobs with no benefits; or she could even be unemployed. The lifetime earnings of a high school graduate are estimated to be 60% of the earnings of a person whose highest degree is a bachelor's degree and 80% of the earnings of a person with a two-year associate degree.[13]

One reason for otherwise excellent applicants being overlooked today is many human resources departments use automated processes or outside contractors to screen candidates, automatically eliminating those lacking specific credentials, like a bachelor's degree. Using this criterion, otherwise qualified or even superior candidates could be eliminated without anyone looking more closely at their experience and qualifications.

Formal education is the most reliable way to get started, but it is not the only way to finish.

LIFE LESSONS

Grace completed two years of college, one year each at two different schools. Half of the courses she took were business-related and the rest were liberal arts. She earned good grades, but lacked that all-important degree.

She entered the workforce at nineteen and worked for fourteen years, starting as a secretary before being promoted to administrative assistant to the director of the city library system. Later she was a senior manager at a software company. During her career, Grace assumed greater responsibility, received regular pay raises, and with benefits she was earning a salary appropriate for the responsibility she assumed and the quality of work she completed. Her pay was equal to or higher than most coworkers who had earned a bachelor's degree.

When the software company consolidated and moved its headquarters to another state and Grace was unable to relocate, she became unemployed for the first time in her life. Grace undertook a job search immediately. With confidence, based on her extensive experience and strong recommendations, she fully expected to find a suitable job well within the six months covered by her severance pay. Even with the help of a job coach, paid for by her employer, aggressively submitting applications, and getting encouragement from all who knew her, it took Grace the full six months to find work. Moreover, while the job she landed is satisfactory, the pay is less than she earned at the software company and the job requirements are below Grace's skill level.

Other job applicants, by simply having a four-year degree, were likely put ahead of Grace. This denied her of even getting called in for an interview in spite of her extensive experience and glowing recommendations.

Grace met the challenge of losing and then regaining her place in the workforce, but not without considerable effort on her part along with a willingness to be flexible when it came to taking on a new position.

People with sufficient intelligence and savvy, and who put themselves in the right place and can recognize when it is the right time, are likely to learn from whatever they are doing and be rewarded for their performance. This includes practical on-the-job training, especially in technical areas, which is invaluable. However, having that all important diploma continues to be a huge asset.

Let's consider the formal education options available as the end of the second decade nears:

Community College

A two-year community college can be the endgame of formal education for some and a bridge to a four-year degree for others. As with most life choices, there are pros and cons when it comes to attending a two-year community college. On the plus side, this school offers lower tuition fees; a greater likelihood of living at home rent-free; possibly a better chance of finding a part-time job; the opportunity to take a lighter class load; and, most of all, the opportunity to learn a skill in two years or less.

> **"Community colleges are one of America's great social inventions, a gateway to the future for first-time students looking for an affordable college education, and for mid-career students looking to get ahead in the workplace."**
> Barbara Mikulski

Community college can be a good choice for students from low-income families and/or who were challenged by the more difficult courses they took in high school. Success at a community college can provide these youth with not only a boost of confidence, but also a sense of accomplishment. Other students may choose a community college as a more economical choice for their first two years of college before transferring to a four-year college where they hope to earn a bachelor's degree.

Students from families making less than $30,000 a year are twice as likely to enroll in a two-year community college compared to those from a median-income family, and are ten times more likely than students from high-income families. A community college education is made possible, in part, by scholarships and grants that cover tuition and fees; and possibly with some money left over for books.[14] About 16 percent of those who graduate with an associate degree from a community college go on to earn a bachelor's degree at a four-year college.[15]

Ivy Tech Community College in Indiana is in many ways typical of the more than 1,600 community colleges in the United States. Because the thirty regional campuses of Ivy Tech are combined into a single statewide system, it is the largest with 200,000 students enrolled. Ivy Tech offers more than thirty associate degrees, ranging alphabetically from agriculture to visual science. In addition, nine- to twelve-month certificates can be earned in dozens of areas, like accounting, real estate, dental assistance, paralegal studies, and more. Typical of most community colleges, Ivy Tech also has more than 350 online courses available.[16]

One of the perceived disadvantages of attending a community college is that the typical atmosphere of "college life" is lacking on social, athletic, and higher academic and research levels. Another potential drawback of the community college could be related to the type of students who attend. Classes are apt to include older students who have been away from school, and others taking advantage of lower admission and retention requirements. The makeup of such a class can result in slower progress, which holds back those students who are better prepared.

Moreover, prestige for these schools is lower with the likelihood there will be fewer contacts with influential alumni. In addition, many community college students are also working with family obligations that can sidetrack them, leading to dropping out. It has been shown, and is understandable based on the

LIFE LESSONS

Zak, an enthusiastic, no-nonsense fellow in jeans and a printed tee shirt with a tattoo peeking out from under his right sleeve, works alongside the proprietor and one other employee at a fast sign shop. When given a sheet containing amateurishly assembled material with the right words, but not delivering the best message, Zak sits down at his computer and applies the magic of a skilled designer. In just a few minutes, the words and a simple diagram are transformed into a clear message describing a variety of delicious frozen soups for sale. On questioning, Zak said he studied graphic design at a respected four-year university, adding, "But I didn't graduate."

Good at what he does, steadily employed, and making $22 an hour plus benefits, Zak is happy at work. He completed five semesters at a traditional four-year college and left in the middle of his junior year. He ran out of money (or at least the willingness to go further in debt) and felt that he had learned enough to do what he wanted to do. In the process, Zak spent $25,000 in tuition alone, and left school with a feeling of failing because he didn't get his degree.

Instead of enrolling in an expensive four-year college, Zak could have enrolled in a graphic design program at the local community college and completed an associate degree in two years; doing so at less than one-third the per-semester cost of the four-year university. He would have met his goals faster and graduated with a sense of accomplishment—a degree. Better counseling while still in high school would have saved Zak time, money, and the risk of lower self-esteem.

school's makeup, that students who enroll in a two-year college with the intention of eventually getting a bachelor's degree are less likely to do so compared with a student who begins in a four-year school, but there are offsetting advantages to a community college.[17]

The negatives associated with selecting a community college notwithstanding, several compelling reasons remain for attending this type of school. First and most important is that anyone with a high school diploma or a GED (See ch. 6) can enroll either directly out of high school or after being away from school for months or years.

Another reason for selecting a community college is that students are more likely to avoid building up large debt from student loans.

This is especially so for youth who are eager to enter the workforce with just the amount and type of formal education and training needed for the job they select, have an idea of what they want to do, and find the courses they want available at a community college.

The combination of lower costs and abundance of job-related training opportunities are significant plusses for attending a community college.

Successful community college students with an associate degree or a certificate have an advantage over high school graduates simply because they have acquired a skill and have a degree to show for it. The community college graduate succeeds in this case because he has invested in himself. If your child is not sure what he wants to do, a community college could be a good place to start.

A community college also offers selected classes for students who qualify for more challenging courses that proceed at a faster pace. Students in these classes can become eligible for Phi Theta Kappa honors (the Phi Beta Kappa equivalent for community college).[18]

Thomas J. Snyder, President of Ivy Tech Community College in Indiana and author of *The Community College Career Track*, regularly advises students who intend to complete the four years required for a bachelor's degree to consider spending their first two years at a community college. His reasons are the following: community college credits for courses that have been selected properly and completed with satisfactory grades are fully transferrable to 90 percent of colleges (at least in Indiana); the cost of a two-year community college is about one-third that of a typical four-year college; scholarships and grants are available, especially on the basis of need; those who transfer and graduate receive a diploma granted by the four-year institution.[19]

Tara's success story (see Life Lessons on page 103) is typical of one that could be repeated by any high school graduate who knows what she would like to do, and is eager to acquire a skill that will enable her to join the workforce immediately at a good job. But there are other characteristics of the typical student body of a community college.

According to an administrator at Ivy Tech Community College, many of their students are actually four-year college graduates who return to school, usually at night or part-time, so they can obtain a certificate of competence allowing them to move ahead with their careers.[20] Earning a specialty certificate at a community college requires satisfactory completion of a short course in a defined discipline; such as, real estate, accounting, financial brokerage, human resources, paralegal, hospitality, and more.

Four-Year College or University

A four-year college can be a liberal arts institution that offers what essentially is a pre-graduate school or pre-professional degree in the humanities, or it can be the type, usually larger, that also offers a "job ready" degree in disciplines like engineering, business, journalism, architecture, chemistry, computer

LIFE LESSONS

Tara is thirty years old and works as a dental assistant. She has worked in the same office for ten years. She is happy working as a carryover employee after a young dentist and two colleagues recently bought the practice where she worked for an older dentist who retired. In addition to Tara, there are two dental hygienists, two dental technicians, and two receptionists in this busy office.

After graduating from high school, Tara decided she wanted to be a dental technician or assistant. Although several dental assistants she knew had been trained on the job, Tara felt she would have an easier time finding a job and would be better qualified if she sought formal training. She enrolled in a local community college, studied for nine months, and earned her Dental Assistant certificate. With many changes in clinical dentistry, Tara has had to keep up by reading journals and attending seminars. She is happy with her job, and earns $35,000 a year with additional health and retirement benefits. Although she is confident that she will keep her job, Tara' skills are portable and there are potential job opportunities with more than 300,000 dentists in the U.S., each needing one or more people with skills like hers. Tara is happy at work and is satisfied with the career path she chose.

science, interior design, etc. A four-year college offers more than a community college, but also costs more.

Students at a four-year college are exposed to "college life," with Greek society, athletics, living away from home and parental supervision, etc. The quality and richness of campus life can have significant plusses both short term and in the long run; and most significantly it offers that first step toward self-sufficiency. Students can enter the workforce after obtaining a bachelor's degree or continue with their education to earn a master's degree, a doctorate, or earn a professional degree.

On the downside, in the past fifty years, the cost of a bachelor's degree has increased dramatically. This greater cost is mostly because of higher tuition, which in some cases has risen from the hundreds per semester to the thousands with an overall increase of nearly ten times in the cost of college![21]

Greater cost has had an adverse effect on some graduates, especially those who remain unemployed and underemployed while at the same time being saddled with high student loan debt. More than one graduate in ten polled recently said that they regretted the decision to go to college because they now have a debt that they find difficult to repay.

When it comes to reducing the need for school debt while attending a four-year college, a city campus can offer a money-saving advantage by allowing a student to live at home. In this case, there also might be a better chance of securing a part-time job in familiar territory making it possible to offset tuition and living expenses.

Private universities can have total costs more than double a state school; however, those with large endowments provide lucrative scholarships for qualified students.

This scholarship aid can be based on grades and test scores, but financial aid is also available to assist students who meet enrollment requirements and are from low-income families. These scholarships can mean that in a few cases, a private college or university will cost only slightly more than a state university.

If your child plans on attending a four-year college, two things are likely to be uppermost in your mind: How much will it cost, including how much debt will be incurred, and, will my child be able to find a good job upon graduation? It is a good idea for any parent, who hopes to see their child attend college, to explore tax free 529 college savings accounts by inquiring at: www.sec.gov/investor/pubs/intro529.htm

In 2015, the answers to these questions, posed above, for the average student are not encouraging. The average left over debt for a bachelor's degree is $35,000; including $26,000 in government-subsidized loans.[22] The total cost for tuition, books, fees, and spending money for an in-state student for one year at a typical state university is around $26,000. An out-of-state student and most students attending a private college or university would expect to pay double this amount or even more per year![23] Moreover, according to Jordan Wasserman, senior business and economics correspondent for *Slate* magazine:

> "Today's crop of new BAs are starting at roughly 8.5 percent unemployment and 16.8 percent under-employment. Close to half of those who land work won't immediately find a job that requires their degree, and for those stuck in that situation, there are fewer 'good' jobs to go around."[24]

This is sobering, but these numbers are averages and include all people.[25] Your child's fate is his alone; subject to what he can do, how hard he works, and how much luck he has along the way. When considering this, remember the old saying "The harder I work, the luckier I get."

Doctorate Degree

Let's look closely at the educational requirements for achieving the most advanced degrees (PhD, MD, DO, OD, JD, etc.). But first, I want to be clear that the cost of tuition is likely to increase for graduate education, and the financial impact of living expenses and time away from the workforce continue to accumulate.

Once you have decided to pursue a doctorate or professional degree several issues have been dealt with. First it takes a lot of classroom time, along with serious "book work," and study at home to earn any of these degrees, but that's not all. Especially toward the end of training, these professions, no matter how exalted the degree might *sound*, require the practical application of skills you have attained in a way that is similar, in my opinion, to the final years of studying a trade. For example, an MD takes a lot of academic courses and studies theory in school to get ready, but once on the job, she works at tasks enabling her to learn skills under the tutelage and guidance of an experienced professional, often one-on-one—not unlike an apprentice learning a trade. After eight years of school, an intern joins the medical team on the bottom rung, and has a long haul before he will eventually enter practice.

Realize that attending university for eight years is not necessarily better; look at it as being simply different—a personal choice. Compared to Bill Gates, who dropped out of Harvard; or Frank McKinney, who never enrolled in college (see appendix B), a person with a degree might feel less accomplished compared to a person who didn't finish college or even go to college at all. Remind your child to focus on his skills and interests—be inspired by others but don't compare. We can't all be Bill Gates!

Study for a profession begins with an undergraduate enrolled in a pre-professional program. (For me it was pre-med.) The pre-professional program, usually resulting in a bachelor's degree in liberal arts, prepares a person for little more than additional schooling. (In fairness, this is the stated purpose of a liberal arts education.) As education for a more advanced degree progresses, courses become focused and practical. In medicine, it eventually turns into a form of on-the-job-training with steadily increased responsibility during an internship, residency, and fellowship.

Now, let's look at the scenario for a typical medical specialist. This is about the longest formal education program pursued today. You might want to share this with your child as she nears the end of her Second Decade and begins planning for her life's work. This might help her decide how many years she expects or wants to devote to formal education before venturing into the world of work.

All individuals must decide how many years they are willing to attend school, what type of work they want to do, and at what stage they want to start working at their career.

1. **Bachelor's degree:** This typically entails four years of exposure to a wide variety of course material both elective and required. Students learn to think and employ their brain as a tool not just a repository. During undergraduate study, students are typically exposed to the humanities, including English, literature, history, and anthropology, philosophy, social studies, psychology, science, and foreign languages. In addition, students have time to take sufficient courses, including required science courses, to qualify for a specific pre-professional area or in disciplines such as education, nursing, engineering, business, architecture, and a wide variety of others enabling them to graduate in four years with a specific skill that could equip them to join the workforce immediately. For those who intend to continue their formal education, a bachelor's degree with the proper pre-requisites can prepare a student to progress in their chosen field of study pursuing a master's degree in the disciplines described above, a doctorate, or a professional degree. Approximately 30 percent of the U.S. population has a bachelor's degree.[26]

2. **Master's degree:** This academic degree is awarded by a university to a person who has successfully completed an advanced course of study in a specific field, for example: MBA (master of business administration), MPH (master of public health), MSW (master of social work), etc. These courses are usually completed in one or two years after

receiving a bachelor's degree. Approximately 8 percent of the U.S population has a master's degree or higher.[27]

3. **Doctorate:** This is the highest academic degree and it usually requires three or four additional years of college after receiving a bachelor's degree. A doctorate prepares a person to be better trained and more knowledgeable when it comes to gathering, using, and expanding information in a specific field, and this includes teaching and reserch. This could be in history, psychology, English, science, and almost any course of study or discipline that awards a doctorate. A person with a PhD may work at a well-defined discipline, be an administrator, or she may teach and carry out research in her field of interest. Less than 2 percent of the U.S. population has earned a doctorate.[28]

4. **Professional degree (Doctorate):** This doctorate takes three to four years of formal education after receiving a bachelor's degree. These professional degrees include MD (medical doctor), JD (Juris doctor), DO (doctor of osteopathy), OD (doctor of optometry), DDS (doctor of dental surgery), DVM (doctor of veterinary medicine), and others. Each has a period of practical training after professional school before a license to actually practice can be obtained. The combined total of the population that holds a professional degree and or a doctorate is approximately 3 percent.[29]

Practical training following the attainment of a professional degree varies, but some professions, like medicine, have a period of time when the graduate is gradually exposed to more responsibilities in the workplace, with some supervision, before obtaining the right to assume complete responsibility for his practice and independent decision-making.

The following describes the years of education and training required for a typical medical specialist—but a path like this, formal or informal, exists for many professions and occupations. Medical specialists are required to complete an additional two, three, or more years after an internship, and pass a test or otherwise meet the qualification requirements to be certified by a board of their peers.

Internship: As a doctor with a diploma that says "MD," it is time to serve a one-year stint as a physician with a limited license, working in a hospital setting under direct supervision. This is when you apply the knowledge you acquired in medical school while gaining skills through practical experience, including hands-on. An internship, when it comes to the twelve monthly "rotations," tends to be selective and not comprehensive, but the lessons learned are transferrable and applicable to the overall concept of being a doctor.

Residency: Two years or more after internship (as many as seven) as a fully licensed physician, are spent by many young doctors learning to diagnose and treat disease in a specific area of medicine. This is done both with supervision and on one's own. A resident is a licensed doctor who engages in a specialty area of study that is limited to a specific type of patient or healthcare issue. Supervised training is combined with independent practice to gain in-depth knowledge.

A specialist retains all of the rights of a fully licensed physician, but is more likely to keep abreast of the advances in medicine related to the area of his own specialty to some degree at the expense of the broader fields of medicine.

The general practitioner or primary care physician who usually entered practice immediately after internship has largely been replaced, by the doctor who spends three years in a family medicine residency or an equivalent training program with a broader scope than most traditional specialists who concentrate on a limited phase of health care. Much primary care is now provided by specialists in internal medicine or by hospitalists who are often internists taking primary responsibility for any patient admitted to the hospital.[30]

Fellowship: A medical fellow devotes one year or more of selected study under a mentor chosen by the fellow (mentee) in his area of specialty or subspecialty. This period of training has more to do with attitude, style, and is a sort of fine-tuning. You know the moves, now you are learning the subtleties and nuances of the specialty or subspecialty you are pursuing.

Finally, you enter the practice of your chosen profession. Mandatory continuing education for recertification is required for many who hold professional degrees, and most people who earn a doctorate/professional degree maintain a life-long regimen of study while continuing to learn from experience on the job. The typical medical specialist will enter practice when they are in their early to mid-thirties—thirteen to sixteen years, in most cases, after completing high school.

Be Flexible

Sometimes, even with the best intentions and careful planning, when you believe you have made the right choices and you have worked hard—life doesn't work out as you anticipated. When this happens, you need to reassess the situation and be flexible enough to make what can be considered mid-course corrections.

Let me explain.

Mary was a popular student in high school and happy with the way her life was progressing. She was captain of the cheerleading squad, participated in several clubs, and also worked regularly at different jobs after school, on weekends, and during the summer. She earned good grades, participated in several school-related activities, and had what added up to an ideal high school career.

She was raised in a middle-class family and her parents were college graduates. She had two younger brothers and her mother was a stay-at-home mom. Her father was steadily employed at an accounting firm and earned a salary that put him near the top 10 percent when it came to income.

When it was time for Mary to start college, she decided to attend a state university, along with several of her high school classmates. There were many advantages to this arrangement, including a wide variety of courses, Greek society, football games, and the advantage of attending a prestigious school. Mary was a good student, who had easily met the school's admission requirements, but she did not qualify for any academic scholarships and, based on family income, was not eligible for any need-based grants.

Mary chose fine arts as her major. Over the next four years, she enjoyed all the aspects of college life, including joining a sorority; but also worked part-time on a regular basis in the campus bookstore. During the summers, she worked fulltime at a variety of jobs. This included working as a nurse's aide during the summer between her junior and senior years.

By her last semester, it was clear to Mary she could not expect to answer many job calls based on her bachelor's degree in fine arts. And, although she had received some support from her family and worked regularly at a variety of jobs to help pay school expenses, she was more than $24,000 in debt, just below the national average. Her family had done what they could and Mary worked hard but there was not enough money from home and her work to fully pay for the $26,000 annual cost of school.

Hardworking and resilient, Mary decided that, based on her positive experience as a nurse's aide, she would pursue a career in nursing. This meant a semester at a local four-year college to complete the science pre-requisites for nursing school, and two more years at a nursing school located in her home town. The two and a half additional years of school and living at home were "all business" for Mary. The dividend was that she gained a marketable skill and would earn a good salary working at a job she enjoyed.

After graduating with a nursing degree, Mary's total school debt was $30,000 and she was six and one half years out of high school. The élan of college life came at a high cost for her. But Mary was prudent enough to make a midcourse change in her plans and came out a winner.

Earning Power

When it comes to earning power, the importance of education is tangible.

The single most important (but not the only) factor determining the wages people are likely to earn is the level of education achieved *before* starting their life's work.

The U.S. Department of Labor regularly reports the relative scale for annual income in terms of education and also the relative ratio of lifetime income. The ratio of lifetime income does not take into consideration time out of the workforce while going to school or studying in a lower paying training position or the length of time actively in the workforce.[31]

Annual Income	Ratio Life Income	Reference HS Grad
High school dropout	$25,100	0.72
High school diploma	$35,400	1.00
Some college	$40,400	1.13
Associate degree	$44,800	1.27
Bachelor's degree	$56,500	1.56
Master's degree	$70,000	1.96
Doctoral degree	$91,000	2.43
Professional degree	$102,200	2.92

Note that the biggest relative difference in income, based solely on formal education, is between a high school graduate, who makes 30 percent more than a high school dropout.

The next greatest difference is between those with a bachelor's degree, who make 20 percent more than a person with an associate degree. Moreover, the unemployment rate for high school dropouts is 50 percent greater than for high school graduates.[32]

These numbers are only averages. Individual statistics can differ greatly; so no blanket assumptions should be made about how much your child will earn. People at each education level, working fulltime and considered successful in their field, can earn much more than these averages; for example, the 2014 median income for cardiac surgeons, one of the higher paid professionals ranged from $142,000 at the low end to $617,000 at the highest.[33] Bolstered by the extremes, these statistics clearly show that the more education a person achieves, the more money she is likely to make. Making the very highest income, in seven figures and even more, is not achieved by a person who works at a job based primarily on their level of education but is limited almost exclusively to the businessman or entrepreneur.[34]

Going to school longer and earning lots of money doesn't guarantee happiness—nor should it be the sole measure of success.

A fruitful and satisfying life is based on many things. I believe the minimum goal for youth finishing their Second Decade should be finding their place in the "major leagues of life." (See ch. 14) The characteristics of which are:

▼ Work you enjoy at a job that you have a reasonable chance of keeping.

▼ Time for family and outside activities.

▼ Enough money to meet the needs of the family.

▼ Freedom and confidence to plan for the future.

▼ Satisfaction with a life that frees you from envy of those with more material things.

Parents and mentors can help teens research their options while encouraging them to make the best choices—but you must also realize that the final decision and the work needed to accomplish these goals is not yours. Ultimately, success in higher education is dependent on the youth's effort.

Next, we will discuss the value of meaningful work and what youth can derive from this activity.

8

W-O-R-K

"Without ambition one starts nothing. Without work
one finishes nothing. The prize will not be sent to you.
You have to win it."
RALPH WALDO EMERSON

AN IMPORTANT MILESTONE IS WHEN A CHILD HAS HIS FIRST chance to work outside of the home. It is likely this opportunity will come through the efforts of a parent, teacher, or other adult who knows the child. After all, a ten- to twelve-year-old doesn't have much in the way of a network when it comes to employment opportunities. (Parents who give their child chores around the home are also the ones most likely to determine the best time and place for their child's first job away from home.)

Help from a parent in obtaining a first job in no way diminishes the value a child can receive from the experience. Once at work, your child is on her own, earning money for the work being accomplished, and as a bonus learning practical skills and lessons that will add to and complement what she is being taught in school. The combination of formal education and life lessons from meaningful work outside of school can have a positive and far-reaching effect on your child's future.[1]

However, when it comes to hours spent at a job while attending high school, there should be limits. Working too many hours can put a student at risk for lower grades—though studies have shown that between 15 and 23 hours of work per week should not interfere with schoolwork or adversely affect grades. However it is important to monitor the teen's grades and take action if classwork is slipping.

Moreover, work should not rule out extracurricular school activities such as sports and clubs. School, study time, activities, and work should all be balanced.[2]

Over the last seven decades, I have observed the positive influence that working can have on a young person. This includes my personal experiences as a youth and what I learned from my parents, my children, my grandchildren, and my grandchildren's friends. In addition, during my more than forty years as a physician, I had the opportunity to interact with thousands of adolescents and their parents. My experience is anecdotal but it is supported by others:[3, 4]

Children between the ages of ten and twenty who have the benefit of working at a meaningful job will learn new skills, develop confidence, assume responsibility, and gain maturity faster.

According to the United States Department of Labor, there are no mandated age restrictions for overall youth employment. However, there are specific federal guidelines when it comes to hazardous jobs. Most of the jobs a teenager would be likely to perform require that they have attained the age of fourteen as a minimum. The intention of any state child labor law is to safeguard children at work, but each state has its own specific set of rules. This includes a few states that require a child to obtain a state-issued work permit, but in most states that responsibility resides with the employer. For particularly hazardous work, both Federal and state regulations require that the worker is between eighteen and twenty. Most of the earliest jobs for a teenager are safe, start around age fourteen, and therefore fit within most state guidelines.[5, 6]

Meaningful work for ten- to fourteen-year-olds is not regulated. Usually this work consists of projects around the home or in the neighborhood. These tasks can be compensated with money or a sincere thank-you, especially those chores that are done around the home. It isn't necessary or even a good idea to pay your son or daughter for routine tasks like drying the dishes and taking out the garbage.

There is a wide range of safe, simple, informal (freelance) work opportunities for children in this age group.

Common jobs include: babysitting, pet care (walking, sitting, and feeding), yard maintenance, newspaper delivery, shoveling snow, washing cars, handyman and helper, etc. Larger home projects, like painting the garage, power-washing the deck, or cleaning the eve troughs could save the family money because they will not be hired out and, therefore could justify payment, but that is a family decision.

An allowance for overall good behavior and to help children gain some practice in handling money is okay, but the family is a team and should work this out together.

Some unpaid activities that also provide useful experience for this younger age group include: 4-H, Boy Scouts, Future Farmers of America, Boys and Girls Clubs (Girls Inc.), Big Brothers/Big Sisters, YMCA, school clubs and sports, church activities, etc.

Work and participation in activities like the above contribute to *Positive Youth Development*, conceptualized by Karen Pittman and described as the 5 C's:[7]

Competence
Confidence
Connection
Character
Caring

Structured activities, including having a paying job, are more likely to be associated with positive youth development than unstructured after-school activities aka "hanging around."[6]

If you want to instill the 5 C's in your child, a good way to start is to help him find a job that fits in with his other obligations; foremost of which is school.

Later, when your child is older, work opportunities should expand beyond the neighborhood to employment that demands greater responsibility and offers appropriate financial compensation. This could include: childcare (good idea to get training from an organization like Safe Sitter, founded by Patricia Keener, MD, an academic pediatrician,[8] or the American Red Cross), doing errands for the elderly and homebound, carwash attendant, managing clubs and carts at a golf course (caddies are still used at some courses), restaurant work, lawn care and landscaping, tutoring, retail clerk, bagging groceries, stocking shelves, lifeguard, pet care, teaching at pre-school or youth activities, painting, and many more. One of the more interesting jobs suggested for teens is to be a videogame tester, a job that could offer good pay and flexible hours.[9]

Some of the expensive lessons you have paid for— tennis, golf, sailing, singing, etc.—can help your teen get a job teaching this skill to younger children at a camp or a recreation facility.

The responsibility and discipline required to land and keep a job teaches children respect for meaningful work along with the satisfaction of earning money.

Helping children get a job outside the home is one of the best practical gifts you can give!

Unfortunately, the current, almost manic, emphasis on grades and test scores has altered the ground rules when it comes to combining work with high school. Success in school is now emphasized to the point where grades are becoming *everything*.[10, 11] Of course, work at the expense of school performance willy-nilly should be avoided. Feeling the need to work at all costs is not right either. Work is important, but never if it results in less participation in school activities or becomes a threat to health or grades. However, I believe a well-grounded student with an otherwise busy schedule can, with the help of a supportive family, find time for work, even intermittently, during the school year and surely during vacation time.

It takes a resourceful and motivated person to do well at both school and work—which is also what it takes to be a success in life.

Work helps teens gain experience interacting with people who may be quite different from those they are used to. They will also be required to follow directions from a boss, learn how to cooperate and function effectively with fellow employees, interact with customers, and develop problem-solving strategies when confronted with new situations.

The varied interpersonal relationships your child will develop on the job, and the skills he learns, will be different than those he confronts elsewhere, including at school and in social interactions at home and with friends.

Think about the last time you went to a fast-food or self-order restaurant. You stood in line and when it was your turn, you placed your order with a young man or woman. How much did you expect from the person behind the counter? You expected polite, friendly, and businesslike communication; neat attire and cleanliness; prompt and courteous service; an accurately filled order and correct change if you paid in cash, or proper use of the machine if you were using a credit card. Even though these youth are earning low wages, they are expected to meet a minimum standard to keep their jobs. They are not born with these skills. They learn and benefit from them. Where? On the job!

In some ways, work is no less important than algebra or any other class at school; it's just different. Both are essential. Work offers a learning experience that complements academic study and, in turn, those things learned in school can be applied effectively in the workplace. Moreover, students who work earn money and learn the value of managing their money, as well as putting some in savings.

Learning the value of money is priceless.

Children who work hard for it will appreciate its value in relation to the effort it took to earn it. This could help them decide which items are worth spending their hard-earned money on and which are not. The difference between money earned at a job and money provided by Mom and Dad becomes apparent to the teen with a job.

Your child should learn the benefits of saving some of his paycheck now. There will always be something to spend his money on later. This is another example of the aforementioned "future time preference." In this case, the value of saving will be realized when money is available at a future date and is used for something absolutely needed or for something memorable or longer-lasting than a spur-of-the-moment purchase.

Studies show that teens who work part-time and earn wages while in high school and college not only develop a healthy regard for money, but are more likely to have a satisfying job as an adult.[12]

That job later in life is also likely to provide a higher income. Specific job-related skills and important life lessons dealing with responsibility and people skills are assets that last a lifetime.

But there are exceptions to almost every rule; Henry represents one. As an exceptional young golfer, Henry made practicing golf his main job, with only a few brief stints working at a golf course. This resulted in Henry gaining a scholarship to an NCAA Division I university. For members of his team, their summer job was playing in golf tournaments, essentially full-time, leaving little time for other work.

When the summer before his senior year of college arrived, Henry decided to accept an internship in Silicon Valley at a high-level tech firm. Heeding the call that 98 percent of Division I athletes make a living at something other than their sport, Henry decided his future was in the business world—he has not looked back since. His skill as a golfer and the lessons he learned while competing, enabled Henry to land a position as a volunteer assistant coach for a Division I college golf program while he started working fulltime at the Silicon Valley Tech Company where he had interned the previous summer. Henry was able to pursue his interest and skill at a sport he loved while building his future at work.

There can be no doubt that work and education complement each other. Knowledge acquired in the classroom can be used on the job to increase the skill level and enhance effectiveness of young workers. At the same time, what is learned at work can add meaning and enhance the credibility of so much that is being learned in the classroom.

For example, in mathematics, children learn that multiplying length by width equals the area of an object. But that's not all, they also learn to pay attention to the units of measure! This knowledge is shown to be practical in the following scenario:

> *Nate works at a flooring store that is having a sale on rugs. From what he learned in school, Nate knows that a 9 x 12-foot rug is three yards by four yards, which means the area of the rug is twelve square yards. If the sale price of a rug is $30 a square yard, a customer would pay $360 plus 7 percent sales tax for a total cost of $385.20.*
>
> *One day, a customer tells Nate that thirty dollars a yard sounds like a lot of money, especially because she saw a sign in the window of a competitor with the same rug on sale for only $3.50 a square foot. She asked Nate if his employer would give her a better price or at least match the other store.*

Nate did the math and explained that at $3.50 per square foot, a 9 x 12-foot rug was 108 square feet. At the price the other store was charging, it would cost $378 for the same rug. With sales tax added, the cost of the rug would be $404.39 or nearly 10 percent more than the price Nate's employer offered.

After hearing Nate's explanation, the customer was pleased she would actually save money and Nate was proud he had made the sale. And Nate's boss was happy because his young salesman didn't let the customer get away.

Soft Skills

On-the-job training can provide soft skills. These are essential character traits for a rounded and successful life. Moreover, success at work plays a significant role in what your child learns in the classroom. A young person in a business setting must be able to use the English language correctly. He must be able to listen attentively, understand directions, and both dress and behave appropriately for the situation. Punctuality, accuracy, responsibility, and honesty, are all necessary traits. It is certain any young

---

Jobs for youth between the ages of ten and twenty should have all or some of the following characteristics:

▼ Be outside of the home

▼ Safe (avoiding hazard)

▼ Not interfering with schoolwork and activities

▼ Pay a wage *(volunteer activities are okay if they the meet other criteria see appendix C)*

▼ Require responsibility (for attendance and quality of work performed)

▼ Accountable to boss or supervisor

▼ Offers satisfaction beyond payment (does not dread the work)

---

person will be judged on these characteristics by a prospective, current, and any future employer, and anyone else he might deal with in his life ahead.

Let's consider the following scenario.

Seventeen-year-old Hannah is employed at a local retirement home. She works twenty hours a week in the grill, earning $10.25 an hour plus a $300 bonus at the end of the year. When asked about her job, she said:

"My main interest in high school is art. I hope to become a graphic designer. I have always been shy, and sometimes have a hard time relating to people. This didn't hamper my art, which I do alone, but I knew I eventually had to do a better job with people. My responsibility at the grill is greeting people, taking their meal order, and entering it into the computer. I also pour drinks, select desserts from the display case, and deliver meals to the residents. I work with a team of coworkers, including teenagers and adults.

"Many of our residents are older and have difficulty hearing, have sight problems, and they don't always understand the menu. It is part of my job to offer a clear explanation of the options and, above all, to be patient and to listen.

"This experience has helped me improve my communication skills. I love my job, and I feel it has helped prepare me not just for college, but also for life."

Decline in Youth Employment

Between 2000 and 2013, the employment rate for youths between sixteen and nineteen decreased almost 50 percent, with just 25 percent in this age group said to be working. This is the lowest participation rate since records have been kept, beginning just after World War II.

Current teenagers have been described as "the first generation that will not have major work experience as part of their adolescent development."[13] This is not good. Based on what we know, those teens who gain work experience are the ones most

"We often miss opportunity because it's dressed in overalls and looks like work."

Thomas A. Edison

likely to benefit by developing soft skills like: dependability, punctuality, confidence, and the ability to communicate effectively in a variety of situations.

Recent research also indicates that teenagers who work in high school and college end up with higher salaries, or a higher hourly rate of pay, as an adult compared with teens who didn't work.[14]

The reason there are fewer teens working today than in the past is not clear; most likely the decline is due to a combination of: more automation, including the use of robots; outsourcing to countries with cheap labor; immigrant labor coming into our country; and decreased mobility for teens.[15]

Many workers who are employed by small and independent contractors, and virtually all unskilled workers in landscaping and lawn care, are from Latin America. These immigrants have successfully competed for and are filling unskilled and entry-level jobs, many of which in past years were either filled by high schoolers working part-time or by recent high school graduates wanting to enter the workforce.

Today's youth can be characterized as being "trapped" in the suburbs. They don't have easily accessible and safe transportation. They are picked up and delivered back to their door by a school bus, or parents manage the "delivery" of their children for after-school and weekend activities until the youths are well into their teens and can finally use the family car, get a ride with a friend, or maybe even use a car of their own.

124

This limitation in transportation makes it challenging for many teens to work outside the home; especially so for the ones too young to drive. This means the youth of today must be more creative. The jobs are there. Finding one is limited only by a youth's imagination, perseverance, and desire. Following are some of the lessons to be learned by w-o-r-k.

Learning How to Save

Caroline developed sound work habits, mostly by baby-sitting during high school.[15] In the summer after her freshman year of college, at age nineteen, she earned more than $2,700 babysitting and working at a variety of small jobs at a private club, including teaching tennis to youngsters and handing out towels at the pool. She spent some of this money for clothes and fun but managed to save most.

When an opportunity to go on an exciting overseas school trip came up during winter term of her sophomore year, her family said she could go, but she had to pay for half. She did, which all but wiped out her savings.

It was fun to travel with schoolmates and Caroline learned a lot about a different area of the world, the Galapagos Islands. Equally important, she learned that these opportunities don't just happen. By spending $2,000 of her hard-earned money for this four-week study tour, she also learned to weigh the cost of something (hard work) against the value received. The result was that for the next school trip, she decided on a less exotic but equally worthwhile and lower-cost study session closer to home. By doing this, she would have another worthwhile experience but spend less of her savings.

Earning money gave Caroline the opportunity to learn the difference between money she received from her supportive parents and the money she earned by working. This included determining the relative value of something that would require her to spend her *own* money. Caroline was accustomed to having everything she needed and a lot of what she wanted from her parents—without a keen appreciation for how hard her parents might have worked to make her life possible. It took earning and spending her own money for Caroline to learn an important lesson: someone must work for the money.

For some teens, what is gained by working isn't always money—there can be other significant benefits and lessons to be learned.

Charlie's decision to purchase a house-painting franchise is an example of this. He gained more from his experience of hiring, firing, soliciting jobs, signing up customers, collecting money, answering complaints, and paying insurance claims than he ever would from any money that he might have earned that summer. After more than three months of hard work as a painting contractor, Charlie actually lost several thousand dollars!

His "profit," if you can call it that, was learning that business promises that sound too good to be true, probably are; and that operating a small business is challenging.

Dealing with Adversity

Travance is an eighteen-year-old high school senior. His grades are good and his favorite class is Japanese, which he has studied for four years. He hopes that his skill with Japanese can be used in the future, but for now his story is an unusual one. He moved out of his family home when he was seventeen and into a small apartment with a friend. He continued to pursue a full schedule in high school, expects to graduate on time, and is paying all of his living expenses by working at a part-time job.

Travance works as a member of the wait staff at a large retirement living facility. His work week is twenty hours at $10.25 an hour, plus he will receive a $300 bonus at the end of the year. He works at bussing, helping in the kitchen, and stocking. He has frequent informal contact with the residents, always with a smile.

In addition to paying for all of his living expenses, Travance is saving money in anticipation of entering community college after high school graduation.

This young man has succeeded both in school and at his job. He has lots of energy and still finds time to enjoy music and other social activities with his friends.

His story is neither usual nor ideal. It is the story of a young man who must deal with adversity—teenagers don't leave home if everything is okay. He is making the best adjustments he can, and is succeeding on the basis of energy and ambition. In spite of pursuing a non-traditional course, Travance, in my opinion, is on the road to success.

For children who don't have these special concerns or a *need* to earn money, having a job remains a good way to develop sound work habits, meet new and interesting people, and simply do something productive.

Absent a real need for money, young people can pursue volunteer efforts—there are many nonprofits looking for able-bodied young people who want to help.

Of course, to be a good volunteer, a person must take the job just as seriously and work as diligently as if it were a job for pay.

A word of caution: serving in a food kitchen once or working one day on a Habitat for Humanity project isn't going to provide much more than a résumé enhancer. Sure, your child was phys-ically present, but not much more. Any effort expended would likely be minimal and maybe not even useful. Brief volunteer activities like this are at risk of being more "where I was and who I was with" than "what I helped accomplish."

Lessons to be Learned

Where your child starts in the workforce will not be where he ends up. After a person starts a life of work, a pattern for future employment evolves. I believe working during the Second Decade is more about what your child *learns* than what he *earns*.

Every job I had in the Second Decade taught me something, and I believe that will be true for your children as well. The jobs I had during high school were my choice. Working after school and on the weekends was how I wanted to spend my time, albeit sometimes with the urging of my father. I liked the money and enjoyed the experiences I was exposed to. I did not feel that work took away from my studies. My grades were good enough and, to be honest, I did all of the studying I was going to do anyway. My social life and athletic experiences were all that I could hope for. For me, life in high school was a combination of formal education, lessons learned on the athletic field, socialization in many school and after-school activities, and both learning and earning on the job.

As an example, I will recap some of the work experiences I had between the ages of ten and twenty:

Boat livery: This was my first job outside of the environs of our neighborhood, and it came at age ten, which was young then and today. I did well enough at this job to encourage my dad, who had arranged for it, to keep finding work for me. Luckily, working at the boat livery was more like an adventure or attending summer camp than hard work. But I did work, and found out that I liked working. This was my first opportunity to be judged by my actions and ability and not as being my parents' child. My lifelong love for boats started here, but I never became much of a fisherman. (See appendix A.)

Laying carpet: This brief but significant encounter turned out to be the most meaningful and influential one-day job I ever had. For a start, it was my first definitive career opportunity. I could have been a carpet layer, and that would not have been all bad. The second was that I made a good enough impression on the job, both with the carpets in the store, and when sent out to work with the carpet installer, that I was considered worthy to be offered the chance to become an apprentice.

Also significant was that to show respect and appreciation for the offer, I had to say that I had already committed to a career and so made my first public announcement, outside the home that is, that I had decided to become a doctor.

Caddying: This job provided my first exposure to very wealthy people, to the etiquette of the game of golf, and the importance of appropriate behavior and respect for your elders. Some of the people I dealt with were famous enough for me to have read about them in newspapers and magazines, see them on TV, or hear them or about them on the radio. The job also gave me the opportunity to observe these people in otherwise unguarded moments. I had a chance to learn about people who had totally different lives than mine.

I didn't feel like I had much in common with most of the other caddies. For this reason, I stayed out of cliques and tried to mind my own business. Many of the caddies were rougher than the kids I had dealt with so far in my life. I was a good caddy and that meant I spent very little time in the caddy shed because I was always up for a bag.

Furniture store: This was my first experience working closely with an adult partner. I learned that being older doesn't necessarily make a person smarter or make him someone who imparts a positive message. Frank had some lessons to share, but most of them turned out to be examples of what not to do. Mr. Van, the owner, was aloof but frequently in the store and he was nice to me. He wore a suit coat and tie. He left most of the selling up to Les, the floor salesman, but it was clear who was in charge.

I learned at this job that it was important to keep busy and, if necessary, create your own job. When I wasn't helping on the truck with deliveries, I dusted furniture and made myself otherwise useful.

Managing a carwash: I was only fourteen and had to deal with a difficult boss. He wasn't mean or demanding, just flawed, mostly an object of pity, and never around when there was work to do. The men I worked with were honest, dependable, and hardworking—when they showed up. As it turned out, I was both boss and a coworker on the line of cars that we washed.

In spite of my extra duties, I made the same wage as these adult men, but I had more responsibility. That experience was amazing. These men didn't complain about me being the "boss." In addition to collecting payment from the customers and drying their cars at the end of the line, I balanced the books (sort of), and paid the men. This job helped convince me I was not a "numbers" or a "financial" man.

Gas stations: These were the first of what I considered grown-up jobs. At sixteen, I was required to do mechanical work that mattered, like installing new brake shoes and bleeding hydraulic brake lines, changing oil, lubricating cars, and I even replaced a muffler and tail pipe on one occasion. With these responsibilities, I had to do my job well or there could be serious consequences.

I also ran Walt's Sunoco on Warren Avenue by myself on Sundays, but just selling gas. I was a bit in awe and felt I needed to justify the trust Walt had in me; so I worked extra hard to do a good job. This service station was his livelihood, and for one day a week his financial future was in my hands.

Fraternity kitchen: I started this job at seventeen, as a freshman undergraduate, and continued working through my junior year in medical school, for a total of seven years. There were many reasons why I enjoyed working in a fraternity kitchen at college and during medical school: camaraderie, the need for a job to pay for my meals, sense of family, lack of need to be a fraternity brother at the table, habit, being macho, and satisfaction in doing a job well. The six years I worked in the Nu Sigma Nu Medical Fraternity kitchen, was the longest time I spent at one job until I began my life's work in medicine.

Delivering flowers: This was a great lesson in the realities of owning a small business. I learned that to be successful it takes hard work, the willingness to take risk, and the need for patience when it comes to actually earning a living commensurate with how hard you are working and the investment you are required to make. In my time driving a delivery truck for Woods Florist in Grosse Pointe Woods, Michigan, I developed a genuine respect for the proprietors, Wally and Ceil Shultz.

Other Jobs: Between the ages of seventeen and twenty, I also had several summer jobs working mostly as an unskilled laborer. I was a carpenter's helper on two major construction projects, an assembly line worker at Chrysler Motors and Briggs Body, a forester (laborer) with the Detroit Department of Parks and Recreation, and a laborer (gofer) at a tool and die shop in Hamtramck, Michigan. At each of these jobs it was acknowledged I was just a college kid working as a fill-in and not someone destined to be part of the regular working team. I was at the lowest rung in the chain of command.

Some of the take-away lessons are:

1. It is personally rewarding to feel pride for a job well done—both as an individual and as part of a team.

2. It was in your best interest, as well everyone working with you for the company to make a profit—otherwise your employer couldn't afford to hire you.

3. Hard work and loyalty will be rewarded. It might not be immediate but your good reputation will follow you and assist in you acquiring a different and better job.

4. Having good leadership improves employee morale, productivity, and overall profitability of the enterprise.

It is my hope that by sharing these experiences, I give credence to the argument that **w-o-r-k** is essential for all children in their Second Decade.

Next, let's discover how important it is for teens to acquire skills and accomplishments.

CULTIVATING SKILLS &
ACHIEVING ACCOMPLISHMENTS

"Do something you're good at. Not too many people
are lucky enough to be good at something."
JOHN GREEN

I N THE SECOND DECADE, *TALENT* IS DISCOVERED, *SKILLS* ARE
developed, *accomplishments* are celebrated, and *recognition*
is granted. The most conspicuous, though mostly minor,
accomplishments at this age tend to be those earned in sports.
These activities are fun and are likely to be on display, i.e., have
an audience.

In addition to sports, successes for youth can be in music, the
performing arts, and academics (spelling bees and other competitions like debate), but there are many more. The showcase for
skills can be in school and also in extra-curricular or other non-
school-related activities that are abundant and diverse.

IQ and physical characteristics such as height, weight, body
type, and looks are innate, i.e., people are born with them. They
can be modified, but only to a point. The DNA a person receives
from his parents, and any advantages or disadvantages that
accrue from the circumstances of his birth are a matter of luck.

Talent is a natural endowment. A few people are lucky enough to have a lot of talent at one thing; others might have talent at several things.

Though people are born with talent, this gift must be cultivated to become a noteworthy skill. This can happen after a sufficient amount and specific type of effort—let's call it hard work. In *Outliers*, Malcolm Gladwell invokes the 10,000-hours rule describing the apparent "overnight success" experienced by many.[1] A notable example is the Beatles. This fabulously successful group honed their skills performing for hours on end in the smoky bistros of Germany before attaining smashing and apparently "instant" success on the *Ed Sullivan Show*.[2]

The Williams sisters in tennis and Tiger Woods in golf are extreme and positive examples of cultivation of talent. Larry Bird, one of the greatest basketball players ever, said it this way: "A *skill* (italics mine) is achieved by someone who recognizes his God-given talent, works his tail off to develop them into skills, and uses these skills to accomplish his goals."[3] These goals could be fame, money, a certain lifestyle, or simply the satisfaction of being good (in a few cases even the very best) at something.

"Skills are common, talent is rare."
Colin Clark

All accomplishment, however, does not result in the same acclaim. Winning the hammer throw at the Olympics and the Singles Championship at the U.S. Open are both wonderful individual accomplishments that would result in a great deal of satisfaction for a person, but the external rewards are hugely different in terms of both money and recognition. Each first-place winner is best at what he does for a time. This is a valid measure of success and should be the cause for satisfaction.

But cultivation of talent must be carried out properly. In the case of the football player Todd Marinovich, his talent was squandered by an overzealous training program instituted by

---

Skills are tools that continue to be useful and can be called upon throughout life when needed.

Accomplishments are relative and can produce trophies that need polishing, or may be results that are valuable but time-limited.

Recognition based on accomplishments is okay, but it is conferred by others, can go away as it came, and could become an addiction if not dealt with properly. These comparisons can be considered cliché but are true when it comes to a child's future.

Satisfaction is a sort of personal recognition which, like skill, is yours to use and enjoy.

---

his father who had super-high expectations. The result was a shambles for a young quarterback, not only in his career but in his life.[4]

Talent was best explained to me by my tenth grade football coach. At the beginning of practice that year he gave a talk to the team explaining how we could best develop our talents and how he could help us in doing so. Then he said, "But I can't teach fast. You gotta be born with it."

There is no child without *some* innate talent, and if there is anybody who has it all I haven't met him or her yet. Through discovery, coupled with work and proper instruction, a person's talents can be recognized; and then with some training, just about everybody can achieve at least modest accomplishments. These may be rewarded with something tangible, like a gift or a trophy, or simply a thank-you or congratulations. Recognition can be private, i.e., a family affair: "Johnny, you are the best dishwasher in our family!" Recognition for more noteworthy talents might be acknowledged publicly, i.e., a bumper sticker that announces "My daughter is an honor student at Wyandotte Middle School," or be reported with a brief announcement in the local newspaper or on television.

Or a person's talents might be chronicled widely in the media and recognition can be far-reaching. Modern media has provided the opportunity for people to be seen by millions and is a huge revenue generator, in some cases providing huge financial rewards for those talented people who perform for a mammoth audience.

Skills—for example, the ability to play tennis well or remember the words and sing the melody in a musical performance to the delight of an audience—are learned behaviors built on a natural talent the individual is blessed with. It takes time and effort to turn talent into skills. The smartest person in the world must first learn the moves before he can become a champion chess player.

"Like many highly educated people, I didn't have much in the way of actual skills."

J. Maarten Troost

Some skills can be learned and demonstrated more readily by a person who also has innate physical characteristics. For example, being tall makes it easier to excel at basketball, being a fast runner is a distinct advantage for a person aspiring for a career as a defensive back in football. But lack of either is not an automatic disqualification. There is no better example of this than Tyrone Curtis "Bugsy" Mogues, who at five feet, three inches is the shortest man to play in the National Basketball Association. Not only did he play, he was a member of four different teams over a stellar fourteen-year career. Bugsy Mogues succeeded against all odds because he had the will and the talent to maximize the physical stature he had. His success was achieved according to natural laws. He played the game well in spite of his diminutive stature and likely because of his big heart.[5]

136

Opportunity can be the limiting factor when it comes to successful development of talent, i.e., not all youth are afforded the same chance.

If your child becomes a champion tennis player and regularly wins matches, this is a personal *accomplishment* that requires skill and talent. Accomplishment might also lead to *recognition* that is conferred by others.

But all of these accomplishments are relative. A tennis champion can be the person who wins the state high school championship or the person who wins the U.S Open or Wimbledon. Either level of success is ultimately based on hard work by a person to develop a skill linked to an innate talent.

Many children who are recognized for their accomplishments in sports, music, the arts, and academics "peak out" in their Second Decade; their feats becoming mostly memories by age twenty. These children may have gone as far as they could when it comes to improving and honing skills. Or the limiting factors might be a loss of interest and unwillingness to continue putting forth the time and effort; or a combination of both.

This concept of *relative accomplishment* is a reason to be careful when we laud the behavior of our children. One can feel pity for the child who received too much recognition too early for accomplishments that were time-limited, age-related, and depended on the level of competition. It is not uncommon for children to outgrow a talent they were thought to have, and by the time they are thirteen, they no longer maintain the "elite" status they once had.

I marveled as a fourteen-year-old girl, a golf "phenomenon," won a professional tournament, and to retain her amateur standing declined the monetary prize. The following year, she won her state's high school champion as a sophomore, before turning professional the next year. Facing stiff competition on the professional circuit, she soon realized that she simply could was not competitive at this level. She withdrew from competition, now plays recreationally, is a mother of two, and works as a school counselor. Her accomplishments in high school are memories. They are hers to enjoy, as are the trophies she earned. Accomplishments for any young person, represented by silver cups and engraved plates, must be held in perspective for what they are. This young woman dealt with these issues and has a satisfying and successful life.

Considering the diagram below, let's have a look at how this works for your child. The foundation is talent. At the base is skill, which can be defined as *ability coming from one's knowledge, practice, talent, and aptitude.*

Skill is a foundational asset. It is tangible, usable, worked for, and acquired. It is owned by the individual. Nobody gave talent to a child; she earned it and she can keep it—it is hers. But skills are not static. They can be strengthened and broadened or they can be diminished and lost if not used. Skills are also relative. Your son is a fine baseball player, but compared to whom?

Accomplishments are relative and depend on the difficulty of the task or the level of competition.

Recognition is conferred by another. It is man-made, not enduring, and subject to renewal. Recognition depends on others who give it to you, and it can also fade. The perceived importance and impact of an accomplishment and the recognition received are relative to the level of competition and the inclination of those who comment on the result. The saying "beware the danger of being a big fish (especially a self-proclaimed big fish) in a small pond" is apt here. The summation and the most important part of the "success pyramid" is satisfaction. This is personal, honest for those true to themselves, and it can never be taken away.

A few years ago, I was at a dinner party attended by doctors who were leaders in their fields. Several spouses were also present. Before the event, the hostess told me she had had her grand piano tuned because one of the guests was a distinguished pianist and would be playing for us. After dinner, when the time for the performance came, he played brilliantly. The small audience was impressed. It was a spectacular performance, especially for a person who made his living in medicine, not music.

When the applause died, as an encore, he sat on the floor with his head below the keyboard, and played a short piece with his hands out of sight above his head. Again he performed flawlessly. His efforts were appreciated by all.

I learned later the ophthalmologist had been a child prodigy who was preparing for a career as a concert pianist. By the time he was fourteen years old, he had achieved numerous accolades for his playing and he was flying high. But according to his own assessment, he felt his skills had peaked, and he had not reached

---

Five characteristics are crucial when it comes to achieving success in life:

▼ Natural Ability

▼ Acquired Skill

▼ Opportunity

▼ Desire

▼ Satisfaction with what you have accomplished

---

the level he had set for himself. Thus, he ended his quest for a career in music and he eventually became a doctor.

The skill at playing the piano stayed with him. He played brilliantly, albeit in private settings. His accomplishments were significant, but on a relative basis. I thought he was great, but I am not in the know when it comes to judging a concert pianist. Any "trophies" from his past accomplishments as a teen, I suspect, retain a prominent place in this doctor's home—to be admired and dusted!

When it comes to achieving success in life, children are fortified with their own dose of natural ability and talent. It is theirs. That is what they bring to the table. You, as their parent, should guide them to develop skills and take advantage of their talent and opportunity. Maybe success won't be in a class with the smartest or the richest, but any child who has the help and encouragement he deserves, and uses his talents and opportunities, should be able to find a solid spot in the inclusive middle class—or beyond!

Next, let's look at two very different parenting styles that probably should be combined in some way for the best effect.

10

PARENTING STYLES

"Life affords no greater responsibility, no greater
privilege, than raising the next generation."
C. Everett Koop

I CAN THINK OF ONLY A FEW OCCUPATIONS AS IMPORTANT AS BEING a parent. This obligation starts in the "get ready" prenatal stage and hits high gear when you bring that bundle home. Once started, the need to be the best parent you can be never ends. Once a parent, always a parent.

There is no perfect parent. (My wife comes about as close as anyone I have ever met, and with her coaching and encouragement, I have done my best to follow her example.)

And there is no one parenting style that is right for everybody—but as long as a parent commits to do his best, and comes even pretty close to doing as well as he hopes he can, children should have a sufficient start to finding their own success in life.

I'd like to share one example of what I consider a successful and effective parenting style:

> *There is sound from the room above. Thirteen-year-old Olivia is out of bed. Her dad promised her that if she got*

herself up and dressed, he would drive her to the Racquet Club. Her tennis coach has organized an intense practice clinic to help those players who want to improve their game by developing consistent ground strokes. The students are expected to be dedicated to the task; a requirement that has been reinforced by the time of the clinic. It begins at 6:30 a.m. and ends at 8:00 a.m., three days a week, for three months. Only those young people with the best intentions will start and only those who are serious will stick to the finish. (This dedication also included the parents! They didn't do the work, but they kept the hours.)

His daughter said she wanted to participate in the clinic to improve her chances of making the high school tennis team in the tenth grade. Based on her enthusiasm, and eager to see their daughter get ahead in a sport she seemed to be getting good at, while gaining self-esteem, her dad and mother agreed to do their part.

Olivia needed transportation to and from the clinic. Her dad agreed that he would drop her off on his way to work and her mother would pick her up and take her to school after the clinic. When the three months were finished, Olivia was presented with a small trophy acknowledging her as the most-improved player. She went on to play three years of varsity tennis in high school, and like her sister, a few years later, was named the co-captain of the team her senior year.

The above story is an example of a parenting style called *concerted cultivation*. In *Unequal Childhoods: Class, Race, and Family Life*, Annette Lareau, PhD, describes this parenting style:

"parents tend to adopt a cultural logic of childrearing that stresses ... discussions between parents and children [and] organized activities [that are] established and controlled by mothers and fathers [who] dominate the lives of [their] children. By making certain their children have [a rich array of] experiences [with support] ... parents engage in a process called concerted cultivation. ...Worried about how their children will get ahead ... [these] parents are increasingly determined to make sure their children are not excluded from any opportunity that might eventually contribute to their advancement ... [this is accomplished by engaging in] deliberate cultivation of children and [their] leisure activities ..."[1]

Another example of this parenting style can be witnessed each spring when driving past a youth soccer field or a little league baseball complex with dozens of parents actively supporting their children in these popular pre-teen activities. Other less-public, but equally intense parent/child experiences occur at swimming competitions, music lessons, in scouting, martial arts, and in a long list of other organized activities that promise to enrich a child's life.

A quite different parenting style described by Dr. Lareau is *natural growth*. Parents who practice this style of childrearing do not consider "organized leisure activities" for children, supported by parents, as an essential aspect of good parenting. For them, the crucial responsibilities of parenthood do not lie in "eliciting their children's feelings, opinions, or thoughts. ... They see a clear boundary between children and adults."[2]

Adults who use the natural growth parenting style take care of their children by providing them with shelter, food, clothing, love, etc. However, they do not steer their children along specific lines or go out of their way to alter their own schedules to accommodate an activity that is designed specifically for their child. These parents do not load up the car with kids, gloves, balls, and bats on Saturday morning and sit in the stands cheering at a little league game, or when needed function as a coach, pitcher, or umpire. They don't descend on a child's life to engage them in so-called *enriching behavior*. Maybe to justify their parenting style, those who engage in natural growth parenting mock what they call "helicopter parents," who they describe as hovering and dropping into their child's life from a position of superiority and control.

According to Lareau, children of parents who practice natural growth are more likely to have just one activity at a time, i.e., children are neither programmed nor fully scheduled. She describes these children as "free to go out and play with friends and relatives who typically live close by." This style of parenting, also called *accomplishment of natural growth*, is paraphrased by Lareau: "Let kids be kids; they will grow up soon enough."[3] Lareau adds this about the attitude of parents who support natural growth for their children: "let parents be parents; *they are doing the right thing for children, at least in the parents' mind*, if they let their children grow up as kids and not as programmed robots." (Italics mine)

What are some differences?

Children reared by parents who practice concerted cultivation may acquire social and other skills that will be valuable to them when they enter the workforce.

Parents who support natural growth are likely to raise children who experience a more childlike and some might call "more normal" childhood. These children may have their own unique advantages when they enter the workforce; and these advantages are likely to be different from children reared with concerted cultivation. Children raised with natural growth are likely to be less idealistic and more practical—attitudes that could be especially helpful for the work they choose, which is likely to be as a tradesman or skilled worker, but possibly much more.

According to sociologists, there is a greater likelihood of a child from the solidly middle to upper middle class being reared with concerted cultivation.[4] Children in the lower middle class and/or working class are more likely to be reared with an expectation and practice of natural growth.

Those in the Greatest Generation, and the early baby boomers, are more likely to have been reared with natural growth. Generations late X, Y, and Z, and especially those born after the

1990s are more likely to be reared with the policy of concerted cultivation. This is evidenced not only by crowded sports fields, but by an emphasis on grades and success in school.

Parents today are more likely to obtain help for their children by hiring a tutor for difficult school subjects, and also to prepare them for the college entrance examinations, SAT and ACT, helping them to get into the college of their choice. A comment on how early these preparations for school can start is offered by sociologist Jacob Cheadle who states: "research … points to the need for effective early childhood policy interventions to reduce disparities in children's academic skill levels [even as early as] at kindergarten entry."[5] Such children, even at this early age, are organized preemptively!

Regardless of parenting technique, how a child turns out ultimately resides with the child.

Each of these parenting styles has advantages and disadvantages. I suspect that if these styles were entirely independent of the income or social status a child is reared in, results for the children growing up could essentially result in a toss-up with an equal amount of success for each style.

However, since concerted cultivation tends to be a practice of the more affluent, all other things being equal, a child in this type of family might have an advantage at least in the society where they function. But that is only with all other things being equal. The most likely expectation remains that neither parenting style guarantees success nor portends disaster. It is possible, and even likely, that most parents eventually practice both styles, but selectively. The best use of this mix of styles might provide children with the benefits derived from both, while avoiding the pitfalls that extremes of either could produce; that is, under-stimulation resulting from minimal parental involvement or over indulgence and spoiling from too much.

There are cases where parental involvement paid great dividends. As mentioned earlier, Venus and Serena Williams excelled in tennis, Tiger Woods in golf, and the Manning brothers in football. They are superstars and legends because of talent *and* the skills developed through the intense involvement of their fathers—an example of concerted cultivation to the extreme.

> **"If you want children to have their feet on the ground, put some responsibility on their shoulders."**
> Abigail Van Buren

Bottom line: parental attention and guidance play a significant role in forming the attitudes, behaviors, and work ethic of children. Too much of either parenting style is not in the best interests of the child or the adult; instead a mixture of concerted cultivation and natural growth may be the best.

Next, is joining the armed services a viable option for your child?

11

THE ARMED SERVICES

"Parents can only give good advice or put them on
the right paths, but the final forming of a person's
character lies in their own hands."
ANNE FRANK

A T THE AGE OF EIGHTEEN, TEENS CAN ENLIST IN THE ARMED
services without parental consent. With few exceptions,
a high school diploma or GED is required to be considered for military service. Additionally, enlistees must pass
a pre-induction physical examination specific to the branch of
service they are applying for. It is then necessary to attain a passing score on the Armed Forces Qualifying Test (AFQT) and the
Armed Services Vocational Aptitude Battery (ASVAB) which
explores skills in special areas. Both of these tests measure the
skill level of prospective enlistees in the areas of math, reasoning, vocabulary, basic understanding of mechanics, etc.

These evaluations are similar to an IQ test, but are more heavily weighted toward practical application of skills while still
testing a person's fund of knowledge. The various branches of the
armed services—Army, Navy, Air Force, Marines, Coast Guard,
and National Guard—each has its own unique requirements in

addition to the standard tests. Once in the service, personnel are required to pass a physical fitness test at least once every two years to be eligible for re-enlistment, promotion, or to qualify for officer training.[1]

The decision to join the military is an individual one.

Why do teens consider joining the military after high school instead of getting a job or going to college?

There are no cut-and-dry answers to whether or not joining the armed services is best for your child.

Some join the military out of patriotism and a desire to protect a way of life. In recent history, these motives were apparent after 9/11. For others, the military is a transitional job, but with potentially more stress than a civilian job. And, in a few cases, young people join the military to carry on family tradition.

For example, Mary Scott's father and husband were U.S. Army officers. She now has six children who serve in some branch of the armed forces. She says, "My children are my heroes. My husband and I always let them know how proud we are of them and how proud they should be."[3] This is not an isolated example of families carrying on a tradition of military service, many do it.

Other reasons for enlisting may be to learn a skill, to travel, or to receive educational benefits both during and after one's period of service. Some people join the military simply because they need income, have not been able to find a job and are able to meet the requirements.

"The army teaches boys to think like men."
Elvis Presley

Romeo Clayton, who served both as an enlisted man and as an officer in the United States Navy, offers ten reasons for joining the Armed Forces.[4]

1. **Jobs.** The military offers training to those who are qualified physically and academically. Working in the military can be an important step toward learning skills and gaining maturity that will help in obtaining employment after your time of enlistment ends; in some cases, allowing you to enter the civilian workforce before you are twenty years old.

2. **Pay and benefits.** A second lieutenant starts at over $36,000 a year plus full benefits, with added monthly allowances of up to $3,000, depending on where he or she is stationed. An enlisted person starts at around $20,000 a year plus full benefits, with added monthly allowances of up to $1,500 depending on where he or she is stationed. Enlistment and re-enlistment bonuses can be over $20,000. After serving only three years, some nuclear-trained enlisted members in the Navy receive bonuses of $90,000 for re-enlisting. Student loans can also be relieved up to a stipulated limit for those who qualify.

3. **Full medical coverage** for you and your family. Military members are immediately eligible for full healthcare benefits for themselves and their immediate family members as soon as they enter the service, and for those who stay through until retirement, the service member and his family retain these benefits after military service.

4. **Skills and training.** The military provides advanced technical training in a variety of career fields and also offers

In December 2013, there were more than 1.3 million men and women on active duty in the armed services. This number is more than doubled by those men and women who make up the active reserves and the National Guard.[2]

opportunities for additional training when you are off-duty. Many military are able to attend college with the benefit of tuition assistance.

5. **Leadership opportunities.** Military leadership is a great way to build a résumé for your next career.

6. **Travel opportunities and vacation time.** The military has installations around the world and pays for you and your family to get there and back. Your off-duty time is yours and you are free to travel and see the world. The military gives you thirty days of paid leave per year, not including weekends and Federal holidays, depending on your job.

7. **A lifetime of benefits for your survivors.** In the event of an active service member's death, the surviving family is given an immediate tax free $100,000 death gratuity benefit, group life insurance benefit of a $400,000 (if elected), social security and indemnity monthly payments for a stipulated time, and the transferability of many VA benefits.

8. **Education opportunities** after you leave the military. The New GI Bill pays veterans who served at least thirty-six months a monthly living stipend and full tuition to pay for college after they leave the military. Depending on how long the service member commits, this GI Bill can be transferred to spouses and children.

9. **Buy a home with a VA loan.** This benefit makes it easier for active service members and veterans to purchase a home while they are serving, or after they have left the service.

10. **A military retirement offers significant benefits.** The military is one of the few places where you can still get a full pension after serving at least twenty years or more and the benefits increase the longer you serve. Military retirement can reach 50 to 75 percent of the average of your final

three years' base salary. In some instances, you can receive more than 75 percent of your base pay in retirement. An officer with twenty years of service, can retire with a life-time pension based on his active-duty salary and retain full healthcare benefits while pursuing a second career.

Even though the conflicts and type of warfare have changed over the decades, each has its own challenges. And it remains clear that, even in peacetime, a military of sufficient size and readiness to maintain national security will be required and recruitment will remain active.[5] Thus, guaranteeing that military service will continue to be an option for youth in their Second Decade.

For young people who see the advantages of service in the military but do not want to give up their job or other aspects of civilian life, serving in the National Guard is an attractive option.

Youth who join the National Guard can combine service with a full-time job or with full- or part-time college studies. Guards-men receive pay for two days of weekend training each month and for an additional block of fifteen days of training at a given time each year. This means that guardsmen will receive as much as six weeks of regular service pay annually. In addition to this money, which could be as much as $2,300, guardsmen are eligible to receive additional money to pay for college. This can

A select few who qualify on the basis of good grades, high moral character, physical fitness, and who secure a U.S. Congressional or Presidential/military nomination can apply for admission to one of the five military academies. The odds are long, but the benefits of securing this kind of placement are significant.[7]

amount to as much as $4,500 a year.[6] In addition to education benefits, guardsmen can qualify for retirement income, health insurance benefits, and home loan assistance.

Teens that have little or no work experience and believe they have no immediate job prospects when they graduate from high school sometimes turn to military service. This is the type of enlistee that has led some people to question the recruitment practices and the soundness of an all-volunteer army. They suggest that the military is made up of misfits representing the underbelly of society, or that they prey on minorities. These opinions notwithstanding, it is a fact that entrance requirements for the military include successful completion of high school or a GED, and enlistees must pass rigorous mental and physical examinations to qualify.

The essence of life in the armed services is discipline, regimentation, loyalty, and opportunity. Moreover, although mortality does not reach the levels of World War II, Korea, or Vietnam, service personnel on average are 2.5 times more likely to suffer death than a comparable civilian—with the infantry being most at risk.[8]

Joining the military is not something that should be taken lightly. Certainly there are significant challenges that go along with the decision to serve and not everyone is well-suited. More questions about joining the armed services can be answered by an armed forces recruiter without the applicant incurring any obligation.

Next, are there ways to maximize opportunity?

12

TAKE ADVANTAGE OF OPPORTUNITY

"Success is where preparation and opportunity meet."
BOBBY UNSER

I SUSPECT THAT MORE TIMES THAN NOT, BENEFITTING FROM BEING in the right place at the right time, even with some measure of planning and responsibility, also takes some luck. But even with luck on your side, really good things don't just happen.

Being able to recognize a once-in-a-lifetime, right-place/ right-time experience that could change your life takes more. That "more" is being alert when something important is in the wind, and being ready to act when the time is right. A person should be able to sense they are experiencing something special—to know they are being offered an opportunity even though it might not be expressed—and then take all the steps necessary to take advantage of it.

The chance to make the most of being at the right place at the right time does not depend on who you are or why you're there. It depends on you *knowing who you* are and how open you are to exploring any worthwhile opportunity that presents itself.

Parents should instill in their children the healthy curiosity that helps them to recognize something potentially good when it comes along.

Teach your children to be aware and alert for people and events that can have positive and even life-changing consequences for them. And show children how to take advantage of these opportunities.

Young children are not equipped to navigate life by themselves. They need a map, a compass, someone in their ear, and a light when things seem dim. Parents, relatives, teachers, mentors (See ch. 13), and other adults should be caring, positive, and available role models for youth in their Second Decade. Adults need to be alert to recognize when they might be the very one to provide that "breakthrough" life-changing experience for a child, grandchild, student, or friend.

Parents have profound effects on their children. Parents can instill, by their behavior and childrearing methods, what a child chooses to do or not do and what they are likely to become. Abraham Lincoln developed his firm belief that "a man's right [is] to own the fruits of his own labor" because he despised working on his father's farm for no pay; and even worse to be hired out to a neighbor with the pay going directly to his father. These and other humanitarian issues added to Abraham Lincoln's profound hatred of slavery.[1]

On the other hand, Lincoln's father was hardworking, temperate, honest, and frugal. These were traits that Abe himself had as a man, and which were likely to have been, at least in part, influenced by a father, who he didn't always agree with. Parents and other adult role models can offer some good and some not-so-good examples, but there is always an effect of some kind on children. Parenting does not take place in a vacuum.[2]

The influence of people and events outside the family are important, especially when children spend more time away from their home—inevitable as the Second Decade progresses.

These influences can have an impact on your child and significantly affect his future.

Formative experiences can take place anywhere, but two likely places are in school and on the job.

As an example, when I was seventeen and a freshman at the University of Michigan, I found myself seated in a large lecture hall for an introductory world history class. This subject was not my first choice, which was political science, but all of those classes were full when I registered. Being a second choice, I was less than enthusiastic about studying world history. Then things got worse. A few weeks into the course, results of my first blue book were returned. (Students completed essay tests in a flimsy tablet with a light blue cover) My grade was a C+. This was not good. I felt I needed an A in this class to help my overall average. I expected a B in English but worried that I could get a C in chemistry and/or French.

While I sat in the lecture hall with more than 200 other students, Professor Dunham, standing on the slightly raised stage and behind a wooden lectern, said he was disappointed to see that some students had performed well below their potential. He hoped "these people" would do better next time.

I swore Professor Dunham was looking directly at me when he said this. I looked around reflexively to see if he was actually engaging someone else, but when I turned back, he was still looking at me (mind you, I was sitting in the middle of a packed lecture hall). The hair on my neck stood up! I knew I had done poorly and I was disappointed in my own performance—but why would Professor Dunham pick me out in front of the whole class?

The next day, I made an appointment with Professor Dunham. This was the first time in my twelve plus years of schooling that I had actually made an appointment to meet with an instructor outside of the classroom. When I entered Professor Dunham's office two days later, I told him who I was. This announcement produced no particular reaction on his part. We began to talk comfortably; so I decided not to mention how I felt when he seemingly singled me out in class. By this time I was convinced there was no way he had been looking only at me.

We talked for what seemed a long time, but it probably was less than a half hour. He told me that he had moved to Ann Arbor, Michigan, from Boston thirty years ago. Then he explained with a smile, "That is where the Lowells talked to the Cabots and the Cabots only talked to God." He said his family considered it both odd and unfortunate that he had chosen a university in the "unsophisticated Midwest" to begin his career in academia. But he told me he was glad he had, and that he felt he had made the right choice. He said he had enjoyed his career as a member of the history department at the University of Michigan. He also told me we would "graduate" together because he intended to retire in the year my class was to graduate.

This patrician educator could not have been much further removed in academia and society than from where I stood as a young man from a working-class family growing up on the east-side of Detroit. In spite of these differences, an unspoken bond was created immediately, at least for me.

Throughout my four years of undergraduate studies, I took the six courses Professor Dunham taught, earned an A in all of them, and would periodically visit with him in his office. In the second semester of my senior year, the class I took from Professor Dunham was The Industrial Revolution in France 1815-1848. In those years, the time and place of the final examination for all courses was listed in the school newspaper, *The Michigan Daily*. I misread the information and missed the final exam! In four years, this was the only time I had done anything that stupid. Ironically, this was my very last final as an undergrad. Panicked, I called Professor Dunham at his home to apologize and explain. He said he understood how something like that could happen and told me I could come to his home after dinner, about 7:30 p.m. and take the test. I could let myself in through the back entrance and go directly to his study where I could complete the test. He said he was not feeling well and would be going to bed early. I could leave my blue book on his desk and let myself out.

I finished the exam and, as was customary, I left a self-addressed postcard on the desk so he could mail my grade directly to me. (This was a regular practice for students because the official university transcripts would not be mailed out for several weeks.) I also left a note on his desk expressing my sincere appreciation for having the opportunity to study under a man who I respected, admired, and who had such a profound and positive effect on my life.

A few days later, the postcard arrived. In the blank area in the center of the card that I left for final grade, an A was prominent. In the lower left-hand corner, Professor Dunham had written a reply to my note. As I write this many years later, I am looking at that very card. On it he said: *"Your note is deeply appreciated. You have always been an excellent student, keen and loyal and that is a teacher's great reward."*

It took 120 credit hours to obtain my bachelor's degree. The courses I took with Professor Dunham represented almost a quarter of these credit hours, and the A's I received made it possible for me to establish a grade point average sufficient to qualify for entrance into medical school. I truly believe that because of Professor Dunham I was able to become a doctor. It took many years of hard work to finally succeed in medical school and in post-graduate training, but having Professor Dunham as a mentor for four years, when I needed it most, gave me the chance to succeed.

My point is, except for a chance encounter in a freshman World History class, I might not have made it into medical school and might not have had the privilege to pursue a career in medicine. Was it only luck that I was in the right place at the right time that morning, attending a history lecture because I was not "lucky" enough to enroll in the political course I really wanted?

Along with recognizing there are events that we seemingly have no control over, I firmly believe it is up to each of us, your child included, to recognize opportunity and be ready to act. I believe it was my parents who instilled this in me and you have the power to instill this behavior and awareness in your child.

**"Every right implies an opportunity,
every opportunity an obligation."**
John D. Rockefeller

Opportunities abound. Teach your child how to recognize them and then do the right thing.

Next, what role can a mentor play in your child's life and how can you help your child find a mentor?

13

FIND A MENTOR

"The mind is not a vessel to be filled
but a fire to be kindled."
PLUTARCH

MENTORING IS A TRANSACTION, STATED OR IMPLIED, AFFECTING two people who have a common purpose. Teaching. Guiding. Leading. A mentor can benefit a young person academically, socially, and professionally; especially as the Second Decade is coming to an end. The value of a mentor cannot be over emphasized.

What this means is that rather than being guided mostly by you, the parent, and other family members, children in their late teens spend more time away from home with other adults: employers, teachers, coaches, etc.—all of whom can have a profound influence on their future.

Before we go further, let's establish the meaning of the word *mentor*. The following definitions are from www.FoundersCorp. org:

"A *mentor* is a person who has had professional and/or life experience that can be used to help others learn and develop.

The mentor is willing to share these experiences in a manner that the mentee (student or disciple) can react to and understand. ... At its best, the advice and help is offered freely without expectation of immediate reward. The mentor is the 'vendor' of the mentor/mentee relationship. For the mentee, the value of the relationship is driven by the quality and objectivity of the mentor's advice and assistance.

"A *mentee* is a person who receives the help and assistance of a mentor. The mentee is willing to be engaged and respectful of the mentor's time and accomplishments. The mentee should understand that the mentor is motivated by personal satisfaction. The mentee is the 'customer' in the mentor/mentee relationship and for the mentor the value of the relationship is driven by the ultimate value that the mentee places on the mentor's help.

"*Mentorship* is not merely advice. It is a bilateral commitment between two people based on mutual trust and commitment. The commitment of the mentor is to provide advice and help to the mentee with the mentee's best interests in mind. The commitment of the mentee is to be ready to listen to the advice and take the help and act upon it. The currency of the mentor/mentee relationship is personal satisfaction and shared accomplishment.[1]

"You can only mentor somebody if they want to be."
Phil Ramone

Establishing a mentor/mentee relationship is ultimately the child's responsibility; that is, the mentee must be ready for the experience and know what he wants to gain from the relationship and what he, as the mentee, has to offer. As a parent, your responsibility is to teach your child how to recognize the opportunity to establish a mentor/mentee relationship when it arises.

There is positive behavior your child can develop to increase both the need for and the likelihood of finding a mentor. The first is to develop an interest and be serious about attaining a reachable goal. This requires preparation and preliminary work on the youth's part. To put it succinctly, the prospective mentee should have some "skin in the game." A serious person who has paid his dues, in so far as possible, is the kind of person who is most likely to attract the attention of a mentor.

Finding a mentor is mostly a matter of being ready, receptive, and lucky on the part of the prospective mentee.

The concept of being at the right place at the right time has already been discussed (See ch. 12). The best way for your child to begin his search is first identifying what he wants to gain from a relationship with a mentor. Your child needs to be aware of his specific needs and wishes; and then be open and receptive when meeting potential mentors. Note: this search should not consume your child's life. He will know when he has met the right match. Let serendipity do its work.

When it came to approaching the three professional mentors I had, I did the work. I knew I wanted to learn from someone's experience, so I was actively aware and looking. Each of these men was well known in his particular field. I simply recognized the opportunity, showed an interest, and took advantage.

To maintain the relationship, it takes much more effort on the part of the mentee than the mentor, i.e., the youth has to want it and be actively engaged. Additionally, these relationships are not stagnant. They change over time, which is healthy. For a mentor/mentee relationship to be at its best, both parties should feel a certain level of satisfaction, accomplishment, and responsibility.

"God deposited someone out there who is expected to mentor you."
Israelmore Ayivor

A mentor must be older and more experienced than the mentee. I cannot think of any exception to this rule. While there is no rule about how much older, a mentor must have sufficiently greater experience than the mentee to make the relationship fruitful for the mentee and satisfying for the mentor. It is, however, appropriate and common for the mentor to have broader experience and extensive knowledge in areas beyond the specific mentor/mentee relationship. Ideally the mentee should be seeking help and guidance in what may be only a small part of the scope of his chosen mentor.

At this point it is important to point out the difference between a mentor and a teacher. Both impart knowledge. A teacher tells you how to do something, while focusing on the task at hand. My nineteen-year-old granddaughter introduced me to Netflix and was a wonderful teacher. The young woman in the ATT store showed me where the "do not disturb" button is on my phone. And the list goes on. I have had the pleasure of having hundreds of teachers and learned from each.

A mentor imparts a *process* for managing information and establishing behavior that can be used as a tool to reach a desired end. The mentee listens and then adds his own contribution,

---

Characteristics of a Mentor

▼ A mentor is likely to be a recognized authority and of high professional standing, or she could be a person with estimable qualities that can be shared.

▼ A mentor should be accessible, approachable, receptive, giving, involved, and free of conflict.

▼ A mentor should consider the best interests of the mentee as tantamount.

▼ A mentor should be honest and have a commitment and loyalty that is enduring.

---

making the result not rote but a hybrid. A mentor sees new life given to his own ideas by someone he has invested in.

In addition to Professor Dunham (see ch. 12), the following are examples of three other men, two professional and the other a family member, who fundamentally changed my life in positive ways. I connected with all of them at just the right time—as I said, serendipity plays a role in meeting mentors, but in each case I was ready and did something about it!

My Father-in-Law

Florian Howard Hiss proved to be a memorable human being. Our first meeting was a bit strained, but what else would you expect when a father meets a "bozo" who intends to "steal" his daughter? Over the next two years, I got to know Florian Hiss well. In the process, I became convinced that no two people could have been less alike than he and I. He was short, bald, precise, an excellent businessman, and completely unfamiliar with the likes of a hammer, screwdriver, pliers, paint brush, or anything related to being a handyman. To my future father-in-law, who was a high-end jeweler, any man who could change a tire, prune a tree, or paint a house possessed a kind of magic and was very special. Quite by luck, that was me.

Florian Hiss steadfastly remained the consummate businessman as well as doting father. His store, Herman Hiss and Company, was the epitome of fine jewelry and a match for any of the jewelry stores in Chicago, Detroit, Minneapolis, or anywhere in the Midwest.

In addition to the jewelry business, Florian Hiss understood investments in stocks and bonds and certificates of deposit, the importance of profits, and how to avoid financial losses. He was generous and kind, willing to embrace new things, but always respectful of tradition. He understood the value of hard work and, above all, the responsibility that went along with taking care of a family. His dedication to business was such that when his own daughter was married, the ceremony was held on a

Monday. He felt it would be a disservice to his customers to close on a Saturday in June. He was, indeed, a man of strong principle.

As he got to know me better, I think he was able to recognize that I had a few qualities in my favor; not the least of which was that one day I would be a doctor. Also to my credit, I could back up a two-wheel trailer, and did a reasonably good job painting the "old cottage" where my future father-in-law had grown up as a boy at Linwood Beach!

While these qualities may have characterized me as a somewhat resourceful young man, he also recognized that I didn't know much about handling money. The truth was, the only thing I knew about money was how to work hard to earn it and how to spend it. For the past seven years, I had spent every cent I earned paying for tuition, clothes, and other basic living expenses. I had no skills at managing money because I never had any to manage. Every penny had a place to go before I was even paid.

Not knowing much about me, my father-in-law guessed correctly that I could use some sound advice when it came to finances and financial planning. To this end, we spent many hours sitting around the kitchen table in the breakfast room at 603 Green Avenue in Bay City, Michigan. During these sessions, he explained to me that my first responsibility as a breadwinner was to pay myself. "The only other thing you can do with your money, besides save it," he explained, "was to give it to somebody else. First in line to take your money was the government. Then, you must pay for your living expenses. Any remaining money is what you paid yourself to be set aside for a time when it was needed, including an unforeseen rainy day." His recommendation was to start a savings fund to provide economic security for my future family.

Without actually using the term *safety net*, he explained to me how important it was to have financial integrity and that a family that supported each other generationally made it so much easier for individual members to succeed, especially those who were younger. Children in families that remained close and stood ready to support each other had confidence and a sense of security, even while they were getting started with their careers and planning families. Even without actually having the money, people in this kind of family knew they would not be left without money, high and dry, in a time of need.

This philosophy explains how much more creative a trapeze artist can be when he knows there is a safety net below. No aerialist wants to fall, but if something happens, it is significant comfort to know a safety net is there.

During these discussions, my father-in-law also stressed the importance of life insurance. He recommended Northwestern Mutual as a high level company, and started me out with a small policy that cost only a few hundred dollars a year. He urged me to buy more policies when I could and to make whole life insurance an important part of my savings program. He stressed that whole life insurance could be an important component of my family's safety net. I took his advice, and it has paid off.

Probably the funniest and most memorable thing that my father-in-law did was "sell" an engagement ring to me. As a junior in medical school and paying my own way, I had absolutely no money. Barbara understood this and said she would not have an engagement ring. I could make it up later. I grudgingly agreed.

When her dad got wind of this, he must have decided there was absolutely no way a jeweler's daughter could be engaged without a ring. This subject never came up and therefore no open discussion took place. However, in the Hiss family circle I am sure the ring issue was a matter of great concern and much thought was given to solving this problem. The solution played out one Saturday morning when I was in Bay City. I was in the jewelry store picking something up for Mrs. Hiss. Barbara's dad greeted me and we exchanged pleasantries. Then he steered the conversation around to diamonds. Before long he asked, "How much could you spend on a ring?" I said sixty dollars was all I had to my name. He responded, "I just made a very good purchase on a one-carat emerald-cut ring. I can sell it to you for sixty dollars." He went on to say the stone would be in a platinum setting with two full-cut baguettes. He asked if I would be interested in buying the ring. I said yes.

We completed the transaction on the spot. Of course, I knew this ring would retail for thousands of dollars, and that he would have made that ring available to me at any price. He gave me a chance to accept the ring without either of us commenting on the obvious. He had "sold" me a ring for less than the tax for the setting alone! This transaction was never discussed between us or with any member of the family other than my wife. My father-in-law died sixteen years later.

Florian Hiss's most profound effect on me was instilling the importance of financial peace of mind and all of the benefits that go with it. Of the mentors I have had, none has been more important than he.

Setting My Course as an Ophthalmologist

I met Malcolm A. McCannel in 1962, in Minneapolis, Minnesota, where he had established a busy ophthalmology practice. He was forty-six, not quite old enough to be a father figure.[2] I was twenty-eight and an ophthalmology resident whose training had been interrupted by the pre-Vietnam War doctor draft; working as the Chief Medical Examiner at the Armed Forces Examining Station. After a few days on the job, I was able to arrange my schedule so that I could complete all of the 200 physicals by midday and still have four hours free each afternoon. Because I was an ophthalmologist in training, the commander told me the Army would allow me to pursue my medical studies during any free time I might have as long as it didn't interfere with my assigned Army duties.

With this information, I checked the yellow pages to find an ophthalmologist with an office within walking distance of the

Examining Station. My aim was to find out if it would be possible to make arrangements for me to be an observer in the office of an ophthalmologist. My second call netted Dr. McCannel. We met in his office the next day and without much in the way of small talk, he told me I could come to the office as often as I wished every weekday and Saturday morning. I could start by observing, and then when I was comfortable, begin doing preliminary work-ups and refractions on his patients. My responsibilities would increase when I demonstrated I could do the job. He offered me five dollars an hour. I jumped at the opportunity. I had a job!

This began a nineteen-month experience that was truly life changing. Mac, as I was told to call him, shared all of his office secrets and taught me a lot about how to run an ophthalmology practice. Mac was outgoing and had many talents. One that was unique and that he was especially proud of was office efficiency. His concept of an efficient office included succinct recordkeeping, efficient examining room configuration, an eclectic approach to examination and treatment equipment, smooth patient flow, and reliable communication. In addition to all of this, he was a fine clinician and a gifted surgeon.

Mac had a lot to offer and I had a lot to learn. Mac was accustomed to having young associates who were already finished with their training; my being a resident with just eight months of training made me a bit of an oddity. This didn't concern Mac though. His solution was to offer me the opportunity to finish my training with him as a preceptor after my military duty was completed. I could take a three-month basic science course at the University of Minnesota, sit for the boards, and join him in practice when this training was completed and I was Board Certified. This would take about three and a half years. I was honored he asked, but I was too much of a traditionalist. I told him I would work in his office as long as I could, but would return to Indiana when I got out of the Army.

While working for Mac, I completed a scientific paper based

on data I had collected at the Examining Station. It described the incidence of amblyopia in the men I was examining. *Amblyopia* is a type of vision loss that occurs when an eye is not stimulated in a normal way early in life. I also published a paper about an office-based glaucoma-testing technique from data I recorded while using a new glaucoma testing instrument in Mac's office. In a typical Mac move, he rose during a luncheon meeting of the Minneapolis Ophthalmology Club and announced: "My young associate would like to deliver a paper he has written called 'Office Tonography.'" Needless to say, that was the first I heard of my giving a talk! The good part was that I gave my first medical paper presentation without the remotest chance of having time for stage fright.

Mac also sponsored me for the Eye Study Club, a group of ophthalmologists who were both serious doctors and fun-loving fellows. This introduced me to some nice people and was the occasion for me to be selected twenty-five years later to deliver the Reudemann Lecture at the club meeting in honor of its founder.

Dr. McCannel also recommended me for a Heed Fellowship for post-residency study. I succeeded in obtaining the award which made it possible for me to complete a year of study at the Wilmer Ophthalmological Institute at Johns Hopkins Hospital. While completing my studies there, I worked with my next mentor, who prepared me for a career in academic medicine.

Preparing for Academic Medicine

In the fall of 1961, I may have been the only first-year eye resident in the country whose chief interest was amblyopia. Five years later, by the time I had finished my residency, Army duty, and nineteen months with Dr. McCannel, I had written two papers about this type of vision loss that affected children but persisted for life if untreated.

I had also kept up with new information about the causes and treatment of this condition. The most important papers I had read were written by Gunter K. von Noorden, MD, an ophthalmologist who was a clinician and clinical researcher on the cutting edge of this science.[3]

Based on this interest, I was able to publish my first paper, "Preventable Disuse Blindness," in the *Journal of the Student American Medical Association* in 1963. A second, and more significant paper, "The Incidence of Amblyopia in Inductees at the AFES Minneapolis Minnesota" was published in the prestigious *American Journal of Ophthalmology* in 1964. In the fall of 1965, during my last year of residency, I attended the annual meeting of the American Academy of Ophthalmology (AAO) in Chicago where Dr. von Noorden was presenting a course on amblyopia. I purchased a ticket and joined the group of attendees in one of the small, crowded hotel room that was specifically converted for AAO courses at the Palmer House. Dr. von Noorden, not knowing who I was or that I was in the audience, referred to my paper from the examination station, and used my name. I felt about ten feet tall!

After his lecture, I cornered Dr. von Noorden outside the room and asked if he would consider me studying under him the following year. I told him I had been awarded a Heed Fellowship, and was eager to study with him. He told me to make an appointment and come to Baltimore for an official interview. Ugh, that would be a thousand miles roundtrip. I made the drive and was accepted at the interview—later discovering I was his only applicant. At just thirty-five, and only seven years older than me, Dr. von Noorden was only at the beginning of what proved to be a distinguished academic career.

Starting in July 1966, he and I began what became a lifelong association that also transformed into a fast friendship. Over the next half century, until Dr. von Noorden's full retirement, we regularly connected professionally; and my wife, Barbara, and befriended Betty, Gunter's wife of more than fifty years.

Early in my career, Gunter included me in several international programs that he was asked to help organize. I would never have had these opportunities without him. These included professional meetings in Bogotá, Damascus, Marrakesh, Geneva, Montevideo, Rome, Saudi Arabia, and at many institutions throughout the United States. We collaborated on a three-hour instruction course each year at the American Academy of Ophthalmology meeting, a course that ran for twenty-five years, one of the longest of its kind in the organization's history. We also co-authored a textbook that was translated into Chinese, Hungarian, and Czech. Today, we still talk by phone several times a month.

Each of the four principal mentor relationships in my life came at crucial times for me, and each profoundly influenced my life.

If you want your child to have the best possible chance to find a mentor, give the following advice to him:

1. Do your best to identify who you are, i.e., your traits and personality.

2. Figure out what you enjoy doing and the career choices you want to pursue.

3. Pay attention to where you are in your life path.

4. Always have something to offer. And show interest.

5. Look for a mentor who is outside your family circle, but don't exclude those who are in.

6. Be aware of the people around you; especially those you relate to and who can help you.

7. Notice the people you admire and try to figure out what it is that you admire about them.

8. Don't be afraid to approach someone you believe could be a mentor—but don't ask them to be your mentor. Just talk with them and ask for their advice or apply for a class or job the prospective mentor teaches or supervises. Then do things that will make you be noticed in a positive way.

9. Don't be discouraged if an attempt to make contact with a possible mentor doesn't work. In the long run, this may be the best because this relationship needs to be a two-way street.

10. Recognize there is no one kind of mentor and no one kind of mentee.

11. You will do better if you choose a mentor for a particular time of life and for a particular endeavor. You can have more than one mentor, but they should be influencing different phases of your life.

12. There is not likely to be a mentor that you want to copy completely. They are individuals and you are too. Be yourself, then take from your mentor something that can help make you even better.

Next, we'll review what should be a universal goal of children.

14

THE MAJOR LEAGUES OF LIFE

"Bliss resides in the heart, confidence is in the mind
and these are more valuable than anything that can
ever be seen, touched, or heard."
ANONYMOUS

A TOUGH REALITY OF BEING A PARENT IS THAT THE WAY WE might define success for our children isn't necessarily what they achieve or even want. Whatever their aims, we naturally want the best for our children. But, there is only so much a parent can do to help make this happen. Parents soon become aware that as the Second Decade begins to wind down, a child's horizons broaden and their lives become truly their own.

The young children parents held almost total sway over will be increasingly more influenced by their peers, the media, other adults, and events as they approach their twentieth birthday. Parental control, nearly total with the pre-adolescent child of ten, gives way to mostly listening, suggesting, and encouraging as children move relentlessly toward chronological adulthood around the age of twenty. No matter what you have done or what you would like to continue doing, the end of the Second Decade essentially ends that phase of your child's life when you, the parent, are in complete control. You can retain influence and be asked for advice as your child goes forth, but that might be it. And, as "sad" as this might be for some parents, I say it is better to have raised an independent adult than one who can't think or decide for himself.

A common denominator for all parents should be the fervent hope for their children to reach their full potential as they proceed with their own lives.

The problem is, there is no foolproof formula for achieving success, and no reliable definition of when success is achieved for a given individual. Parents who have done their best raising kids are not guaranteed that older children will follow the path you wished for. But this doesn't mean that parents can't grade their own efforts; a grade based on two important things that parents should have done in a steady and unwavering way while their child was soaring, stumbling, gliding, and sometimes simply enduring his way through the Second Decade.

First, you should have exercised all of the positive influence you could muster to help your child get a solid education. A minimum is for your child to graduate high school and earn diploma. Again, let me emphasize: this is the starting point; the minimum goal. Post high school, kids must further their education or training to attain independence (financial and otherwise) and happiness as adults. There are many options available. It is not the number of years of the education or the training a young adult receives after high school that matters. What is critical is that the college education, vocational training, or work experience is right for your child.

There is no foolproof path that suits all children.

Second, you should have made sure your child learned the value of meaningful work while in high school—if not sooner. In addition to teaching hard work related and soft social skills, working outside of the home teaches independence, responsibility and the value of money. These traits will benefit children for a lifetime. (See ch. 8)

This tandem of school and work during the Second Decade provides children first with an academic fund of knowledge from pursuing a well-executed plan in the classroom and second it teaches important practical skills and responsible behavior from meaningful work at a job.

Helping your child attain success, both in her educational pursuits and at meaningful work, is the best gift you can give as she prepares for a productive and self-sustaining life in the inclusive middle class—or as a baseball fan, what I like to call the "Major Leagues of Life."

I define the Major Leagues of Life as:

▼ A satisfying job with reasonable assurance of keeping it.

▼ An income adequate to meet a person's and the family's needs while sustaining a comfortable lifestyle.

▼ Freedom to make decisions with confidence and optimism for the future.

These criteria must be interpreted in relative terms as there are many landing spots and a wide range of accomplishments that fall within the parameters of the Major Leagues of Life. At one end are those with a lower income and, frankly, a simpler life that will not include many of the things that might be expected or considered standard for someone at the upper levels of the inclusive middle class.

"Men go abroad to wonder at the heights of mountains, at the huge waves of the sea, at the long courses of rivers, at the vast compass of the ocean, at the circular motion of the stars, and they pass themselves without wondering."
St. Augustine

A unifying factor characterizing anyone in the Major Leagues of Life is that they can manage their own life, are confident that they can sustain that way of life, and they feel free to make plans for their future. It is not just income level, number of cars, size of a house, school district, or where they shop that defines success. Achieving the Major Leagues of Life depends on attitude; not solely on income or the material things you have acquired.

How one behaves and accepts financial responsibility fills out the picture of the Major Leagues of Life. So many of life's joys and problems revolve around money; so it is important for income to meet expenses, and preferably, to have some to spare and put in savings. Maybe a better way to say this is: Don't let what you perceive as your needs exceed what you have as income.

A place in the Major Leagues of Life is not guaranteed. (See ch. 2) A person can reach the inclusive middle class and later lose the critical aspect of that status: satisfaction and confidence. One way this happens is when lifestyle "needs" exceed actual income. In other cases, people and families face loss of income because of misfortune. When this happens, people need and deserve help in their time of distress from a compassionate society—that is *us*.

Talking about class means speaking in generalities and not specifics.

Circumstances and life choices are different for everyone. No two people are exactly the same.

We are each just one dot on that curve that describes who is average, who is above average, and who is below. The criteria for placement according to income level is objective and can be determined for us. But that is not the whole story.

This book in not intended to support or deny macro societal or economic approaches when it comes to defining or molding life, especially life in the inclusive middle class. This book aims to point out the ways you, as a parent and mentor, can help children get a solid foothold on life and attain happiness and self-sufficiency as adults.

When I talk about the major leagues of life, I see a parallel with the major leagues of baseball. The twenty-seven players of each team put on the same uniform, sit on the same bench, and play on the same field. The "clean up" hitter or the twenty-game winner might make fifty times the salary of the utility player, but each is giving his all—and I don't think I ever heard of a major league baseball player who was not happy to be on that bench. Each position player knows that if he raises his batting average fifty points and each pitcher knows that if he develops a 95 mph fastball with good control, he will not only retain a place on the bench but he will move up.

The Major Leagues of Life is that "bench." We can all sit on it somewhere, virtually, as we take our place in the inclusive middle class. We won't all have the same start. We don't all have the same talents. And we won't all land at the same place on the field—but the rules of the game are the same for everyone.

Each parent, and that goes for the single parent as well as the one with a spouse, and each child in any family, can work as a team, play by the rules, and do what it takes to build the best life possible.

If you want to raise your child to be a happy, self-sufficient adult, encourage your child to get the best education he or she can and w-o-r-k at meaningful jobs.

177

IN SUMMARY

.

THE MAN WITH A PLAN WILL DO BETTER THAN THE MAN WITHOUT a plan every time. If you want your child to do well, to be better off as an adult, then you need a plan for your child's Second Decade. This plan should not be a manifesto dictating your child's every move. Instead it will suggest steps your child can take in the right direction.

It should also include a plan of action for you on behalf of your child. Consider these questions:

▼ When should you assert your parental authority?

▼ When should you hold back and let events unfold as they will?

▼ How can you best introduce opportunities but not cram them down your child's throat?

▼ How can you suggest possibilities without making demands?

It is up to each parent to decide which decisions children need help with because they simply lack perspective and wisdom.

This can include decisions like choosing a high school or college, what courses to take in high school and college, when a tutor might be beneficial, and how to manage the costs of college.

Along with formal education, never lose sight of how important it is for your school-age child to engage in meaningful work outside the home.

As children progress from age ten to twenty, the parent-child relationship will be assuming a crescendo. Just think of it, your child goes from the fifth grade to the sophomore or junior year in college or their third year in the working world. It can be a challenging experience, anything but placid, and definitely eventful.

What occurs in this all important Second Decade is a predictor of the quality of life your child will experience as an adult. Do the best job you can.

Good luck to you and your child!

Appendix A

MY FIRST REAL JOB

SOMETIMES WE DON'T REALIZE THE IMPORTANCE CERTAIN EVENTS will have for us until much later. For me, it was the summer I worked at Uncle Carl's. It wasn't until many years later when the full impact of this experience really struck home.

I was young that summer. Very young. I had fun doing things that shouldn't have been all that much fun really, but they were new to me. (The fact they might not have been legal or safe was not evident to me at the time.)

Adults were objects of authority. I believed they should be trusted and obeyed. I was only ten years old and, while I was big for my age, I was just a kid. What I am about to tell you is the story of my first real job, how I got it, what I did, and what it meant to me for years to come. It starts like this:

"Are you awake?" The voice from the bottom of the stairwell was Carl Issel—Uncle Carl to me. It was six a.m.

Of course I am, I thought. How could I still be asleep with your bellowing?

In a softer voice, Uncle Carl continued. "You don't have to get up now if you don't want to, Genie, but I have a couple customers who want to go fishing." (I was called Genie or "Little Gene" until I started high school. My dad was Big Gene.")

Okay. This meant I was expected to get out of bed, put on my swim trunks, walk down to the break wall, and wade into Lake St. Clair's 65-degree water to retrieve a sixteen-foot wooden rowboat that probably had four inches of water in the bottom, and then bail out the water before pulling it back to the dock.

This was my first real job. It was 1944, The War was winding down. My father had arranged it for me. My criteria for *real*: I was expected to work every day, it was outside the neighborhood, I had stipulated responsibilities, and I would be paid!

Carl Issel was a friend of my father's from the 1920s, during prohibition and before the Great Depression. Uncle Carl and my dad met when they were both bachelors. Each went his own way during the decade-long economic downturn of the 30s, staying in touch occasionally. In the spring of 1944, Carl called my father to say he was beginning a new venture. This was not unexpected news. When my father lost his sales job with the National Cash Register Company in 1932, he fell back to the more secure tool and die trade he had learned a decade earlier when he first arrived in Detroit. Carl, also a salesman, had no other special skills. He remained a salesman at heart and continued to live, more or less, the life of a free spirit, albeit with the help of a steadily employed spouse. His current wife, his second or possibly third, taught second grade.

Carl's news was that he had purchased a small house at Thirteen Mile Road and Jefferson Avenue in St. Clair Shores, a small town at the east edge of the Detroit city limits. His lot had a sixty-foot frontage on Lake St. Clair with a solid concrete break wall separating the property from the lake. Carl's new venture was a boat livery. His operation would cater to fishermen willing to try their luck at catching perch, blue gill, and an occasional walleye. He would be opening in a few weeks and needed a helper. My dad found him one—me.

The St. Clair River flows into Lake St. Clair from the north.

From the lake, water flows south into the Detroit River. Lake St. Clair is a round bulge about twenty-one miles in diameter. East to west it separates Michigan from Ontario, Canada. On the map with a skinny river at each end, it looks like the belly of a boa constrictor that has just swallowed a goat. This lake has long been a popular recreational waterway for boaters and fishermen in the area. In the bigger picture, Lake St Clair lies between two of the Great Lakes, Lake Huron to the north and Lake Erie to the south.

Carl's narrow slice of the lake's shoreline had a wooden dock that projected twenty feet from the break wall into the lake. Next to it was a launch ramp with wooden rollers and a winch suitable to retrieve and launch the small boats that made up his fleet. The dock and ramp took up half of the width of the break wall separating the yard from the lake. This left only thirty feet available for tying up the fishing boats. Part of this was obstructed by a small outbuilding at the water's edge. It was called the Hoosegow. The limited space remaining for tying up boats was not the only problem. Lake St. Clair is very shallow with an average depth of just over eleven feet. The prevailing northeast wind frequently piped up to 25 MPH. This wind was capable of creating waves that could crash into and over the break wall. Any boat moored there would sustain significant damage from the pounding of a "Noreaster." Carl's wooden boats would be turned into matchsticks in an afternoon. For this reason, the dozen or so rowboats in Carl's fleet were secured offshore with a light anchor and short anchor line. Scattered between fifty and a hundred feet into the lake, this offshore location was the main reason for me. Carl needed a boat retriever. Later when he realized all of them leaked, he needed a boat caulker and painter; again, that was me.

My dad didn't have to hear much about this scheme to make up his mind about me being Carl's "man" in the water. All of this was decided without consulting me. For the summer of 1944, I would live upstairs in the house Carl shared with his wife, Mildred, the school teacher. I would be right there, in the house, on hand to retrieve and later tend to Carl's fledging "fishing fleet."

I had no way of even suspecting it at the time, but this was only the first of many jobs my father would arrange for me; even less did I recognize that this was the first step on a path that would convince me that to be happy I had to keep busy—to have a job. The chance to earn some real money for the first time was also important. In those days, whatever money I earned I gave immediately and willingly to my parents. My satisfaction at doing so, and the praise I received, was compensation enough.

My routine started early each morning with a cold plunge into Lake St Clair. It continued with an apology and a lie. Once in the water, I retrieved the anchor of the nearest boat. I stowed the anchor and pulled the boat in with the line, walking chest deep in the water. I jumped on the dock, secured the boat, and started baling and cleaning. While I was doing this, the fishermen made arrangements with Carl. This usually included a cup of coffee and some bogus information from Uncle Carl about where the fish were biting. When the fishermen arrived on the dock, I made sure I *apologized* for any water still in the bottom. I then *lied*, telling them that any water still in the bottom of the boat had splashed in and I assured them the boats didn't leak. Each passenger was given a serviceable life vest and was told how to use it. I then supplied them with minnows and worms and wished them good luck.

When all of the fishermen were out on the lake, I began the never-ending chore of caulking and painting any leaky boats that were not in use. For the entire summer there was at least one boat on shore needing this attention. This was absolutely necessary to make sure the boat didn't fill with water while out on the lake. Being wooden, the boats would float, at least for a while, but it would be pretty dicey with a couple of fishermen onboard, even if they had life preservers.

At the end of the season we took pride in the fact that we

had avoided calamity. All of our fishermen returned safely that summer. I don't know if we ever had a truly satisfied customer. In those days, the greater Detroit area had more than a quarter of the state's population. We had enough people to realistically expect a steady flow of new business. That was good because I didn't recognize many repeat customers.

One of the highlights of the summer was Carl's cooking. He grilled huge steaks on a charcoal grill on the lawn in back of the house. The medium-rare T-bone and porterhouse steaks were wonderful. I had never eaten so well, and hadn't experienced anything cooked on a grill except hotdogs at picnics and in the Boy Scouts. For me, this was absolutely living high— even exotic—compared to anything I had ever eaten at home. To my delight, I was always given a whole steak, which I ate with gusto.

Another example of what I interpreted as Carl's hospitality took place in the aforementioned Hoosegow. This building measured about twelve by twenty feet. It was wood-framed, painted white, with almost continuous windows, green shutters, and screens. One wall came right to the water's edge. There were a few chairs, a table, lots of ashtrays, glasses, and a large cooler. At almost any time of the day, and any day of the week, Carl could be seen pouring generous drinks and regaling his visitors. Only a few were fishermen. Most were people who just dropped by. This group even included the priest from the Catholic Church across the street. He was there often, although never on Sundays.

It was many years later when I realized Carl's income must have been primarily from this "blind pig," a name carried over from prohibition days. It was used to describe an establishment where booze was sold illegally. In Carl's case, the illegality was that he had no license and sold alcohol on Sundays. It is not too great a stretch that the boat livery may have been nothing more than a cover. By 1944, it was just a decade after the repeal of prohibition. Lake St. Clair was a virtual superhighway for delivery of alcohol from Canada to the United States, and there were many former bootleggers around. As I think back, it is very likely that Uncle Carl was one of them.

This was a summer that passed quickly. It was fun and it was misery, but most of all it was an experience with some sense of a job well done. Like many such experiences, the pain gradually drifted to nothingness, and the good times kept getting better.

Appendix B

AN UNORTHODOX PATH TO SUCCESS

FRANK MCKINNEY IS A SELF-DESCRIBED "REAL ESTATE ARTIST" WHO builds multimillion dollar homes, costing in one case more than $22 million. He has written five bestselling books and is the founder of Caring House Project that provides unique housing for the homeless in the United States, Latin America, and the Caribbean. He attended four high schools in four years in Indianapolis, finishing with what he reports as a 1.8 GPA, but also a diploma (maybe awarded to get rid of him!).

Moving to Florida at age eighteen, with fifty dollars in his pocket, he got a job digging sand traps by hand for $180 a week at the Deerfield Golf Club.

Now, more than a quarter of a century later, he is a millionaire known for building some of the world's finest and most expensive and imaginative homes. All of this was accomplished with hard work and dedication to a dream. McKinney never spent a day in school after his star-crossed high school experience, but has become a legend in his field.

His father and grandfather were successful bankers in Indianapolis. His father was an Olympic swimmer and his grandfather, at one time, owned the Pittsburgh Pirates baseball team and was Chairman of the Democratic National Committee.

Frank McKinney chose a unique path in life. He stayed true to himself and made maximum use of his innate talent.

Frank McKinney's story tells us that while the educational level attained by a person is the most reliable predictor of success—brains, hard work, and luck are the most reliable way to *achieve* success.

Appendix C

VOLUNTEER WORK

C ALEB BROWN IS SMALL FOR HIS AGE, BUT NOT WHEN IT comes to his heart. He told me about a project he completed as a requirement to earn his rank of Eagle Scout. Caleb considered several ideas before deciding on Christmas trees for the needy. Here, in his own words, is his story about volunteering:

"I had never made a Christmas tree out of a wire tomato cage before, so I first had to learn how to make one," he explained. Once he knew how to make the Christmas trees, Caleb had to figure out who he would give the trees to.

"I met with Shelia Morton, the Food Pantry co-manager. She loved my idea and was excited to know that a lot of people were going to receive a Christmas tree this year. We set up a date for the trees to be delivered … December 4, 2013."

Caleb then needed approval from his Boy Scout leader.

"I met with my eagle coach, scoutmaster, and an assistant scoutmaster to go over the project proposal process. On October 3, 2013, Steve Heath approved my project. After it was approved, I felt relieved and exhilarated at the same time."

Now, it was time for Caleb to acquire the necessary materials.

"A large amount of materials and supplies were donated. I counted and sorted all of my useable materials and supplies. My mom helped by making bows and my sisters made a bag for each tree filled with ornaments. My dad helped by teaching and assisting me with the repairing of the lights."

Next was assembling the trees.

"My first workday was November 15. The first weekend was a lock-in. The first weekend we made 148 Christmas trees, but only forty fit into the storage unit. The other 108 trees were kept at our house. We had trees in our garage, basement, front room, hallway, and kitchen."

Finally, it was time to deliver the trees.

"Wednesday, December 4, was delivery day. I made three trips to the Inter Church Food Pantry. When we arrived with the second and third loads, people were lined up to get a free tree. I was able to meet some of the people who were getting a Christmas tree. Most people said that this was the first Christmas tree they had had in a long time. Some also said they would not have any presents and this tree was going to be the only Christmas decoration they had. People were crying, and thanking me for the trees. One lady said that her and her husband had jobs, but had to walk to work. She also said that this was the first Christmas tree they had had in about six years."

Caleb finishes his story succinctly and modestly. "Giving to others made my Christmas more enjoyable. I am glad I chose this project."

Caleb learned many lessons and skills at a volunteer job that makes most of the real jobs I have done pale in comparison.

Appendix D

SUITABLE JOB PROSPECTS

Don't believe it when people say there aren't jobs available for today's youth. Following is a brief list of suitable jobs for kids in their Second Decade. And, I am confident there are others where you live! Some of these jobs can be done on a freelance basis, while others require being hired by an employer.

1. Retail (including clothing, hardware, food, etc.)
2. Fast-Food Restaurant
3. Wait staff & kitchen help (in restaurants, delis, retirement communities, hospitals, etc.)
4. Painting (residential and commercial buildings)
5. Golf Course
6. Car Wash
7. Grocery store/supermarket
8. Stock boy or girl
9. Cashier

10. Babysitting

11. Kennel Worker

12. General laborer/handyman

13. Lifeguard at Swimming pool/Beach/Waterpark

14. Pizza delivery

15. Supervising/teaching/tutoring children in sports, music, academics

16. Landscaping/yardwork/Pool maintenance

17. United States Post Office (for applicants who have attained the age of eighteen)

If nothing in the list above is of interest to your child, then send her to Google, where she might find something that is of interest.

I will make this wild and unfounded statement: There are as many jobs for teens today as there have been in previous generations but it takes creativity to find them!

NOTES

Most of the notes have been garnered from material available on the Internet; accessible with a Google search. The material comes in two categories. First are statistics. These are at best approximations even in the published form and are subject to interpretation, but even with this, they tell the essential story. They are fluid and will change over time. Fortunately, if you care, the most up-to-date statistics will be available online. Very little of what is in this book is something that could be subjected to rigorous scientific scrutiny.

The second level of references are opinions from people who are considered reliable and not spouting propaganda.

Preface

1. Adolescence—Puberty, Cognitive transition, Emotional transition, Social transition Laurence Steinberg, Ph.D. http://psychology.jrank.org/pages/14/Adolescence.html
   "Sometimes referred to as teenage years, youth, or puberty, adolescence covers the period from roughly age 10 to 20 in a child's development" Alfred Adler *(with permission)*
   In the study of child development, adolescence refers to the second decade of the life span, roughly from ages 10 to 20. The word *adolescence* is Latin in origin, derived from the verb adolescere, which means "to grow into adulthood." In all societies, adolescence is a time of growing up, of moving from the immaturity of childhood into the maturity of adulthood.

2. *How Children Succeed: Grit, Curiosity, and the Hidden Power of Charac-*
ter Paperback; July 2, 2013 by Paul Tough http://www.amazon.com/
How-Children-Succeed-Curiosity-Character/dp/0544104404
Q and A with author
Q. What made you want to write *How Children Succeed*?
A. In 2008, I published my first book, *Whatever It Takes*, about Geoffrey
Canada and the Harlem Children's Zone. I spent five years reporting
that book, but when I finished it, I realized I still had a lot of questions
about what really happens in childhood. *How Children Succeed* is an
attempt to answer those questions, which for many of us are big and
mysterious and central in our lives: Why do certain children succeed
while other children fail? Why is it, exactly, that poor children are less
likely to succeed, on average, than middle-class children? And most
important, what can we all do to steer more kids toward success?
Q. Where did you go to find the answers?
A. My reporting for this book took me all over the country, from a
pediatric clinic in a low-income San Francisco neighborhood to a
chess tournament in central Ohio to a wealthy private school in New
York City. And what I found as I reported was that there is a new
and groundbreaking conversation going on, out of the public eye,
about childhood and success and failure. It is very different than the
traditional education debate. There are economists working on this,
neuroscientists, psychologists, medical doctors. They are often working independently from one another. They don't always coordinate
their efforts. But they're beginning to find some common ground, and
together they're reaching some interesting and important conclusions.
Q. A lot of your reporting for this book was in low-income neighborhoods. Overall, what did you learn about kids growing up in poverty?
A. A lot of what we think we know about the effect of poverty on a
child's development is just plain wrong. It's certainly indisputable that
growing up in poverty is really hard on children. But the conventional
wisdom is that the big problem for low-income kids is that they don't
get enough cognitive stimulation early on. In fact, what seems to have
more of an effect is the chaotic environments that many low-income
kids grow up in and the often stressful relationships they have with the
adults around them. That makes a huge difference in how children's
brains develop, and scientists are now able to trace a direct route from
those early negative experiences to later problems in school, health,
and behavior.
The problem is that science isn't yet reflected in the way we run our
schools and operate our social safety net. And that's a big part of why
so many low-income kids don't do well in school. We now know better
than ever what kind of help they need to succeed in school. But very
few schools are equipped to deliver that help.
Q. Many readers were first exposed to your reporting on character
through your article in the *New York Times Magazine* in September 2011,

which was titled "What If the Secret to Success Is Failure?" How does failure help us succeed?

A. That's an idea that I think was best expressed by Dominic Randolph, the head of the Riverdale Country School, an exclusive private school in the Bronx where they're now doing some interesting experiments with teaching character. Here's how he put it: "The idea of building grit and building self-control is that you get that through failure. And in most highly academic environments in the United States, no one fails anything."

That idea resonated with a lot of readers. I don't think it's quite true that failure itself helps us succeed. In fact, repeated failures can be quite devastating to a child's development. What I think is important on the road to success is learning to deal with failure, to manage adversity. That's a skill that parents can certainly help their children develop— but so can teachers and coaches and mentors and neighbors and lots of other people.

Q. How did writing this book affect you as a parent?

A. My wife and I became parents for the first time just as I started reporting this book, and our son Ellington is now three. Those are crucial years in a child's development, and I spent a lot of them reading papers on the infant brain and studies on attachment and trauma and stress hormones, trying not to get too overwhelmed.

In the end, though, this research had a surprising effect: it made me more relaxed as a parent. When Ellington was born, I was very much caught up in the idea of childhood as a race—the faster a child develops skills, the better he does on tests, the better he'll do in life. Having done this reporting, I'm less concerned about my son's reading and counting ability. Don't get me wrong, I still want him to know that stuff. But I think he'll get there in time. What I'm more concerned about is his *character*—or whatever the right synonym is for character when you're talking about a three-year-old. I want him to be able to get over disappointments, to calm himself down, to keep working at a puzzle even when it's frustrating, to be good at sharing, to feel loved and confident and full of a sense of belonging. Most important, I want him to be able to deal with failure. That's a difficult thing for parents to give their children, since we have deep in our DNA the urge to shield our kids from every kind of trouble. But what we're finding out now is that in trying to protect our children, we may actually be harming them. By not giving them the chance to learn to manage adversity, to cope with failure, we produce kids who have real problems when they grow up. Overcoming adversity is what produces character. And character, even more than IQ, is what leads to real and lasting success.

Introduction

1. *The Decline of Childhood Mortality* by Kenneth Hill, Department of Population Dynamics, School of Hygiene and Public Health at Johns

Hopkins University (https://jhir.library.jhu.edu/...2/.../WP90-07). Over the last three or four centuries, child mortality has fallen dramatically. In developed countries, this transition from high to low mortality is essentially complete; whereas prior to the decline, a child had only about a 60 percent chance of surviving to age five; today a newborn has better than a 99 percent chance of reaching age five. The decline occurred through reduced exposure to pathogens, largely as a result initially of public health measures, and later as a result of living in a healthier population, through improved nutrition and reduced crowding, and through specific preventive and therapeutic medical interventions.

As the decline has progressed, the medical effects have become increasingly important. In developing countries, the transition is largely incomplete, though it has started everywhere. In a few countries in Africa, the risk of dying by age five is still over 300 per thousand; in parts of South Asia, it is still over 200 per thousand; in parts of Latin America, it is still over 150 per thousand. Practically everywhere, barring civil wars or natural disasters, it is declining at a fairly steady pace, and in some countries (Chile, Costa Rica) has reached levels of which Europe was proud only three decades ago. This decline is much more strongly associated with medical knowledge and medical practice than was the earlier decline in Europe. Indeed, the development and implementation of cheap and effective preventive measures has probably been the decisive factor in child mortality decline in LDC's over the last two decades.

2. http://www.catholic.com/quickquestions/how-did-the-church-decided-that-seven-is-the-age-of-reason-and-the-age-for-first-comm. The Church does not define the age of reason as seven years old. Rather, the Church does not obligate Catholics under the age of seven to observe laws which are merely ecclesiastical. Even once the age of seven is attained, children who do not possess the use of reason generally are not bound. *Code of Canon Law* states, "Merely ecclesiastical laws bind those who have been baptized in the Catholic Church or received into it, possess the efficient use of reason, and, unless the law expressly provides otherwise, have completed seven years of age" (CIC 11).

In the case of First Communion, there is no age restriction. The Church simply requires that children possess the use of reason, know and understand what the Eucharist is, and are properly disposed. (Jim Blackburn)

3. Sorabella, Jean. Independent Scholar (http://www.metmuseum.org/toah/hd/birt/hd_birt.htm). Iconic pictures of the Christ Child with his mother are very common in Italian art (2004.442), but other scenes from his childhood are considerably rarer. A small panel by Cosimo Tura (49.7.17) depicts the Flight into Egypt, when Joseph, Mary, and the infant Jesus fled for safety from Herod's massacre of young children thanks to an angel's warning. The strange pose of the sleeping child,

with his hand to his side and his legs tightly crossed, anticipates the end of his earthly life and the state of his corpse after crucifixion.

4. https://www.google.com/#q=barbizon+school+of+art+showing+children. Although the Barbizon School depicted Nature and people doing ordinary things, including work, the picture of "A Girl with Cat" is one of the relatively few paintings that depict a child. Although a few others can be seen, they are not in abundance. In contrast to the old school, the girl with a cat is shown as a child (http://www.mfa.org/node/9523) while a girl of roughly the same age painted 200 years earlier has a stern countenance and wears adult clothing and appears only as a little adult.

5. https://industrialrevolution.wordpress.com/category/child-labor/. Children made up a large number of workers in factories and mines during the Industrial Revolution. ... Their small statures allowed them to climb into tight spaces in mines. Their nimble hands could work machines easier than adults. These advantages gave factory owners and mine operators every reason to hire children like this.

6. http://www.dickmeister.com/id366.html. Even the most casual students of the history of American labor undoubtedly have come across the appalling accounts of child labor, accompanied by photos of exhausted, grime-covered teen and pre-teen children staring sad-eyed into the camera. The children stand outside the mines, mills, farms, and other highly dangerous places where they worked ten, twelve, and fifteen hours a day, sometimes even more. They worked at home as well, in their impoverished families' dilapidated tenement flats, rolling cigars, stitching garments, and doing other tasks for long, miserably paid hours.

7. http://rarehistoricalphotos.com/child-laborers-news boys-smoking-cigarettes-1910/. Young children at work in adult occupations were likely to smoke, aping their adult co-workers.

8. Whaples, Robert. Wake Forest University (https://eh.net/encyclopedia/child-labor-in-the-united-states/). The low value of child labor in agriculture may help explain why children were an important source of labor in many early industrial firms. In 1820, children aged fifteen and under made up 23 percent of the manufacturing labor force of the industrializing Northeast. They were especially common in textiles, constituting 50 percent of the workforce in cotton mills with sixteen or more employees, as well as 41 percent of workers in wool mills, and 24 percent in paper mills. Goldin and Sokoloff (1982) conclude, however, that child labor's share of industrial employment began its decline as early as 1840. Many textile manufacturers employed whole families and—despite its declining share—child labor continued to be an important input into this industry until the early twentieth century.

9. U.S. Department of Education, Institute of Education Sciences, National Center for Education Statistics (http://nces.ed.gov/programs/coe/indicator_coi.asp). In school year 2011–2012, some 3.1

197

million public high school students, or 81 percent, graduated on time with a regular diploma. Among all public high school students, Asian/Pacific Islander students had the highest graduation rate (93 percent), followed by whites (85 percent), Hispanics (76 percent), and American Indians/Alaska Natives and Blacks (68 percent each).

10. http://www.mcclatchydc.com/news/nation-world/national/economy/article24755047.html. According to the McClatchy Report, for the fourth consecutive summer, teen employment has stayed anchored around record lows, prompting experts to fear that a generation of youth is likely to be economically stunted with lower earnings and opportunities in years ahead.

11. http://nces.ed.gov/fastfacts/display.asp?id=372. U.S. Department of Education, Institute of Education Sciences, National Center for Education Statistics. In fall 2015, some 20.2 million students are expected to attend American colleges and universities, constituting an increase of about 4.9 million since fall 2000. About 7.0 million students will attend 2-year institutions and 13.2 million will attend 4-year institutions in fall 2015. Some 17.3 million students are expected to enroll in undergraduate programs and about 3.0 million will enroll in postbaccalaurate

Chapter 1

1. Frey, Thomas. (http://www.futuristspeaker.com/2013/09/life-as-a-teenager-in-1994-2014-and-2034-what-a-difference-a-generation-makes-part-2/). Our teenage years have always been a time of great awkwardness, super hormones, and bad decision-making. But lately these years have moved even further down the path of supreme weirdness. Puberty is now kicking in at an increasingly early age, yet because jobs are harder to come by, today's adolescents are taking on adult roles much later in life. The same hormone overload that turns meek ten-year-olds into restless, exuberant, and emotionally intense teenagers desperate to attain every goal, fulfill every desire, and experience every sensation, is the same body-morphing system that later transitions them back into relatively placid adults. It's just that these "limbo years" are getting longer.

Researchers have found that teens do not underestimate the risks that they take; rather they overestimate the reward. A study at Temple University with MRI brain-imaging scans revealed that teens simply find rewards more rewarding than adults do.

For this and many other reasons, 2014 is ushering in a vastly different teenager than those in 1994. Both internal and external influences are causing today's youth to think and act very differently, leaving past experts on teen psychology in a quandary.

So will the teens of 2034 be even more difficult to define? Are they trending towards becoming a different grade of human?

2. Scheff, Sue. http://www.msn.com/?cobrand=asus13.msn.com &ocid

=ASUDHP&pc=ASU2JS. Sue Scheff lists the following benefits from a teen working:

Time management: Having to balance school and work will teach teens early on the importance of prioritizing responsibilities and managing their time. The sooner they learn how to do this the better off they'll be when they leave for college and eventually branch out into the real world of fulltime jobs and responsibilities.

Help build a resume: Being able to list work experience on a resume will help your teen get ahead of the crowd when it comes time to apply for college or find a fulltime job. It will show prospective colleges and employers that your teen is a motivated, hardworking individual and will set them above the people who have no prior work experience.

Financial independence: There is a certain satisfaction that is brought about by being able to buy something you want with your own hard-earned money, and having a job that brings in a paycheck will allow teens to learn how to effectively manage their money and rely on themselves and not their parents for different purchases. Learning to manage money is a life skill that everyone needs to have, so learning it early on will only benefit your teenager.

Develop indispensable life skills: Your teen will learn very quickly the importance of working as a team and having solid communication skills, two talents that are transferrable into almost any industry or experience. The experiences that they have, both good and bad, from a part-time job will help them to become better-rounded as an individual.

Learn the value of hard work: Unfortunately hard work is becoming more under-valued these days, especially with teens, and it's important to teach our kids that hard work is a trait to be admired and respected. Learning to work for what you want is an advantageous tool to have.

3. The Heritage Foundation (http://www.heritage.org/initiatives/first-principles/primary-sources/the-declaration-of-independence). The *Declaration of Independence* is the founding document of the American political tradition. It articulates the fundamental ideas that form the American nation: All men are created free and equal and possess the same inherent, natural rights. Legitimate governments must therefore be based on the consent of the governed and must exist "to secure these rights."

As a practical matter, the *Declaration of Independence* announced to the world the unanimous decision of the thirteen American colonies to separate themselves from Great Britain. But its true revolutionary significance—then as well as now—is the declaration of a new basis of political legitimacy in the sovereignty of the people. The Americans' final appeal was not to any man-made decree or evolving spirit but to rights inherently possessed by all men. These rights are found in eternal "Laws of Nature and of Nature's God." As such, the Declaration's meaning transcends the particulars of time and circumstances.

Declaration of Independence: A Transcription
IN CONGRESS, July 4, 1776.

The unanimous Declaration of the thirteen united States of America,
When in the Course of human events, it becomes necessary for one people
to dissolve the political bands which have connected them with another, and
to assume among the powers of the earth, the separate and equal station to
which the Laws of Nature and of Nature's God entitle them, a decent respect
to the opinions of mankind requires that they should declare the causes which
impel them to the separation.

We hold these truths to be self-evident, that all men are created equal, that
they are endowed by their Creator with certain unalienable Rights, that
among these are Life, Liberty and the pursuit of Happiness.--That to secure
these rights, Governments are instituted among Men, deriving their just
powers from the consent of the governed, --That whenever any Form of
Government becomes destructive of these ends, it is the Right of the People
to alter or to abolish it, and to institute new Government, laying its founda-
tion on such principles and organizing its powers in such form, as to them
shall seem most likely to effect their Safety and Happiness. Prudence, indeed,
will dictate that Governments long established should not be changed for
light and transient causes; and accordingly all experience hath shewn, that
mankind are more disposed to suffer, while evils are sufferable, than to right
themselves by abolishing the forms to which they are accustomed. But when
a long train of abuses and usurpations, pursuing invariably the same Object
evinces a design to reduce them under absolute Despotism, it is their right, it
is their duty, to throw off such Government, and to provide new Guards for
their future security.--Such has been the patient sufferance of these Colonies;
and such is now the necessity which constrains them to alter their former
Systems of Government. The history of the present King of Great Britain
is a history of repeated injuries and usurpations, all having in direct object
the establishment of an absolute Tyranny over these States. To prove this, let
Facts be submitted to a candid world.

He has refused his Assent to Laws, the most wholesome and necessary for the
public good.

He has forbidden his Governors to pass Laws of immediate and pressing
importance, unless suspended in their operation till his Assent should be
obtained; and when so suspended, he has utterly neglected to attend to them.
He has refused to pass other Laws for the accommodation of large districts of
people, unless those people would relinquish the right of Representation in
the Legislature, a right inestimable to them and formidable to tyrants only.
He has called together legislative bodies at places unusual, uncomfortable,
and distant from the depository of their public Records, for the sole purpose
of fatiguing them into compliance with his measures.

He has dissolved Representative Houses repeatedly, for opposing with manly
firmness his invasions on the rights of the people.

He has refused for a long time, after such dissolutions, to cause others to
be elected; whereby the Legislative powers, incapable of Annihilation, have
returned to the People at large for their exercise; the State remaining in the

meantime exposed to all the dangers of invasion from without, and convulsions within.

He has endeavored to prevent the population of these States; for that purpose obstructing the Laws for Naturalization of Foreigners; refusing to pass others to encourage their migrations hither, and raising the conditions of new Appropriations of Lands.

He has obstructed the Administration of Justice, by refusing his Assent to Laws for establishing Judiciary powers.

He has made Judges dependent on his Will alone, for the tenure of their offices, and the amount and payment of their salaries.

He has erected a multitude of New Offices, and sent hither swarms of Officers to harrass our people, and eat out their substance.

He has kept among us, in times of peace, Standing Armies without the Consent of our legislatures.

He has affected to render the Military independent of and superior to the Civil power.

He has combined with others to subject us to a jurisdiction foreign to our constitution, and unacknowledged by our laws; giving his Assent to their Acts of pretended Legislation:

For Quartering large bodies of armed troops among us:

For protecting them, by a mock Trial, from punishment for any Murders which they should commit on the Inhabitants of these States:

For cutting off our Trade with all parts of the world:

For imposing Taxes on us without our Consent:

For depriving us in many cases, of the benefits of Trial by Jury:

For transporting us beyond Seas to be tried for pretended offences

For abolishing the free System of English Laws in a neighboring Province, establishing therein an arbitrary government, and enlarging its Boundaries so as to render it at once an example and fit instrument for introducing the same absolute rule into these Colonies:

For taking away our Charters, abolishing our most valuable Laws, and altering fundamentally the Forms of our Governments:

For suspending our own Legislatures, and declaring themselves invested with power to legislate for us in all cases whatsoever.

He has abdicated Government here, by declaring us out of his Protection and waging War against us.

He has plundered our seas, ravaged our Coasts, burnt our towns, and destroyed the lives of our people.

He is at this time transporting large Armies of foreign Mercenaries to compleat the works of death, desolation and tyranny, already begun with circumstances of Cruelty & perfidy scarcely paralleled in the most barbarous ages, and totally unworthy the Head of a civilized nation.

He has constrained our fellow Citizens taken Captive on the high Seas to bear Arms against their Country, to become the executioners of their friends and Brethren, or to fall themselves by their Hands.

He has excited domestic insurrections amongst us, and has endeavored to bring on the inhabitants of our frontiers, the merciless Indian Savages, whose known rule of warfare, is an undistinguished destruction of all ages, sexes and conditions.

In every stage of these Oppressions We have petitioned for Redress in the most humble terms: Our repeated Petitions have been answered only by repeated injury. A Prince whose character is thus marked by every act which may define a Tyrant, is unfit to be the ruler of a free people.

Nor have We been wanting in attentions to our British brethren. We have warned them from time to time of attempts by their legislature to extend an unwarrantable jurisdiction over us. We have reminded them of the circumstances of our emigration and settlement here. We have appealed to their native justice and magnanimity, and we have conjured them by the ties of our common kindred to disavow these usurpations, which, would inevitably interrupt our connections and correspondence. They too have been deaf to the voice of justice and of consanguinity. We must, therefore, acquiesce in the necessity, which denounces our Separation, and hold them, as we hold the rest of mankind, Enemies in War, in Peace Friends.

We, therefore, the Representatives of the united States of America, in General Congress, Assembled, appealing to the Supreme Judge of the world for the rectitude of our intentions, do, in the Name, and by Authority of the good People of these Colonies, solemnly publish and declare, That these United Colonies are, and of Right ought to be Free and Independent States; that they are Absolved from all Allegiance to the British Crown, and that all political connection between them and the State of Great Britain, is and ought to be totally dissolved; and that as Free and Independent States, they have full Power to levy War, conclude Peace, contract Alliances, establish Commerce, and to do all other Acts and Things which Independent States may of right do. And for the support of this Declaration, with a firm reliance on the protection of divine Providence, we mutually pledge to each other our Lives, our Fortunes and our sacred Honor.

Chapter 2

1. http://www.americanforests.org/our-programs/urbanforests/ urban-forests-case-studies/detroit-introduction/. In the late nineteenth and early twentieth centuries, Detroit was honored as a "city of trees." But in the mid-twentieth century, Detroit's urban canopy suffered a tremendous blow that urban forest advocates have been struggling to overcome ever since. Elms once dominated the city, but after Dutch elm disease reached Detroit around 1950, the city began losing trees at an alarming rate. Between 1950 and 1980, about 500,000 trees succumbed to the disease, urban expansion, or neglect. Economic constraints prevented the city from replacing those trees, and Detroit's urban forest languished in a state of limbo for decades. Adding insult to injury, a new invasive pest, the emerald ash borer, arrived in Detroit in 2002 and has since decimated the city's ash trees—many of which were planted to replace the lost elm trees.

2. Reynolds, Alan. (http://www.wsj.com/articles/alan-reynolds-the-mumbo-jumbo-of-middle-class-economics-1425340903). The following is an example of one side in the bickering that is, in effect, a "political football" where anyone can prove that his own point-of-view is correct. The White House's Council of Economic Advisers defines "middle class economics" primarily by the average income of the bottom 90%. "Average income for the bottom 90 percent of households," according to the ERP, "functions as a decent proxy for the median household's income growth."
This is absurd. The average income for the bottom 90% is not a decent proxy for the median nor even a decent measure of household income. It is instead a roughly fabricated estimate of pretax "market income" reported on tax returns that falls below some threshold for the top 10% ($114,290 in 2013). But this dodgy number does serve as the basis for CEA Chairman Jason Furman's assertion a day later on the Vox blog that the U.S. has suffered a "40-year stagnation in incomes for the middle class and those working to get into the middle class."
3. https://tamino.wordpress.com/2012/09/14/mitt-romneys-middle-class/. During the 2012 U.S. Presidential campaign, Mitt Romney called the middle class "more of a feeling than a statistic." He was criticized for including people making as much as $200,000 as being middle class at least in attitude.
4. Plummer, Brad. (http://www.washingtonpost.com/news/wonkblog/wp/2012/09/18/who-receives-benefits-from-the-federal-government-in-six-charts/). In 2011, about 49 percent of the population lived in a household where at least one member received a direct benefit from the federal government. A big chunk of these households are retirees. And about 27 percent of households benefited from a means-tested poverty program. A quick breakdown:
—Last year, about 29 percent of households received Medicare benefits and 31.6 percent received Social Security. (Obviously there is a lot of overlap between those two, since those programs mainly benefit retirees.)
—Meanwhile, about 32 million households, or 27.1 percent, benefited from at least one means-tested poverty program. The biggest benefits here were Medicaid (19.5 percent), food stamps (12.7 percent), and subsidized lunches (11.2 percent). Again, there is some overlap.
—Smaller benefits include public housing (5 percent of households), unemployment (4 percent), and veterans' compensation (2.6 percent). Only 7 percent of households receive some sort of direct cash assistance, such as the TANF welfare program.
5. The National Bureau of Economic Research (http://www.nber.org/digest/jun06/w11681.html). The persistence of poverty also depends strongly on individual and family characteristics. Among those beginning a spell of poverty, about 83 percent of white children living in two-parent households headed by someone with at least a high school

education will escape long-term poverty. In contrast, only 10 percent of poor black children in a household headed by a single woman without a high school diploma will avoid it.

6. National Center for Education Statistics (https://nces.ed.gov/fastfacts/display.asp?id=27). Between 1990 and 2014, educational attainment rates among 25- to 29-year-olds increased. The percentage who had received at least a high school diploma or its equivalent increased from 86 to 91 percent, with most of the change (4 percentage points) occurring between 2004 and 2014. The percentage who had completed a bachelor's or higher degree increased from 23 percent in 1990 to 34 percent in 2014; and the percentage who had completed a master's or higher degree increased from 5 percent in 1995 to 8 percent in 2014.

7. http://inequality.org/wealth-inequality/. The vast majority of American families—94.5 percent, the latest Federal Reserve survey data make clear—hold one sort of financial asset or another, from savings and checking accounts to stocks and cash-value life insurance policies. But the overall ownership of these financial assets has become stunningly concentrated. America's richest 10 percent now hold nearly 85 percent of these assets. In 1989, the nation's richest tenth of families held 79 percent of them.

8. https://www.healthcare.gov/glossary/federal-poverty-level-FPL/. A measure of income level issued annually by the Department of Health and Human Services. Federal poverty levels are used to determine your eligibility for certain programs and benefits. The amounts below are 2015 numbers and used for calculating eligibility for Medicaid and the Children's Health Insurance Program (CHIP). 2014 numbers are used to calculate eligibility for savings on private insurance plans for 2015.

$11,770 for individuals
$15,930 for a family of 2
$20,090 for a family of 3
$24,250 for a family of 4
$28,410 for a family of 5
$32,570 for a family of 6
$36,730 for a family of 7
$40,890 for a family of 8

9. Peterson, Kim. *MoneyWatch*, April 1, 2015. (1) Median household income was $54,510 in February, according to the latest estimates from Sentier Research. That's up from just above the $51,000 mark in 2012. Pew Research defines a middle-class household income as two-thirds to double the national median, or between about $36,000 and $109,000 a year. Of course, a middle-class income can vary depending on where you live. In San Jose, California, it ranges between $51,000 and $182,000 a year, according to a recent analysis by NPR. (2) Homeownership has long been a hallmark of the middle class. In a 2013 speech, President Obama called it "the most tangible cornerstone that lies at the heart of

the American Dream, at the heart of middle-class life." (3) When nearly nine out of ten Americans said a secure job is essential to being in the middle class. Only 45 percent said owning a home was important. (4) This was another hot topic in Pew's survey of middle-class characteristics. Two-thirds of adults said health insurance was necessary to be considered middle class. (5) Investing for the golden years is important to America's middle class, but that doesn't mean they do a very good job of it. (6) But generally, when Americans think of middle-class families, surveys show they think of parents who went to college and are saving for a college education for their children. (7) The family vacation "is a middle-class staple." (8) You think you are middle class. This may be the most important distinction of all: For many, being middle class is simply a state of mind.

10. https://www.americanprogress.org/issues/education/report/2013/05/08/62519/the-importance-of-preschool-and-child-care-for-working-mothers/. Most families currently have three options for securing child care. First, parents can stay at home and care for their children themselves. But this is increasingly difficult, as most families now rely on two breadwinners to stay above water. Moreover, mothers are more likely than fathers to take time away from paid work to care for a child, which can exacerbate mothers' lifetime earnings gap. Second, parents can pay for child care out-of-pocket. But this approach is very costly for families, eating up 35.9 percent of a low-income family's monthly budget. The third option for families is to use federal- or state-funded child care, but access to any publicly funded program, let alone a high-quality program, is very limited. Nationwide, nearly three in four children are not enrolled in a federal or state-funded pre-K program.

11. https://www.google.com/#q=minimum+wage. The federal minimum wage provisions are contained in the Fair Labor Standards Act (FLSA). The federal minimum wage is $7.25 per hour effective July 24, 2009. Many states also have minimum wage laws. Some state laws provide greater employee protections; employers must comply with both.

12. Dolan, Kerry. (http://www.forbes.com/sites/kerryadolan/2014/07/08/how-the-stroh-family-lost-the-largest-private-beer-fortune-in-the-u-s/). The Stroh family owned it all, a fortune that *FORBES* then calculated was worth at least $700 million. Just by matching the S&P 500, the family would currently be worth about $9 billion. Yet today Stroh's, as a family business or even a collective financial entity, has essentially ceased to exist. The company has been sold for parts. The Stroh Companies has doled out its last dividends to shareholders.

Chapter 3

1. Baginni, Julian. (http://www.theguardian.com/science/2015/mar/19/do-your-genes-determine-your-entire-life). Research suggests that many of our traits are more than 50 percent inherited,

including obedience to authority, vulnerability to stress, and risk-seeking. Researchers have even suggested that when it comes to issues such as religion and politics, our choices are much more determined by our genes than we think. But heritability is not about "chance or risk of passing it on," says Spector. "It simply means how much of the variation within a given population is down to genes. Crucially, this will be different according to the environment of that population.

2. Kim, Christine. (http://www.heritage.org/research/reports/2008 /09/academic-success-begins-at-home-how-children-can-succeed-in-school). While academic research has consistently shown that increased spending does not correlate with educational gains, the research does show a strong relationship between parental influences and children's educational outcomes, from school readiness to college completion.

3. Gormley, William, Jr. (http://www.edweek.org/ew/articles/2013/ 05/08/30gormley.h32.html). First, a high-quality pre-K program can boost school readiness substantially, for disadvantaged children. This has been amply demonstrated by the Perry Preschool Project, the Abecedarian Project, the Chicago Child-Parent Centers Project, and many others. High-quality universal preschool programs in Georgia and Oklahoma have also demonstrated big gains in school readiness for poor children.

Second, the cognitive benefits from pre-K often decline from kindergarten to third grade. Sometimes the "fade out" is modest, as in the case of the Chicago Child-Parent Centers. Sometimes it is dramatic, as with a 2010 Head Start evaluation. Note, though, that the Head Start evaluation included high-quality, low-quality, and medium-quality programs.

Third, even if some initial fade-out occurs, the long-term benefits of a high-quality pre-K program can be substantial. These include higher high school graduation rates, lower rates of juvenile delinquency, less substance abuse, and higher adult earnings.

Thus, many studies show that high-quality pre-K programs can improve outcomes for disadvantaged children in the short run and generate favorable returns for taxpayers in the long run.

4. Péréz-Peña, Richard and Rich, Motoko. (http://www.nytimes. com/2014/02/04/us/push-for-preschool-becomes-a-bipartisan-cause-outside-washington.html?_r=0). With a growing body of research pointing to the importance of early child development and its effect on later academic and social progress, enrollment in state-funded preschool has more than doubled since 2002, to about 30 percent of all four-year-olds nationwide. In just the past year, Alabama, Michigan, Minnesota, Montana, and the city of San Antonio have enacted new or expanded programs, while in dozens of other places, mayors, governors, and legislators are making a serious push for preschool.

5. Huntington, Marie. (http://smallbusiness.chron.com/difference-between-day-care-center-kindergarten-54625.html). Daycare centers offer developmental programs, and kindergarten schools provide

instructive programs for specific age groups of children. The teacher-child ratio in daycare centers varies depending on the age groups of the children. Most kindergarten programs have one certified teacher and one teacher assistant for each class group. In both types of programs, the teachers and other staff are required to maintain open communication with parents, and to inform parents of the progress and development of their children.

6. Washington State Department of Social and Health Services (http://www.education.com/reference/article/Ref_Child_Center_Nine/) Updated on Feb 17, 2011

7. Lerner, Richard M., Susman, Elizabeth J., Sternbrg, Laurence, and Rogol, Alan. *Puberty and Psychological Development* (published online: 26 JUL 2013). Puberty is one of the most profound biological and social transitions in the life span. It begins with subtle changes in brain-neuroendocrine processes, hormone concentrations, and physical morphological characteristics and culminates in reproductive maturity. The onset and trajectory of the hormone and physical changes that characterize puberty are well documented. Puberty as a social construction is a more complicated concept and entails ambiguity regarding the onset and offset of puberty; social-role passages into new reference groups; perceptions of body, self, and sexual image; and expectations for independent and mature behavior (Alsaker, 1995). Puberty as an integrated biological and social construction has intrigued scholars, artists, parents, and adolescents alike for centuries, and cultures have ritualized puberty to varying degrees. The biological changes of puberty are universal, but the timing and social significance of these changes to adolescents themselves, societies, and scientific inquiry vary across historical time and cultures. Nonetheless, there is widespread agreement on the profound biosocial complexity of puberty and its essential role as a period beginning with reproductive-function awakening and culminating in sexual maturity.

8. Lerner, Richard M. Cited in: *Promoting Positive Youth Development: Theoretical and Empirical Bases*. Institute for Applied Research in Youth Development, Tufts University. White paper prepared for: Workshop on the Science of Adolescent Health and Development, National Research Council, Washington, DC. September 9, 2005. National Research Council/Institute of Medicine. Washington, D.C.: National Academy of Sciences.

9. http://www.pewsocialtrends.org/2014/03/07/millennials-in-adulthood/. The median age at first marriage is now the highest in modern history—29 for men and 27 for women. In contrast to the patterns of the past, when adults in all socio-economic groups married at roughly the same rate, marriage today is more prevalent among those with higher incomes and more education.

10. McNeely, Clea and Blanchard, Jayne, MA, PhD. *The Teen Years Explained*. (http://www.jhsph.edu/research/centers-and-institutes/center-for-adolescent-health/). Gracefully avoiding a scientific debate

about the role of nature vs. nurture, the Guide illustrates that development is both an individual process and one that is significantly influenced by the formal and informal contexts in which it unfolds. Young people move in and out of numerous settings every day—familial, institutional, informal, and virtual. The range of environments they encounter grows with the increasing autonomy of adolescence. Each of these represents an opportunity for development, derailment, or both. Cognitive development doesn't stop when the school bell rings, and social development doesn't kick in upon arrival at the teen center. The Guide challenges us to remember that while we will not and should not always have control over adolescents, we can, in fact, shape many of the settings where they spend time. Creating contexts that nurture growth and minimize risk requires the kind of working knowledge of adolescent development that this guide offers.

11. Klineberg, SL. "Future time perspective and the preference for delayed reward." *JPers Soc Psychol.* 1968 Mar; 8(3):253-7. PubMed PMID: 5645229. It was hypothesized and demonstrated that the capacity to prefer a larger reward, delayed for a short and specified time, over a smaller reward available immediately, is related to (1) the degree to which images of personal future events in general are endowed with a sense of reality, and (2) the degree of everyday preoccupation with future rather than present events. Forty-seven 10.5-12.5-year-old males were individually interviewed. Twenty-five SS who consistently chose delayed larger rewards were compared with the remaining twenty-two SS who preferred immediate smaller reinforcements on measures of five different aspects of their outlook on the future. As predicted, there was no relationship between choices made in these situations and measures of the length of future time perspectives.

Chapter 4

1. Reinberg, Steven. http://abcnews.go.com/Health/Healthday/story?id=4508655. Life expectancy rates in the United States are at an all-time high, with people born in 2005 projected to live for nearly 78 years, a new federal study finds. The finding reflects a continuing trend of increasing life expectancy that began in 1955, when the average American lived to be 69.6 years old. By 1995, life expectancy was 75.8 years, and by 2005, it had risen to 77.9 years, according to the report, released Wednesday.

2. http://www.lingholic.com/how-many-words-do-i-need-to-know-the-955-rule-in-language-learning-part-2/. According to Susie Dent, lexicographer and expert in dictionaries, the average active vocabulary of an adult English speaker is of around 20,000 words, with a passive one of around 40,000 words. The English language has 171,476 words in current use in its largest dictionary. The *Oxford Dictionary* total word count would probably approach three quarters of a million.

3. http://www.study-body-language.com/Body-language-signs.html

and http://www.psychologytoday.com/basics/body-language. What these body language signs can tell us? A lot actually: How comfortable or stressed a person is; does he feel confident or insecure? Where we want to go, or with whom we want to be. Relations and power struggles between superiors and their subordinates. How sociable and approachable someone is. How "in-tune" someone is with us and what is his\her sort interest level. In short, you can get many good indicators about the state of mind simply by observing his posture, lay of head, and the position of his limbs. Head signals, posture and attitude, hand and arm positions, leg positions, sitting.

4. http://www.forbes.com/sites/jacquelynsmith/2012/10/05/steve-jobs-always-dressed-exactly-the-same-heres-who-else-does/ *and* http://www.amazon.com/Steve-Jobs-Walter-Isaacson/dp/1442369051. The late Apple co-founder was best known for his visionary leadership and innovation—but he was also known for his unvarying signature look. Unlike most corporate executives, who wear suits and ties, Steve Jobs was committed to his chosen uniform of a black mock turtleneck, blue jeans, and New Balance sneakers.

5. http://www.wikihow.com/Be-Goth *and* http://fashion-lifestyle.bg/subculture_en_broi3. The dark world of Goths is one of the most diverse and healthy subcultures, flourishing in all kinds of communities worldwide. The spooky, ghoulish look and dark clothes is an instantly striking style. But when other Goths in white-out contact lenses start throwing around terms like "ethereal chill wave" and quoting from *The Moonstone* it can be somewhat intimidating. Starting slow and working your way into the Goth subculture can be an immensely rewarding experience for anyone looking for community.

6. http://www.stopbullying.gov/cyberbullying/. Cyberbullying is bullying that takes place using electronic technology. Examples of cyberbullying include mean text messages or e-mails, rumors sent by e-mail or posted on social networking sites, and embarrassing pictures, videos, websites, and fake profiles.

7. http://www.stopbullying.gov/laws/federal/. Although there are no federal laws that directly address bullying, in some cases, bullying overlaps with discriminatory harassment when it is based on race, national origin, color, sex, age, disability, or religion. When bullying and harassment overlap, federally funded schools (including colleges and universities) have an obligation to resolve the harassment. When the situation is not adequately resolved, the U.S. Department of Education's Office for Civil Rights and the U.S. Department of Justice's Civil Rights Division may be able to help.

8. http://info.character.org/blog/bid/128143/19-Signs-Your-Child-Is-Being-Bullied-and-What-to-Do-about-It *and* http://www.nspcc.org.uk/preventing-abuse/child-abuse-and-neglect/bullying-and-cyber-bullying/signs-symptoms-effects/. Here are possible warnings that a child may be bullied and needs your support. Of course, these signs could indicate other problems, but any of these warrant looking into

further. Every child is different and any child can have an "off" day, so look instead for a pattern of behavior that is not typical for your child.
• Unexplained physical marks, cuts, bruises and scrapes.
• Unexplained loss of toys, school supplies, clothing, lunches, or money.
• Clothes, toys, books, electronic items are damaged or missing or child reports mysteriously "losing" possessions.
• Doesn't want to go to school or other activities with peers.
• Afraid of riding the school bus.
• Afraid to be left alone: wants you there at dismissal, suddenly clingy.
• Suddenly sullen, withdrawn, evasive; remarks about feeling lonely.
• Marked change in typical behavior or personality.
• Appears sad, moody, angry, anxious or depressed and that mood lasts with no known cause.
• Physical complaints: headaches, stomachaches, frequently visits the school nurse.
• Difficulty sleeping, nightmares, cries self to sleep, bedwetting.
• Change in eating habits.
• Begins bullying siblings or younger kids. (Bullied children can sometimes flip their role and become the bully.)
• Waits to get home to use the bathroom. (School and park bathrooms, because they are often not adult-supervised, can be hotspots for bullying).
• Suddenly has fewer friends or doesn't want to be with the "regular group."
• Ravenous when he comes home. (Bullies can use extortion to steal a victim's lunch money or lunch.)
• Sudden and significant drop in grades. (Bullying can cause a child to have difficulty focusing and concentrating.)
• Blames self for problems; feels "not good enough."
• Talks about feeling helpless or about suicide; runs away.

Chapter 5

1. http://medicaldictionary.thefreedictionary.com/Wechsler+Intelligence+Test. The Wechsler Intelligence Scales are standardized tests, meaning that as part of the test design, they were administered to a large, representative sample of the target population, and norms were determined from the results. The scales have a mean, or average, standard score of 100 and a standard deviation of 15. The standard deviation indicates how far above or below the norm the subject's score is. For example, a ten-year-old is assessed with the WISC-III scale and achieves a full-scale IQ score of 85. The mean score of 100 is the average level at which all ten-year-olds in the representative sample performed. This child's score would be one standard deviation below

that norm. While the full-scale IQ scores provide a reference point for evaluation, they are only an average of a variety of skill areas. A trained psychologist will evaluate and interpret an individual's performance on the scale's subtests to discover their strengths and weaknesses and offer recommendations based upon these findings.

2. http://www.assessmentpsychology.com/iq.htm

Measured Intelligence and Education

WAIS Mean IQ	Educational Equivalent
125	Mean of persons receiving PhD and MD degrees
115	Mean of college graduates
105	Mean of high school graduates
100	Average for total population
75	About 50-50 chance of reaching ninth grade

Minimum AFQT

Branch	Tier I ≥ HS Diploma	Tier II = GED
Army	35	50
Navy	35	50
Air Force	40	65
Marines	32	50
Coast Guard	45	50 with 15 college credits
*Army National Guard	35	50
*Air National Guard	35	50

3. Sailer, Steve. http://isteve.blogspot.com/2013/04/almost-100-million-people-arent-smart.html. Standards for enlistment. AFQT required minimum scores for people with a high school diploma as of December 2012 (unless otherwise noted) are:
   Also, if you have a GED and complete a certain number of college credits, you can use the HS Diploma column. Thus, the lowest percentile you can get into the military with is the Marines at the 32nd percentile (if you have a high school diploma, plus the Marines have plenty of physical and other requirements). With 315 million residents in the country, 31 percent aren't smart enough to join the Marines, which is over 97 million.

4. Op. cit. 2.

5. http://www.us.mensa.org/join/testscores/qualifyingscores/. American Mensa accepts scores from approximately 200 different standardized intelligence tests. An IQ of between 130 and 132 is required, depending on the test. This means about 2% of the population is eligible to apply for and take a test required for membership.

6. https://www.google.com/#q=average+iq+of+police+officers. The standard range of scores applied for police officers is a score between 20 and 27. According to ABC News, the average score nationally for police officers is 21 to 22, the equivalent of an IQ of 104, or just a little above average. A perfect score on the Wonderlic is a 50.
7. Op.cit. 3.
8. http://blog.prepscholar.com/celebrity-sat-scores-kesha-bill -gates-and-more
9. http://www.goodreads.com/quotes/335885-i-failed-in-some -subjects-in-exam-but-my-friend

Chapter 6

1. https://www.galottery.com/about-us. Georgia Lottery proceeds are used to fund specific education programs: 1) Tuition grants, scholarships or loans to undergraduate college students for attendance at eligible Georgia colleges, universities, or technical colleges; 2) The Georgia Prekindergarten Program for all 4-year-olds; and 3) capital outlay projects including computer and other technological upgrades for schools, technical institutes, colleges and universities in the state. More than 1.7 million students have been able to attend colleges through Georgia's HOPE scholarship program; more than 1.4 million four-year-olds have attended Georgia's Prekindergarten Program; and all of Georgia's public schools have benefited from over $1.8 billion in capital outlay, computer and technology upgrades.
2. Lareau, Annette. *Unequal Childhoods: Class, Race, and Family Life*. University of California Press, 2003. Numerous studies link family-of-origin class status and later life economic well-being, but none expose the processes through which inequality is reproduced like Annette Lareau's *Unequal Childhoods*. Using observations from two elementary schools, interviews with 88 students' parents, and more than a year of observation in the homes of 12 of these nine- and ten-year-old children, Lareau explores how parenting and childhood vary by social class.
   Some may argue her small observation sample limits cross-class and cross-race comparisons, but what is sacrificed in breadth is more than compensated for with depth. What she and her assistants hear from parents and observe through soccer games, neighborhood play, car and bus trips across town, homework sessions, morning routines, doctor and dentist appointments, and parent-teacher conferences demonstrate striking class-based differences in the organization of children's daily lives, their language development, and their ability to interact with social institutions. Further, these class-based distinctions translate into a sense of entitlement among middle-class offspring and a sense of restraint among children growing up in poorer households. While other studies allude to these class differences, especially in school contexts, this study takes readers even deeper into the lives of children than most. The result is a richer understanding of how cultural

repertoires imparted to children vary by class in ways that entrench class inequality at early ages.

The first of the two approaches to child rearing identified by Lareau is "concerted cultivation." This style is predominant in middle-class homes. Parents using this approach constantly foster and assess their children's talents by involving them in organized activities, molding their reasoning skills, and intervening on their behalf with teachers and coaches. Through rich description of children's daily lives, readers see how middle-class parents challenge children to formulate questions for doctors, teach them to shake hands and look adults in the eye, broaden their vocabularies, and model how to demand action from social institutions. Lareau calls the logic of child rearing among working-class and poor families "natural accomplishment of growth." This approach is more spontaneous, focusing on providing children's basic needs while allowing talents to develop naturally. These children's lives take place near home with fewer structured activities, more interaction with siblings, and more clear boundaries between adults and children. Lareau nicely contrasts the two styles with her detailed descriptions of how working-class and poor children are expected to be silently obedient in the presence of adults while their parents model unease and restraint in their interactions with school officials and medical professionals. These contrasts demonstrate how middle-class children learn to demand what they want while working-class and poor children learn to accept what is.

While children raised with the "concerted cultivation" logic are better prepared to achieve within social institutions like school and work, Lareau also outlines down sides to this approach. Middle-class children are generally more stressed and exhausted, less creative, and fight more with siblings than working- class or poor children. Ultimately, Lareau suggests parents and society should expose all children to the beneficial features of both approaches and be wary of the harmful aspects.

One unsatisfying feature of the book is its limited discussion of race's role in shaping childhood and framing futures. Lareau argues that social class is more determinative of the organization and experience of childhood than race. In her study, middle-class black children's lives are organized more similarly to middle-class white children's lives than to poorer black children's lives. However, one similarity across class categories is that black children all encounter racism. Mention is made of how black children and parents in each class category face discrimination. These confrontations with race make childhood and how children see their futures different for black and white children, regardless of class. Further, the interesting dynamic may be less in comparing the relative impact of two closely intertwined social forces and more about how the two intersect. For example, do middle-class...

3. http://www.magnet.edu/about/what-are-magnet-schools. Magnet schools are built on the foundation of five pillars and are free public

elementary and secondary schools of choice that are operated by school districts or a consortium of districts. Magnet schools have a focused theme and aligned curricula in Science, Technology, Engineering, and Mathematics (STEM), Fine and Performing Arts, International Baccalaureate, International Studies, Micro Society, Career and Technical Education (CTE), World Languages (immersion and non-immersion) and many others. Magnet schools are typically more "hands on—minds on" and use an approach to learning that is inquiry or performance/project based. They use state, district, or Common Core standards in all subject areas, however, they are taught within the overall theme of the school.

Most magnet schools do not have entrance criteria, but rather, embody the belief that all students have interests and talents that families and educators believe are better cultivated in a magnet school. They often use a random computer-based lottery system for admission. There are also "Talented & Gifted" magnet schools that may utilize student assessment data and teacher or parent recommendations for selection. Diversity is an important element of a magnet school. Since student interest in a theme is the only eligibility criteria to attend a magnet school, students from a wide array of backgrounds attend magnet schools. As a result, they promote higher level cognitive and social learning. Magnet schools make the extra effort to create a sense of classroom and school community and cultivate school spirit. Curriculum is also clear and transparent for families so they can more fully engage in the learning of their students.

Magnet schools serve all students including English learners as well as students receiving Special Education services. Transportation is typically also provided for no cost to families.

The five pillars of the magnet school are: 1) diversity, 2) academic excellence, 3) innovation,4) high quality, 5) family and community commitment.

4. Research related to the International Baccalaureate An annotated bibliography of 2014 studies. Laura C. Engel, Dorinne Banks, Jennifer Patterson and Samantha Stehle The George Washington University January 2015

5. http://www.myips.org/Page/32229. What are Magnet/Choice Programs? A magnet program offers families the opportunity to choose a specialized curriculum that enables students to engage with additional resources and innovative techniques that focus on their individual talents and interests. Each IPS magnet program emphasizes an instructional theme or approach. While similar courses may be offered in neighborhood schools, our magnet programs attract students from across the district by offering unique, focused, in-depth study experiences that support specific areas of interest. Families are encouraged to become actively involved in choosing the instructional program most appropriate for their children's interests and abilities.

Magnet schools recruit students with a high interest in their programs, good academic and attendance records, and a willingness to work hard in the programs. Parent/guardian participation in the school is essential in order to help ensure students' success. Applications from students with special needs may be evaluated to verify the program can support students' specific needs

6. https://nces.ed.gov/fastfacts/display.asp?id=
   SOURCE: U.S. Department of Education, National Center for Education Statistics. (2015). *The Condition of Education 2015* (NCES 2015–144), Charter School Enrollment
7. http://thenotebook.org/blog/158505/multiple-choices -how-are-charter-schools-funded. The formula that allocates money to charters is based on each school district's per-student expenses for the prior year. So payments vary widely depending on where a student lives. Each district has a rate for regular education students and one for special education students. Statewide, for non-special education students, payments range from $6,600 to more than $17,000 per student. Special education amounts are much greater, from $13,000 per child to more than $43,000
8. http://www.ncsl.org/research/education/charter-schools-overview.aspx. Since the first enactment of charter school legislation in Minnesota in 1991, 43 states and the District of Columbia have adopted laws allowing charter schools. Alabama is the most recent state to allow charter schools. According to the National Alliance for Public Charter Schools, there were 5,997 charter schools in the 2012-2013 school year, making up 6.3 percent of all U.S. public schools. The most recent data showed 4.6 percent of public school students attended charter schools.
9. The effect of charter schools on charter students and public schools *Economics of Education Review*, Volume 24, Issue 2, Pages 133-147 Eric P. Bettinger. Using school-level data from Michigan's standardized testing program changes in test scores between charter and public school students do not improve, and may actually decline.
10. www.capenet.org/facts.html. Private schools account for 24 percent of the nation's schools and 10 % of students enrolled
11. http:/privateschoolreview.com/tuition-stats/private-school -cost-by-state. Private school tuitions range from just over $5,000 in Alaska to nearly $30,000 in Connecticut with an average of just over $10,000
12. http://www.ncsl.org/research/educat   stat   iones/voucher-law-comparison.aspx. Thirteen states and the District of Columbia provides state-funded school vouchers to qualifying students. While each state approaches school vouchers differently, there are common questions states must address when developing their voucher programs. These include:
    What will the program jurisdiction be? Will it be statewide? Will it be limited to certain areas of the state?

Which students will be eligible for a voucher? Will it be offered to low income students, special needs students, students attending failing schools, etc.? Or, will every student in the state be eligible?

Will the voucher be only for students currently enrolled in public school? Or, will it be offered to students already attending private schools who otherwise meet the eligibility criteria?

What will private schools be required to do in exchange for accepting publicly-funded students? Will they have to administer state assessments? Will they have to share student performance data with parents? Will they have to receive official accreditation? Will private schools have to share their financial reports with the state? For what reasons will participating schools be allowed to reject voucher student applications?

Will there be a cap on the number of vouchers that can be handed out each year?

What will be the maximum dollar value of a voucher?

13. http://www.capenet.org/facts.html. According to a report released in January by the National Center for Education Statistics, tenth-graders in private high schools in 2002 were nearly twice as likely as their public school counterparts to receive a bachelor's degree or higher by 2012. In turn, degree recipients were ultimately more successful in securing a job and realizing higher earnings—considerable consolation in an economy scarred by persistently high levels of unemployment.

14. http://www.parents.com/blogs/homeschool-den/2013 /07/29/must-read/homeschool-questions-answered- why-do-people-homeschool/. People are often curious why homeschoolers have chosen this route. After all, the vast majority of people choose to send their children to public school. On the other hand, there are now more children being home-schooled than are enrolled in charter and voucher schools *combined*. I read recently that there are now over 2 million homeschooled children. In 1999, three reasons for homeschooling were the most frequently cited:
    - 49 percent of homeschooled students had parents who cited the ability to give their child a better education,
    - 38 percent had parents who cited religious reasons, and
    - 26 percent had parents who cited a poor learning environment at school (Bielick, Chandler, & Broughman 2001)

15. http://childrensmd.org/. *18 reasons why doctor and lawyers homeschool their kids*, Kathleen Berchelmann, M.D.
    - We spend less time homeschooling each day than we used to spend driving.
    - We can't afford private education.
    - Our kids are excelling academically as homeschoolers.
    - Homeschooling is not hard, and it's fun!
    - Use whatever public school services you like.
    - I like parenting more, by far.
    - Our family spends our best hours of each day together.

- We yell at our kids less.
- Our kids have time for creative play and unique interests.
- We are able to work on the kids' behavior and work ethic throughout the day.
- Get rid of bad habits, fast.
- Be the master of your own schedule.
- Younger children learn from older siblings.
- Save money.
- Teach your kids practical life skills.
- Better socialization, less unhealthy peer pressure and bullying.
- Sleep
- Teach kids your own values

Homeschooling isn't right for every family or every child. I can't even predict what the future holds for our family—will we continue homeschooling through high school? I don't know. But for now, we've found a way for our family to be very happy growing and learning together.

16. http://www.actstudent.org/faq/actsat.html
The SAT is more of an aptitude test, testing reasoning and verbal abilities.
The ACT is an achievement test, measuring what a student has learned in school.
The ACT has up to 5 components: English, Mathematics, Reading, Science, and an optional Writing Test. The SAT has only 3 components: Critical Reading, Mathematics, and a required Writing Test.
The College Board introduced a new version of the SAT in 2005, with a mandatory writing test. ACT continues to offer its well-established test, plus an optional writing test. You take the ACT Writing Test only if required or requested by the college(s) you're applying to.
The SAT penalizes you for wrong answers, so guessing is discouraged. The ACT is scored based on the number of correct answers with no penalty for guessing.
The ACT has an Interest Inventory that allows students to evaluate their interests in various career options.

17. http://www.bls.gov/opub/ted/2014/ted_20140508.htm. Of the nearly 3.0 million youth age 16 to 24 who graduated from high school between January and October 2013, about 2.0 million (65.9 percent) were enrolled in college in October. The college enrollment rate of recent high school graduates in October 2013 was little different from the rate in October 2012 (66.2 percent).In October 2014, 68.4 percent of 2014 high school graduates were enrolled in colleges or universities, the U.S. Bureau of Labor Statistics reported.

18. www.clasp.org/.../GED-Landscape-2-5-. An ever increasing population of Americans have gone unnoticed once they have left school: former high school dropouts. Today, there are an estimated 39 to 40 million people without a high school diploma, and that number is growing. In fact, if current dropout rates, as well as rates at which

candidates take and pass the GED or an equivalent assessment persist, over 7 million more people will not earn a high school credential by 2021. The impact of this national failure is evident and increasingly severe: high unemployment and low wages are virtually a lifelong sentence for most people without a diploma.

19. http://study.com/articles/A_High_School_Diploma_v_the_GED. html. The GED test is designed for adults over the age of 16 who haven't earned a high school diploma and aren't currently enrolled in high school. For current students who are considering leaving high school early, the GED test can also provide an alternative to graduation. However, unless extreme circumstances are forcing an individual out of high school, it typically makes more sense to earn a diploma. At a minimum, all students should need to meet with a school counselor before choosing to drop out and pursue the GED certificate. Although the GED test represents less of a time commitment than a high school diploma, it's not academically easier. The test is graded on an equivalency scale compared to current high school students. To pass, test takers must perform on a level comparable to or above 60% of high school seniors. Made up of five subject area tests, the GED tests include the following subjects:

> Science
> Social studies
> Mathematics
> Language arts, reading
> Language arts, writing

In addition to short-form answers, the writing test also involves an essay. Individuals considering taking the GED test need to study. Adult education centers across the country offer test-prep courses, and students may also purchase study books or find free practice exams and questions online.

20. http://americanradioworks.publicradio.org/features/ged/. by Emily Hanford, Stephen Smith, and Laurie Stern. The General Educational Development test (GED) is a second chance for millions of people who didn't finish high school. Each year, more than 700,000 people take the GED test. People who pass it are supposed to possess a level of education and skills equivalent to those of a high school graduate. Most test-takers hope the GED will lead to a better job or more education. Statistics for Arizona are typical

> 609,162 (12.4%) of adults did not have a high school credential
> 18,237 took the GED test
> 11,588 passed the test

State policies can have a big impact on the number of people who pass the GED. In New York, for example, anyone 16 or older can take the GED for free. The pass rate is 53 percent. In Iowa, to be eligible to take the test you must demonstrate you have a good chance of passing by getting minimum scores on a GED practice test or other standardized test first. The pass rate is 62 percent.

21. https://www.google.com/?gws_rd=ssl#q=average+income+of+a+high+school+dropout. The average dropout can expect to earn an annual income of $20,241, according to the U.S. Census Bureau (PDF). That's a full $10,386 less than the typical high school graduate, and $36,424 less than someone with a bachelor's degree. Sep 21, 2012

22. http://www.bls.gov/opub/ted/2015/median-weekly-earn-ings-by-education-gender-race-and-ethnicity-in-2014.htm. Median weekly earnings of full-time wage and salary workers age 25 and older with less than a high school diploma were $488 in 2014. The median for workers with a high school diploma only (no college) was $668 per week.

23. http://www.usnews.com/news/articles/2014/02/11/study-income-gap-between-young-college-and-high-school-grads-widens. Among millennials ages 25 to 32, median annual earnings for full-time work-ing college-degree holders are $17,500 greater than for those with high school diplomas only. That gap steadily widened for each successive generation in the latter half of the 20th century.

24. http://mije.org/health/dropouts-graduates-jails-or-jobs. A report pre-sented last year by researchers at Northeastern University found that male dropouts of all races were 47 times more liked to be jailed than their college graduate peers. The rate for Black males was staggering with "23 of every 100 young Black male dropouts were in jail on any given day in 2006-07 compared to only 6 to 7 of every 100 Asian, His-panic or White dropouts."

25. http://www.gifted.uconn.edu/nrcgt/renzpark.html. Joseph S. Ren-zulli and Sunghee Park. *Analysis of Dropout Questionnaire*: Many of the gifted male students left school because they were failing school, got a job, could not keep up with their schoolwork, and did not like school. Gifted female students left school because they did not like school, were pregnant, became a parent, or were failing school. Many of the parents whose child dropped out of school tried to talk him or her into staying in school, but not many of them offered counseling services to their children.
Analysis of Student Questionnaire: Almost half the gifted dropout stu-dents (48.2%) were in the lowest quartile SES level, while only 3.6% of them were in the highest quartile SES level. More Hispanic and Native Americans dropped out of school than White and Asian Amer-icans. A high percentage of gifted dropouts' fathers and mothers did not finish high school (father: 40%, mother: 25.6%) or graduated only high school (father: 23%, mother: 35.9%). Of the gifted students, 5% dropped out of school.

26. Op cit 23

27. Op cit 23

28. http://www.infoplease.com/ipa/A0883617.html

Chapter 7

1. http://nces.ed.gov/fastfacts/display.asp?id=372. In fall 2015, some 20.2 million students are expected to attend American colleges and universities, constituting an increase of about 4.9 million since fall 2000 Females are expected to account for the majority of college students: about 11.5 million females will attend in fall 2015, compared with 8.7 million males. Also, more students are expected to attend full time than part time (an estimated 12.6 million, compared with about 7.6 million). About 7.0 million students will attend 2-year institutions and 13.2 million will attend 4-year institutions in fall 2015. Some 17.3 million students are expected to enroll in undergraduate programs and about 3.0 million will enroll in post baccalaureate programs.

2. http://fivethirtyeight.com/features/more-high-school-grads-decide-college-isnt-worth-it/. The drop in college attendance among recent high school graduates appears concentrated among groups most likely to be deciding between going to school and joining the labor force: Part-time and community college enrollments saw the sharpest decline. Meanwhile, the enrollment rate increased for four-year colleges, where costs have been rising the fastest.1 (For-profit colleges, which have been subject to mounting criticism over their high costs and inconsistent educational value, have also seen enrollment decline.)

3. http://teenadvice.about.com/od/teenlifefaqsandqas/a/postgrad-choices_3.htm. *A Word to the Wise:* While there is nothing wrong with jumping right in to the workforce after high school youth should be wary of accepting just any old job in order to bring home a paycheck. While you are still young you have so many opportunities to take advantage of that working in a dead end job or accepting a seemingly high paying position with no future is simply a waste. This is your life; make the best of it.

4. https://www.census.gov/prod/.../p23-210.pdf. Does going to school pay off? Most people think so. Currently, almost 90 percent of young adults graduate from high school and about 60 percent of high school seniors continue on to college the following year. People decide to go to college for many reasons. One of the most compelling is the expecta-tion of future economic success based on educational attainment.
This report illustrates the economic value of an education, that is, the added value of a high school diploma or college degree. It explores the relationship between educational attainment and earnings and demonstrates how the relationship has changed over the last 25 years. Additionally, it provides, by level of education, synthetic estimates of the average total earnings adults are likely to accumulate over the course of their working lives.

5. http://www.usitc.gov/research_and_analysis/documents/ Pierce%20and%20Schott%20%20The%20Surprisingly%20Swift%20 Decline%20of%20U.S.%20Manufacturing%20Employment_0.pdf. We find that industries where the threat of tariff hikes declines the most

experience greater employment loss due to suppressed job creation, exaggerated job destruction and a substitution away from low-skill workers. We show that these policy-related employment losses coincide with a relative acceleration of U.S. imports from China, the number of U.S. firms importing from China, the number of Chinese firms exporting to the U.S., and the number of U.S.-China importer-exporter pairs.

6. http://www.cccompletioncorps.org/why-students-drop-out.
60% of community college students work 20 hours per week.
25% of community college students work 35 or more hours per week.
23% of all college students have dependent children
62% of all college students who drop out are responsible for paying for their own education
College costs have risen 400% in the last 25 years
Community college costs have risen 200% in the last 7 years and 7.3% since 2000
30% of students who drop out still must repay student loans
Textbook costs have significantly increased in the past 10 years
60% of community college students are enrolled part-time, limiting their financial aid and benefit options.

7. Op.cit. 1

8. http://www.masslegalhelp.org/children-and-families/emanci pation. Emancipation is a legal process through which a minor child obtains a court order to end the rights and responsibilities that the child's parent owe to the child such as financial support for the child and decision making authority over the child. There can be either a partial or complete emancipation. While emancipation relieves both the parent and child from certain obligations, the minor must still follow the law.

9. Dillon, Sam. http://www.nytimes.com/2009/10/09/education/ 09dropout.html?_r=0. On any given day, about one in every 10 young male high school dropouts is in jail or juvenile detention, compared with one in 35 young male high school graduates, according to a new study of the effects of dropping out of school in an America where demand for low-skill workers is plunging.
The picture is even bleaker for African-Americans, with nearly one in four young black male dropouts incarcerated or otherwise institutionalized on an average day, the study said. That compares with about one in 14 young, male, white, Asian or Hispanic dropouts.

10. https://www.ufv.ca/media/assets/institutional-research/HS_ Analysis_2004.pdf. Data agrees that cost, friends' opinions, educational professionals' opinions and parents' opinions and education level are factors that influence a students' decision in pursuing post-secondary education. Moreover, our conclusions correspond with prior research that shows that preparation for post-secondary education is an issue that affects students' pursuits of higher education.

11. Jacob, Joanne. http://www.joannejacobs.com/2007/01/not-smart-enough-for-college/. There is no magic point at which a genuine college-level education becomes an option, but anything below an IQ of 110 is problematic. If you want to do well, you should have an IQ of 115 or higher. Put another way, it makes sense for only about 15% of the population, 25% if one stretches it, to get a college education. And yet more than 45% of recent high school graduates enroll in four-year colleges. Adjust that percentage to account for high-school dropouts, and more than 40% of all persons in their late teens are trying to go to a four-year college — enough people to absorb everyone down through an IQ of 104. This could be a pessimistic view (the glass is half empty) that that could be modified some by taking into account the difficulty of the course of study and the motivation of the student

12. http://www.dol.gov/apprenticeship/. ApprenticeshipUSA offers employers in every industry the tools to develop a highly skilled workforce to help grow their business. For workers, ApprenticeshipUSA offers opportunities to earn a salary while learning the skills necessary to succeed in high-demand careers. ApprenticeshipUSA exemplifies high standards, instructional rigor and quality training. Whether you are an employer looking to hire, train or retain a skilled workforce, or a worker looking for a new career in a well-paying occupation, ApprenticeshipUSA will help you achieve your goals.

13. http://trends.collegeboard.org/education-pays/figures-tables/lifetime-earnings-education-level. The typical bachelor's degree recipient can expect to earn about 66% more during a 40-year working life than the typical high school graduate earns over the same period

14. http://www.usnews.com/news/articles/2015/07/20/americans-making-under-30-000-can-already-send-their-children-to-college-for-free. Full-time students from the lowest family-income quartile (family incomes under $30,000) who were enrolled in public two-year or four-year colleges in their own state received enough grant aid, on average, to cover their tuition and fees during the 2011-12 school year, and have money left over to help cover books and living expenses, according the report. These students, on average, received more than $9,700 for a four-year public university in their state, leaving them with more than $2,200 for books and living expenses. Grant aid includes money from federal and state governments, colleges and universities, employers, other private sources and from estimated federal tax credits and deductions

15. http://qz.com/324023/only-1/6-of-us-community-college-students-go-on-to-earn-four-year-degrees/. A total of 16.2%—or about one in six—community college students went on to get a four-year degree.

16. https://www.ivytech.edu/online/. Today, you don't need to travel to campus to get a college degree. Online programs allow you to take classes on your schedule, at your own pace. You'll still interact with your instructors and classmates—and you'll still have to work

hard—but you'll save time and gas money along the way to graduation. And if you want to go to class in your pajamas, no one will ever know.
Ivy Tech Community College offers more than 350 online courses statewide, and many degree programs can be completed entirely online.

17. Snyder, Thomas J. *The Community College Career Track*. John Wiley and Sons.(2012) Pages 3–5.
18. Ibid., 152, 157.
19. Ibid., 11–26.
20. Personal communication Paul St Angelo January 2014
21. http://www.bloomberg.com/news/articles/2013-08-26/college-costs-surge-500-in-u-s-since-1985-chart-of-the-d. The cost of higher education has surged more than 500 percent since 1985, illustrating why there have been renewed calls for change from both political parties.
22. Touryalai, Hahla. http://www.forbes.com/fdc/welcome_mjx.shtml. Here's an indication of how burdensome student loans have become: About one-third of millennials say they would have been better off working, instead of going to college and paying tuition. That's a according to a new Wells Fargo study which surveyed 1,414 millennials between the ages of 22 and 32. More than half of them financed their education through student loans, and many say the if they had $10,000 the "first thing" they'd do is pay down their student loan or credit card debt. That's no surprise when you consider student borrowing topped the $100 billion threshold for the first time in 2010, and total outstanding loans exceeded $1 trillion for the first time in 2011. Student loan debt now exceeds credit card debt in the U.S. which stands at about $798 billion.
23. http://admissions.indiana.edu/cost-financial-aid/tuition-fees.html

	In State	Out of State
Tuition and fees	$10,388	$33,740
Room and board	$9,794	$9,794
Books and supplies	$1,230	$1,230
Total direct costs	**$21,412**	**$44,764**
Transportation	$1,030	$1,030
Personal expenses	$2,096	$2,096
Total cost of attendance	**$24,538**	**$47,890**

24. http://www.slate.com/blogs/moneybox/2014/05/08/unemployment_and_the_class_of_2014_how_bad_is_the_job_market_for_new_college.html. The bad news is that these recent B.A.s, working in jobs that don't require a college degree, are in occupations that pay far less than in the past. It used to be that more than half of these

overeducated young workers would find themselves in "good" jobs—meaning that they'd pay at least $45,000 in today's market. Today, less than 40 percent do. Meanwhile, more than a fifth of this group were in low-wage jobs, meaning they paid $25,000 a year or less.

25. http://money.cnn.com/2013/05/17/pf/college/student-debt/.The bulk of the class of 2013's debt is in government loans, with graduates owing an average of $26,000. They also had an average of $19,000 in private loans, $18,000 in state loans, $13,000 in personal and family loans and $3,000 in credit card debt.

26. https://www.google.com/?gws_rd=ssl#q=what+percentage+of+the+population+has+a+bachelor%27s+degree. As of last March (2014), 30.4 percent of people over age 25 in the United States held at least a bachelor's degree, and 10.9 percent held a graduate degree, up from 26.2 percent and 8.7 percent 10 years earlier. Feb 23, 2012

27. Ibid.

28. Ibid.

29. Ibid.

30. http://www.hospitalmedicine.ucsd.edu/people/about.shtml. Hospitalists are physicians whose primary professional focus is the general medical care of hospitalized patients. Their activities include patient care, teaching, research, and leadership related to Hospital Medicine.

31. https://www.census.gov/prod/2011pubs/acs-14.pdf. The results of this analysis demonstrate that there is a clear and well-defined relationship between education and earnings, and that this relationship perseveres, even after considering a collection of other personal and geographic characteristic

32. http://everydaylife.globalpost.com/high-school-dropouts-vs-unemployment-11756.html. The lack of a high school diploma affects workers into adulthood. The U.S. Department of Labor reported that from 2012 to 2013, the unemployment rate for those over 25 years of age without a high school diploma hovered between 11 and 12 percent, peaking at 12.5 percent in April 2012. Compare that to high school graduates, whose highest rate during the same time frame was much less, at 8.1 percent.

33. http://everydaylife.globalpost.com/much-money-heart-surgery-doctors-make-10776.html. These salaries place cardiac surgeons among the highest-paid of all surgical specialties. In the AMGA survey, only neurosurgeons, at $656,520 a year, and orthopedic spinal surgeons, at $710,556 a year, reported higher earnings. In comparison, general surgeons reported a median salary of $370,024 a year. In the MGMA survey, neurosurgeons enjoyed the highest salaries at $767,627 per year, with pediatric neurosurgeons earning $643,188 a year. General surgeons were well below those figures, at $368,108 per year. Among hospital-employed surgeons, orthopedic spinal surgeons topped the list at $714,088 a year, with neurosurgeons close behind at $701,927 and pediatric neurosurgeons earning $656,282.

34. http://www.entrepreneur.com/article/230582. It's a safe bet that more ink and paper have been expended in the name of how to make money than just about any topic. In case you're wondering why, here's a hint: Do you know how the dollar sign originated? Try overlapping the letters U and S, as in United States.

    Capitalism and the American Dream are both alive and well, and with good reason. Who would have thought basic staples like food, shelter, transportation and healthcare would cost so damn much? We used to think of a millionaire as rich. Pretty soon that's going to be the poverty level.

    So how do you get ahead—and stay ahead—of the ever-increasing cost of living? Surprisingly enough, there's no secret to making big bucks. The problem is people want it to be easy, like a winning lottery ticket, a magic formula for timing the stock market or a get-rich-quick pill.

Chapter 8

1. Quilty, David. http://www.moneycrashers.com/part-time-jobs-high-school-students/. Finding and keeping a part-time job while attending high school can be a daunting task. Balancing work with classes, homework, extracurricular activities, and just hanging out with friends can be tough, but millions of teens are able to manage part-time work along with their other responsibilities.

    During my first two years of high school I was a paper delivery boy, leaving at 4 am every morning to deliver newspapers. I also went out once or twice a week in the evening to collect money from my customers. For the last two years of school I had a retail job, behind the counter at a mom and pop drugstore. These jobs taught me how to manage money, how to handle responsibility, and how to deal with the general public. They were invaluable experiences and provided me with some much-needed autonomy and spending money, too.

    There are different schools of thought on whether teenagers should have part-time jobs, but I find that the pros easily outweigh any cons. A teenager who works long hours every day after school could see his or her schoolwork suffer, but a less-intensive part-time job can be a wonderful learning experience. If kids can get to school on time, maintain solid grades, and participate in school activities, part-time jobs in high school can be beneficial to their success.

2. http://www.dol.gov/whd/state/nonfarm.htm. State hours limitations on a school day and in a school week usually apply only to those enrolled in school. Several states exempt high school graduates from the hours and/or night work or other provisions, or have less restrictive provisions for minors participating in various school-work programs. Separate work standards in messenger service and street trades are common, but are not displayed in table. Some states have exceptions or special conditions for minors engaged in specific employments, such as street trades, recreation and entertainment, and jobs in establishments offering alcoholic beverages for sale.

Students of 14 and 15 enrolled in approved Work Experience and Career Exploration programs may work during school hours up to 3 hours on a school day and 23 hours in a school week.

3. http://www.ncbi.nlm.nih.gov/pmc/articles/PMC2936460/
Having a paying job at some time during high school has become a near-universal adolescent experience Many youth start to work informally even earlier, at about the age of twelve, most often in their own neighborhoods, babysitting, shoveling snow, cutting grass, or doing various odd jobs. At first, paid work is episodic and generally quite limited. By the age of 16, adolescent workers are more likely to have formal jobs, working in the retail and service sectors of the economy, especially in fast food restaurants, grocery stores, or other retail stores. Employment becomes more regular and more time-consuming during the latter years of high school, with many teens working 20 or more hours per week.

4. http://www.ncbi.nlm.nih.gov/pmc/articles/PMC2936460/
Due to the limited job market for teenage workers, sometimes teens can gain access to a wider range of work settings through volunteering, internships, or various programs sponsored by their schools, including "job shadowing" an experienced worker, or work-study experiences. It is unrealistic to expect teenagers to make firm occupational choices during high school, and relatively few do so in this era of extended higher education and prolonged transitions to adulthood. Nonetheless, it is still worthwhile to begin thinking about work and the kinds of challenges and opportunities that would be most congenial to a teen's nascent interests and capacities. Teens may begin to think about what kinds of rewards at work are most important to them, be they intrinsic (e.g., autonomy, responsibility, opportunities to express creativity, a job that enables them to help other people) or extrinsic (e.g., high income, opportunities for advancement), or some combination of both. It is during high school and the years immediately following that these values crystallize.
Much school and major "shopping" as well as occupational "floundering," could possibly be avoided if young people's work values were sufficiently formed to provide a basis for effective educational and career decision making. Some combination of paid jobs, internships, and volunteer jobs might encourage optimal career exploration and long-term benefits.

5. http://www.dol.gov/dol/topic/youthlabor/hazardousjobs.htm
The Fair Labor Standards Act (FLSA) prohibits minors under age 18 years old to work in any occupation that it deems to be hazardous. Among these occupations are excavation, manufacturing explosives, mining, and operating many types of power-driven equipment. Certain industries allow minors under age 18 to perform certain tasks at worksites whose primary work activity is dangerous, but these tasks are very specific and the state and federal government closely monitor compliance.

Child labor laws vary from state to state. Regulations provide very specific information on these occupations and other safety standards for minor employees. Please consult your state department of labor for this information.

6. http://www.dol.gov/dol/topic/youthlabor/agerequirements.htm. Youth Rules! A gateway providing quick access to information about federal and state labor laws that apply to young workers. The web page includes information designed to educate teens, parents, educators, and employers about the hours youth can work, the jobs youth can do, and how to prevent workplace injuries.

7. http://www.actforyouth.net/youth_development/development/outcomes.cfm. Building on available youth development research and theory, Pittman offered the model of 5 Cs as a framework for understanding positive youth development outcomes:

Confidence: a sense of self-worth and mastery; having a sense of self-efficacy (belief in one's capacity to succeed)

Character: taking responsibility; a sense of independence and individuality; connection to principles and values

Connection: a sense of safety, structure, and belonging; positive bonds with people and social institutions

Competence: the ability to act effectively in school, in social situations, and at work

Contribution: active participation and leadership in a variety of settings; making a difference

In his 2007 book, *The Good Teen*, Richard M. Lerner includes an additional outcome [4]:

Caring: a sense of sympathy and empathy for others; commitment to social justice

8. http://www.safesitter.org/learn-about-us/our-people/founder.aspx. Safe Sitter is a medically accurate, competency-based, highly structured babysitting preparation course designed for young adolescents (11 and up). The curriculum is written by a pediatrician and presented in sections. All sites registered to teach Safe Sitter utilize only Safe Sitter-trained instructors, ensuring compliance with teaching methodologies and a quality educational experience for students. Prior to course completion, students must demonstrate acceptable skills in the care of a choking infant and child, and pass a written exam proving mastery of key concepts.

9. https://gametestingjobsforteenager.wordpress.com/. You can make up to $120 an hour, but you won't start there. Jobs can start at $15 to $20 per hour.

10. https://hphs.dist113.org/Academics/ARL/De-emphasizing%20 Grades%20to%20Emphasize%20Learning.pdf. The scene is a common one for teachers: papers are returned to students who immediately search for the grade, sigh, take out calculators, tabulate quarter grades and then compare grades with their neighbors! The students often ignore rich teacher comments and constructive feedback on the papers Instead they focus on the all-important grade.

11. http://www.alfiekohn.org/article/case-grades/. Grades don't pre-pare children for the "real world" — unless one has in mind a world where interest in learning and quality of thinking are unimportant. Nor are grades a necessary part of schooling, any more than paddling or taking extended dictation could be described that way. Still, it takes courage to do right by kids in an era when the quantitative matters more than the qualitative, when meeting (someone else's) standards counts for more than exploring ideas, and when anything "rigorous" is automatically assumed to be valuable. We have to be willing to chal-lenge the conventional wisdom, which in this case means asking not how to improve grades but how to jettison them once and for all.

12. http://ottawacitizen.com/life/parenting/the-working-life-there-are-benefits-later-in-life-for-teens-who-work. Teens who worked at 15 were more likely to have higher incomes at 17, 19 and 23. The exact amount varied according to the number of hours worked and their age. For example, working 33 hours a week during the school year at the age of 15 led to approximately a 25-per-cent income increase at the age of 23.

13. http://www.childtrends.org/?indicators=youth-employment. A number of factors may account for the recent decline in youth employment. Current economic conditions have aggravated employ-ment prospects for both students and others. Among students, there may be greater pressure and competition for achievement; for example, students are taking more advanced placement courses.[10] Students are also taking more courses; the average number of Carnegie units (a standard measure of the amount of time spent on a subject) earned by public high school graduates rose from 22 in 1982, to 26 in 2004. More stringent academic requirements, often including community service work, have cut into the time otherwise available for paid work. Fur-thermore, college enrollment rates have been rising since 2001. With real wages for this age-group falling in recent years, workers may be motivated to enhance their earning power by acquiring further education.

14. Op. Cit. 12.

15. Op Cit. 13.

Chapter 9

1. http://gladwell.com/outliers/the-10,000-hour-rule/

2. http://www.history.com/this-day-in-history/america-meets-the-beatles-on-the-ed-sullivan-show. It is estimated that 73 mil-lion Americans were watching that night as the Beatles made their live U.S. television debut. Roughly eight minutes before Fred Kaps took the stage, Sullivan gave his now-famous intro, "Ladies and gentlemen... the Beatles!" and after a few seconds of rapturous cheering from the audience, the band kicked into "All My Lovin'."

3. https://careerpivot.com/2013/larry-bird-winners-talents-and-skills/. Comments about Larry Bird: Talents: He had some real natural talents. My guess they were great vision and hands. He could see the court and teammates out of the corner of his eye. He could make the basketball twirl and spin in his subtle hands. Skills: Larry Bird developed into a tremendous shooter and passer. Did this come naturally? No, he worked hard at it. His talents made it seem easy. He could see things on the court that allowed him to leverage the natural skills in his hands to make great passes.

4. http://espn.go.com/page2/s/list/phenomflops.html.
Todd Marinovich: Trained from birth to be a quarterback by his father, Marv (a former lineman with the Oakland Raiders), Marinovich was the 1987 *USA Today* Offensive Player of the Year. After a lackluster college career at USC, the Raiders made him a surprise first-round pick in 1991, but he was out of the NFL after two years after failing a drug test. In March 2001, Marinovich pleaded no contest to heroin possession.

5. http://www.basketballreference.com/players/b/boguemu01.htm-loin possession. Bogues was drafted 12th overall in the 1987 NBA draft by the Washington Bullets, and was part of a talent-laden draft class that also included David Robinson, Reggie Miller, Scottie Pippen, and Kevin Johnson. In his rookie year, Bogues was a teammate of Manute Bol who stood 7 ft 7 in (2.31 m) tall. They were the tallest and shortest players in NBA history at the time, with 28 inches (71 cm) difference between them. Bol and Bogues appeared on three magazine covers together. Despite his height, Bogues managed to block 39 shots throughout his NBA span including one on 7 ft.... tall Patrick Ewing. This happened on April 14, 1993, in the first quarter when Ewing was pulling the ball back to go up for the shot and Bogues stripped him of the ball. Bogues reportedly had a 44-inch (110 cm) measured vertical leap, but his hands were too small to hold on to a ball to dunk one-handed.[

Chapter 10

1. http://www.criticalpages.com/2013/unequal-childhoods/. A review of *Unequal Childhoods*: Annette Lareau's ground-breaking *Unequal Childhoods* shows us what social stratification consists of in the United States and how it perpetuates itself. In effect, the process of sorting ourselves by social/cultural/economic class begins in childhood and never really ends. We may be unaware that we are nudging the process along, but in fact we are doing precisely that.
As parents, we practice, basically, one of two types of child rearing, "concerted cultivation" or "the accomplishment of natural growth." (More about these terms and concepts in a moment.) Lareau draws her thickest line of socio-economic demarcation between the middle class, on the one hand, and the working class and poor, on the other. For Lareau, only two classes count in American society, shape how most of

us actually live our lives. She proposes the two different styles of child rearing she has identified as distinguishing the first mode of living from the second, as dividing us into two distinct socio-cultural groups. She concedes that family income and assets play a large role in directing our lives, but the determining factor for her is how parents view and carry out their responsibilities as parents. This, in turn, reflects the parents' own education and occupation, as well as their aspirations for their children. Here is where "concerted cultivation" and "the accomplishment of natural growth" enter the picture:

Unequal Childhoods, 2nd edition, contains the now classic analysis of how social class shapes parenting in unexpected fashion in white and African-American families. A decade after the original study, Lareau revisited the families to examine social class in the transition to adulthood. The second edition has 100 pages of new material.

Social Scientists have shown that the social class position of a child's parents matters. It matters for school success, and ultimately, occupational success. But the mechanisms have been poorly understood. *Unequal Childhoods* was an "instant classic" as it showed in riveting detail how families with children ten years old went through their daily routines. Middle-class families, black and white, aggressively sought to develop their children's talents and schools through a series of organized activities, extensive language training, and by overseeing their children's experiences in institutions such as schools. By contrast, working-class and poor families, black and white, used very scarce resources to take care of their children, but they then gave them free time to hang out, gave them clear directives, and turned over responsibility to schooling. Lareau argued that both of these cultural logics of child rearing had merit, but the middle-class strategy had payoffs in institutions.

Now, Lareau has gone back and found all of the families featured in the book. She interviewed the young adults as they were 19 to 21 years of age; she also interviewed their parents and siblings. As children are transformed into young adults, it is possible that the actions of their parents might matter less. But Lareau found that the power of social class that she witnessed when the children were ten only grew in importance through time. Middle-class parents continued the process of gathering information and intervening in their children's lives ... even when the children had moved hundreds of miles from home. As young adults repeatedly turned to their parents for guidance, the parents treated them, in key ways, as children. In working-class and poor families, the parents saw the young adults as "grown," which was a view shared by the young adults themselves. Nonetheless, when the kids ran into problems in school or other institutions, the middle-class parents were heavily involved in managing situations to maximize opportunities. The working-class and poor parents loved their children very much, but as when their children were younger, it was harder for them to comply with the demands of professionals. Thus, the trajectories began when the children were ten continued to unfold over time. The middle-class kids generally achieved much more educational success than the working-class and poor kids. Since education is the "800 pound gorilla" for shaping labor market chances, the career prospects of the middle-class young adults are much brighter than their less privileged counterparts. Still, the working-class and poor young adults express much more appreciation for all that their parents have done for them than do the middle-class young adults. And the power of extended family is a guiding force in shaping the lives of working-class and poor lives in a way absent from the middle-class young adults in the study. While we have a language for race in America, on the subject of social class we remain blind and.nearly mute. Lareau's work helps us open our eyes and our minds to how much children's life paths are structured when they are only ten years of age.

2. Ibid.
3. Ibid.
4. Ibid.
5. http://www.sciencedirect.com/science/article/pii/ S0049089X08001282. Drawing on longitudinal data from the Early Childhood Longitudinal Study, Kindergarten Class of 1998–1999, this study used IRT modeling to operationalize a parental educational investment measure based upon Lareau's notion of 'concerted cultivation.' The analysis used multilevel piecewise growth models regressing children's general knowledge achievement from kindergarten through the first grade on a measure of concerted cultivation and indicators of the family context. The measure of concerted cultivation explained over 30% of the SES gradient and an additional 20–25% of the race/ ethnic general knowledge gaps at kindergarten entry after controlling for SES, and was larger than the SES coefficient in magnitude. These findings (a) lend partial support to Lareau's contention that concerted cultivation explains SES learning advantages; (b) contradict the argument that net of SES, concerted cultivation is mostly unrelated to race/ ethnic gaps; (c) and raises questions about the importance concerted cultivation for learning disparities after school entry.

Chapter 11

1. http://todaysmilitary.com/joining?source-. When it comes to learning about the Military, knowing where to start your research may seem daunting. Don't worry—we're here to help. The first steps to considering service include understanding the Military's basic entrance requirements, exploring the different Service branches and deciding between enlisted and officer career paths. The eligibility requirements for joining the armed forces can differ between branches. Knowing what the requirements are can help you avoid wasting time and effort. An issue that may make you ineligible for one service may be acceptable for another service

2. http://us-military-branches.insidegov.com/app-question/443/How-many-people-are-there-in-the-US-military

3. http://www.npr.org/templates/story/story.php?storyId=127217846

4. http://themilitarywallet.com/reasons-to-join-the-military/

5. http://www.goarmy.com/

6. http://www.nationalguard.com/benefits

7. https://www.whitehouse.gov/administration/vice-president-biden/academy-nominations/steps

Mission Statement: The mission of the U.S. service academies is to provide instruction and experience to all cadets so that they graduate with the knowledge and character essential to leadership and the motivation to become career officers in the U.S. military.

Eligibility: To be eligible to enter an Academy, you must be:

A citizen of the United States

Of good moral character

Unmarried with no dependents

At least 17, but less than 23 years of age by July 1 of the year you would enter.

Selections: It takes a well-rounded program of leadership, academic, and athletic preparation to be one of the few who can meet the Service Academies high admission standards and the fierce competitions for appointment. Carefully consider the characteristics of dedication, desire to serve others, ability to accept discipline, sense of duty, and morality, and the enjoyment of challenge in deciding if you want to pursue an Academy education.

Academic Preparation: It is recommended that young persons who aspire to go to one of the service academies take a college preparatory curriculum in high school that stresses English and Math. Also, they should plan on taking the ACT and SAT test as early as possible and more than once.

Physical Preparation: During the admissions process prospective cadets will be given the Candidate Fitness Assessment. All three academies have the same physical fitness events: the basketball throw; pull-ups (men & women) or flexed-arm hang (women); shuttle run; modified sit-ups; push-ups; and the one-mile run. The purpose of these tests is to evaluate a candidate's upper body strength and endurance. Please check with each academy on their specific requirements for the Candidate Fitness Assessment.

General Information: The minimum SAT scores for the academies are 500 verbal and 500 math. The average SAT scores at the academies are 540-620 verbal and 630-710 math. The minimum ACT scores for the academies are 21 English, 19 Social Studies, 24 Mathematics, and 24 Natural Science. The average ACT scores are 23-27 English; 24-29 Social Studies; 27-32 Mathematics; 28-32 Natural Science (minimum and average scores are slightly higher for the Naval Academy). Virtually all cadets are from the top 25% of their high school class.

8. http://www.rand.org/pubs/research_briefs/RB9195/index1.html. In 1969, four years before the United States eliminated the draft and moved to an all-volunteer force, a member of the President's Commission on an All-Volunteer Armed Force wrote to its chairman that "while there is a reasonable possibility that a peacetime armed force could be entirely voluntary, I am certain that an armed force involved in a major conflict could not be voluntary."[1] So far, his reservations have not been borne out. However, given the ongoing war in Iraq—with casualties rising, enlistments dropping, and a majority of the American public no longer believing that the war is worth fighting—the issue of recruiting enough volunteers to maintain the U.S. military at required levels is again relevant

Chapter 12

1. Basler, Roy P. [editor] *The Collected Works of Abraham Lincoln*, Volume I, "Fragments of a Tariff Discussion" (December 1, 1847), p. 412.
2. http://www.abrahamlincolnonline.org/lincoln/news/thomas.htm. The sad tale of Thomas Lincoln: Lincoln's comments about his father were "scornful statements that his father grew up 'literally without education,' that he 'never did more in the way of writing than to bunglingly sign his own name,' and that he chose to settle in a region where 'there was absolutely nothing to excite ambition for education.'" Lincoln's cousin, Dennis Hanks, doubted whether "Abe loved his father very well or not," and concluded "I don't think he did," according to noted historian Michael Burlingame in his book *The Inner World of Abraham Lincoln*. Records indicate that in his early manhood Thomas was a reasonably respectable citizen. The records indicate that he was a wage earner, jury member, petitioner for a road and a guard for a county prison.

Chapter 13

1. http://foundercorps.org/content/mentorship-best-practices
What is Mentorship? The mentor/mentee relationship is a unique and personal relationship, which transcends a mere advisor or board relationship. It is one of the most rewarding things people can be involved in outside of their family relationships. Mentorship doesn't happen by accident. Both the mentor and the mentee have their parts to play in a successful mentor/mentee relationship.
A "mentor" is a person who has had professional and life experience that can be used to help others learn and develop. The mentor is willing to share these experiences in a manner that the mentee can react to and understand. While there may be commercial aspects to a mentor's engagement, at its best the advice and help that is offered is provided freely and without expectation of immediate reward. The mentor is the "vendor" of the mentor/mentee relationship and for the mentee the

value of the relationship is driven by the quality and objectivity of the mentor's advice and assistance.

A "mentee" is a person who receives the help and assistance of the mentor. The mentee is willing to be engaged and respectful of the mentor's time and accomplishments. While there may be commercial aspects to the mentor's engagement, the mentee should understand that the best mentors are not motivated by money but by personal satisfaction. The mentee is the "customer" of the mentor/mentee relationship and for the mentor the value of the relationship is driven by the ultimate value that the mentee places on the mentor's help.

Mentorship is not merely advice. It is a bilateral commitment between two people, based upon mutual trust and a commitment. The commitment of the mentor is to provide advice and help to the mentee with the mentee's best interests in mind. The commitment of the mentee is to be ready to listen to the advice and take the help and act upon it. The currency of the mentor/mentee relationship is personal satisfaction and shared accomplishment.

2. http://www.eyeworld.org/article-in-memoriam-malcolm-a-mccannel-m-d-. ASCRS founding member Malcolm A. McCannel, M.D., died on December 30, 2012, in his home in Indianapolis. He was 96 years old. "'Mac' was a special man," said Richard L. Lindstrom, M.D., adjunct professor emeritus, ophthalmology department, University of Minnesota, Minneapolis, and founder, Minnesota Eye Consultants, Minneapolis. "He pioneered practice management methods, including the use of ophthalmic technicians to take histories, perform refractions and other testing prior to being placed in one of multiple surgeon consultation rooms at a time when most ophthalmologists were performing all testing themselves. This allowed him to see a large number of patients per hour and develop a high volume surgical practice." Dr. Lindstrom said Dr. McCannel was an early adopter of IOL implants. "The famous McCannel suture was developed, in part, to manage the subluxations associated with early iris clip intraocular lenses implanted after intracapsular cataract extraction," he said. "Amazing to me, he was an avid reader of the ophthalmic literature 20 years after he retired from clinical care and could astutely discuss both advances in technology and technique, as well as the societal impact of the changing care delivery models. A humble and caring man, he was loved by his patients, employees (including my wife Jaci Lindstrom who was a COMT and scrub tech for him), colleagues, family, and innumerable friends. He will be missed, but his impact on how we interact with patients today lives on in hundreds of practices worldwide." According to his obituary printed in the *Indianapolis Star Tribune*, Dr. McCannel was born in Minot, N.D., earned his bachelor's degree in 1937 at the University of Minnesota, his M.D. in 1941 from Temple University School of Medicine, Philadelphia, and his M.S. in 1946 from the University of Minnesota School of Medicine. He practiced ophthalmology

with his father, Archibald D. McCannel, M.D., in Minot for several years before moving to Minneapolis in 1949 and establishing Ophthalmology, P.A., where he remained for 42 years until his retirement in 1991. From 1957 to 1983, Dr. McCannel traveled with Project Hope, Medico-Care International, and Project Orbis to administer free eye surgery to the less fortunate around the globe, the obituary said. He was the author of numerous articles and textbook chapters including a definitive paper describing a surgery technique he developed called the McCannel suture. He is survived by his wife, four daughters, and five grandchildren. Dr. McCannel was cremated and his final request was for no memorial service.

3. http://www.ascrs.org/node/21409. Dr. Gunter K. von Noorden has been one of the preeminent leaders in ophthalmology and strabismus surgery for the past 40 years. Most recently, in 2010, he retired as distinguished emeritus professor at the Baylor College of Medicine. Dr. von Noorden began his career as a resident at the University of Iowa in 1957, which was followed by a fellowship at the University of Tuebingen Eye Clinic in Germany. He then returned to the University of Iowa, spending two years as an assistant professor of ophthalmology. In 1963, Dr. von Noorden became a professor at the Wilmer Eye Institute at Johns Hopkins in Baltimore, Maryland. In 1972, he moved to Houston, Texas to serve as a professor and director of the Ocular Motility Service at the Baylor College of Medicine. Born in Germany in 1928, Dr. von Noorden's family moved to Berlin in 1937. This had a profound impact on his life—exposing him to Adolf Hitler's dictatorship and Nazi propaganda. Following his involvement in Battle of Berlin in 1945 and the end of WW II, Dr. von Noorden was determined to dedicate his life to healing others and worked his way through medical school at the Johann-Wolfgang Goethe University. Dr. von Noorden is charter member and former president of the American Association of Pediatric Ophthalmology (AAPOS), the International Strabismological Association (ISA), and the American Orthoptic Council (AOC). He also served as former president of the American Association of Research in Vision and Ophthalmology (ARVO). He has published 310 scientific papers and is the author of 4 books, including **Ocular Motility and Binocular Vision: Theory and Management of Strabismus**. The book has been heralded as the "gold-standard text for ocular motility disorders for the past 30 years." Dr. von Noorden has presented 21 named lectures worldwide and is the recipient of numerous awards. His awards include the Franceschetti Prize, the Proctor Award, the Bowman Medal, and the Jackson Memorial Lecture Award from the American Academy of Ophthalmology (AAO).

ABOUT THE AUTHOR

EUGENE M. HELVESTON, MD, is emeritus professor of ophthalmology; founder of the section of Pediatric Ophthalmology; and former Chairman of the Department of Ophthalmology at Indiana University School of Medicine, where he provided patient care and teaching, and carried out clinical research.

During his career, he taught in forty-five states and also served as a volunteer surgeon and lecturer in fifty countries. In 2002, he founded an award-winning international telemedicine program to serve doctors and their patients in developing countries.

After authoring hundreds of professional papers and three medical textbooks on pediatric ophthalmology and surgery for strabismus, he turned his attention to writing about the two things he felt had the most meaningful impact on his life: getting the best education for the career you want to pursue and working at a meaningful job starting at an early age.

A native of Detroit, Michigan, and a graduate of the University of Michigan, Dr. Helveston has worked since early in his Second Decade. He believes this was the mortar that held together the bricks of his formal education—or maybe it was the other way around!

He believes that helping children earn a high school diploma and encouraging them to find a job early in their Second Decade are two of the most important things parents, grandparents, and mentors can do to prepare youth for becoming happy and self-sufficient adults.

INDEX

Page numbers beginning with 193 refer to notes.

Symbols

4-H, 117
5 C's, 117–118, 227

A

academic skills, xxiii, 31
accomplishment(s), 69, 133–135,
    137–138
    relative, 137
ACT (*see* American College
    Testing)
adversity, 6, 126–127
AFQT (*see* Armed Forces
    Qualifying Test)
after-school activities, 4, 81, 118,
    128
Air Force, 6, 61, 147, 211
alcohol, 36

allowance, 117
American College Testing (ACT),
    61, 83, 145
American dream, 3
apprenticeships, 85, 89, 96
Armed forces, 33, 60, 89, 89, 147-
    152
Armed Forces Qualifying Test
    (AFQT), 60–61, 147, 211
Armed Services Vocational
    Aptitude Battery (ASVAB),
    60, 147
Army, 61, 147
associate degree, xxii, 85, 89–90,
    95–96, 99–101, 113
athletics (*also see* sports), xi, 2,
    103
attire, 47–49
attitude, xxiii, 3, 6, 11–12, 21–22,
    24, 28, 49, 110, 144, 176, 203,
    209

B

bachelor's degree, xxii, 77, 85, 87,
    95–99, 101–102, 104–108, 111,
    113, 157, 216, 219, 222, 224,
    234
    cost of, 104
Barbizon School of Art, xx
basic knowledge of U.S. and
    world history, 51–52
basic knowledge of U.S.
    government, 52–53
basic life skills, 41
Big Brothers/Big Sisters, 117
Bird, Larry, 134
birth status, 5
body language, 41, 43–45, 209
Boy Scouts, 28, 117
Boys and Girls Clubs, 117
bullying, 53–54, 209–210, 217

C

campus life, 103
character, 3
charter schools, 74, 75, 76, 80, 215
Cheadle, Jacob, 145
checkpoints, 1–2
childcare costs, 22
child labor, xx1–xxi, 116, 197
chores around the home, 2, 9, 115
    allowance, 117
church activities, 4, 117
civic groups, 33
Clayton, Romeo, 148
clubs, 2, 4, 33, 79, 110, 116–118
Coast Guard, 61, 147, 211
cognitive skills, xiii, 208, 214

college, 34
    campus life, 103
    community/two-year (see
        community college)
    cost of, 104, 223
    debt, 101
    four-year/university, xxii, 72,
        85, 87, 89–90, 92–93, 95,
        98–104, 111, 222
    government-subsidized loans,
        105
    liberal arts college, 39
    private universities, 104
    reasons for not going to, 94–95
    scholarship aid, 104
    state university, 90
communication, 41
    body language, 41, 43–45, 209
    clear, 42
    e-mail, 10, 46–47, 209
    first impressions, 36
    Gmail, 46
    profanity, 42
    proper word usage, 44
    slang, 42
    texting, 27
    vulgarity, 42
community college, xxii, 15, 34,
    72, 76, 83, 85, 87, 89–90, 92–93,
    95, 98–103, 127, 220–222
Community College Career Track,
    xvi, 102
concerted cultivation, 69, 76, 142,
    144, 145–146, 213, 229–231
Cub Scouts, 28
curiosity, 154
cyber-bullying, 53, 54

D

daycare, 29, 30
debt from student loans, 101
Declaration of Independence, 5, 51, 199–200
decline in youth employment, 123
Department of Labor, 25, 112, 116, 217
desire, 139
diploma, xii, 2, 14–15, 20–21, 33–35, 40, 58–60, 67–70, 75, 82–91, 101, 147, 204, 211, 217–220, 224
DNA, 29, 69, 133, 195
doctorate degree, 85, 105, 108
driver's license, 33, 35
dropout of high school, 2, 34, 67, 82–83, 85, 112
    reasons for, 84
drugs, 36
    signs of possible use, 36

E

earning money, 115
eighteenth century, xix-xx
e-mail, 10, 46–47, 209
enriching behavior, 143
entry-level job, 34
equal rights, 29
ethical behavior, 53
extracurricular activities, ix, 33, 79, 116, 225

F

Facebook, 10, 46
failure, 5

family
    chores, 2, 9, 115
    parents' economic status, education level, 29
    stable and loving, 6–7, 29
fellowship, 110
financial security, 25
first impressions, 36
five most important "checkpoints", 1–2
formal education, xi, xxi, 11, 20, 23, 25, 36, 83, 87–88, 90–91, 95, 98, 101, 106–108, 112, 115, 128, 180
formal training, 95
formative years, 3, 28
four-year college, xxii, 72, 85, 87, 89–90, 92–93, 95, 98–104, 111, 222
freelance work, 9, 117, 191
free public education, 67
friendships, 2
Future Farmers of America, 117
future time preference, 37–38, 120

G

Gates, Bill, 62, 70, 106
GED, 15, 60, 82–84, 89, 101, 147, 152, 211, 217–219
generational leap, 15, 20
Generations late X, Y, and Z, 144
GI Bill, 150
Gladwell, Malcolm, 134
global society, xxi
Gmail, 46
Golden Rule, 53
government-subsidized loans, 105
graduating high school, 33–34

Greatest Generation, 144
Greek society, 103
grit, xiii, 36, 195

H

hard work, 3
helicopter parents, 143
high school, 67–86
  checklist when considering a
    high school, 79
  diploma, xii, 2, 14–15, 20–21,
    33–35, 40, 58–60, 67–70, 75,
    82–91, 101, 147, 204, 211,
    217–220, 224
  dropout, 2, 34, 67, 82–83, 85,
    112
  extracurricular activities, xi,
    33, 79, 116, 225
  graduating, 33–34
  high school opportunities, 71
  reasons for dropping out, 84
  types of, 72
    charter schools, 74, 75, 76,
      80, 215
    International Baccalaureate
      (IB), 73
    magnet schools, 72–73, 81
    parochial, 71
    private high schools, 71, 75,
      77
    public, 71–72
  vouchers, 78
Hiss, Florian Howard, 163, 166
homeschooling, 67, 77, 216, 217
  associations, 78
household chores, 2, 115
  allowance, 117

I

immigrants, 124
inclusive middle class, xxiii, 7, 9,
  13, 19–21, 25, 140, 175–177
income based on education
  level, 112
Industrial Revolution, xix–xx,
  156, 197
informal attire, 48
innate level of intelligence, 29
innate talent, 135
inner cities, 10
Intelligence Quotient (*see* IQ)
International Baccalaureate (IB),
  73
Internet, 36
internship, 109
interpersonal relationships, 119
IQ, 57–62, 95, 133, 147
Ivy Tech Community College,
  99, 102

J

jail, 84
job interview, 43, 45, 47–48
jobs
  entry-level, 34
  freelance, 9, 117, 191
  manufacturing, 88
  part-time job, ix, 79
  technical, 88

K

Keener, Patricia, MD, 118
kindergarten, 29, 67

knowledge of basic U.S. and
    world history, 51
knowledge of U.S. government,
    52–53

L

landmarks, 39
Lareau, Annette, PhD, 69, 142,
    144
liberal arts college, 39
life skills, 31, 41
lifetime earnings, 96, 112, 205
Lincoln, Abraham, 154, 233
LinkedIn, 46
lower class, 21
low(er) income, 20–21

M

magnet schools, 72–73, 81
major leagues of life, 113,
    173–177
manufacturing jobs, 88
Marine Corps, 61, 147
Marinovich, Todd, 34
marriage, 34
master's degree, 85, 87, 90, 104,
    107–108
McKinney, Frank, 106, 187–188
meaningful work, xix, 2, 23, 28,
    81, 114–116, 118, 174–175, 180
media, 36
median annual household
    income, 12, 22, 85, 113
medical specialist, 106
Mensa, 60, 211
mentee, 160

mentor(s), xi, xvi, xxi–xxii, 35,
    54, 68, 86, 88, 94, 110, 114, 154,
    157–163, 166, 168, 170–171,
    176, 195, 233–234
    characteristics of, 162
mentorship, 160
middle class, xxiii, 7, 9–25, 69,
    110, 140, 144, 175–177, 194,
    203–205, 212–213, 229–231
middle school, 36, 68
Mikulski, Barbara, 98
military
    Air Force, 6, 61, 147, 211
    Armed Forces Qualifying Test
        (AFQT), 60–61, 147, 211
    Armed Services Vocational
        Aptitude Battery (ASVAB),
        60, 147
    Army, 61, 147
    Coast Guard, 61, 147, 211
    GI Bill, 150
    job counselors, 60
    Marine Corps, 61, 147
    National Guard, 147, 151
    Navy, 61, 147–149, 211
minimum wage, 25
mobility, 10
Mogues, Tyrone Curtis
    "Bugsy," 136
money, value of, 120, 175
music, 133

N

National Guard, 147, 151
natural ability, 139–140
natural growth, 69–70, 76, 143,
    144, 146, 229, 230
Navy, 61, 147–149, 211
nineteenth century, xix,–xx
nurturing skills, 29

O

on-the-job training, 21, 83, 87, 89, 95, 98, 122
opportunity, 6–7, 137, 139–140, 153, 158
optimism, 12, 20
Outliers, 134

P

parenting styles, 69–70, 76, 141–146
   concerted cultivation, 69, 76, 142, 144, 145–146, 213, 229–231
   helicopter parents, 143
   natural growth, 69–70, 76, 143, 144, 146, 229, 230
parents' economic status, education level, 29
parochial high schools, 71
part-time job, xi, 79
patience, 37
peer pressure, 35–36, 54, 217
performing arts, 133
Phi Beta Kappa, 101
Phi Theta Kappa, 101
picking the right battle, 39
Pittman, Karen, 117, 227
pivotal landmarks, 39
Positive Youth Development, 117
poverty, 19–20, 25
practical skills, xxiii, 68, 115, 175
pre-kindergarten, 29, 67
preparation, 3
pre-school, 29
primary school, xii, 29–31, 68, 71–72, 76–77
prison, 84
private high schools, 71, 75, 77

private universities, 104
profanity, 42
professional degrees, 59, 85, 105, 108
proper word usage, 44
puberty, xii, 32, 69, 193, 207
public high school, 71–72

R

reading to a child, 44
recognition, 133–138
relationships, interpersonal, 119
relative accomplishment, 137
Renaissance, xix
residency, 109

S

Safe Sitter, 118
SAT (*see* Scholastic Aptitude Test)
satisfaction, 135, 139
scholarship aid, 104
Scholastic Aptitude Test (SAT), 61–62, 145
school debt, 104
school vouchers, 78
Scott, Mary, 148
self-confidence, 94
self-esteem, 84, 94
sex, 36
"shock" behavior, 50
signs of possible drug use, 36
single parents, 34
skill(s), 133–136, 138, 146
   acquired, 139
   basic life, 41
   cognitive, xiii, 208, 214
   practical, xxiii, 68, 115, 175

skill set, 15, 68
slang, 42
Snyder, Thomas J., xvi, 102
social activities, xi
social media, 54
    Facebook, 10, 46
    LinkedIn, 46
    Twitter, 10, 46
    YouTube, 10
social networking, 54
soft skills, 122
sports, 2, 4, 33, 68, 117, 133, 137
state university, 90
status of birth, 5
Stroh Brewery, 25–26
student loan debt, 101
suitable attire, 47

T

table manners, 50
talent, 2, 134–137, 140, 146
    innate, 135
technical jobs, 88
technology, 27
ten-year-olds, description of, 30
texting, 27
tobacco, 36
trade school, 21, 85, 96
travel, 4
twentieth century, xx, 197, 202
Twitter, 10, 46
two-year college (*see* community
    college)

U

*Unequal Childhoods: Class, Race,
    and Family Life*, 69, 142
unskilled workers, 124
upper class, 21
U.S. government, basic
    knowledge of, 52–53
U.S. Constitution, 24

V

values, 7
vocational school, 71
vocational training, xxii, 68, 80,
    89–91, 95, 174
volunteering, 2, 33, 127, 189, 226
voting, 33, 93
vouchers, 78
vulgarity, 42

W

Wechsler Adult Intelligence Scale
    (WAIS), 57–58
Williams, Venus and Serena, 134,
    145
Woods, Tiger, 134, 146
work ethic, 14, 19, 24, 66, 146, 217
working-class families, 69
working poor, 20–21

Y

YMCA, 117
youth employment, decline in,
    123
YouTube, 10

—